Marx's 'Capital' and Capitalism Today

Other publications

Marx's 'Capital' and Capitalism Today, Volume One
   Routledge & Kegan Paul 1977

B. Hindess
The Decline of Working Class Politics
   MacGibbon & Kee 1971 and Paladin
The Use of Official Statistics in Sociology
   Macmillan 1973
Philosophy and Methodology in the Social Sciences
   Harvester 1977
(editor) *Sociological Theories of the Economy*
   Macmillan 1977

P. Q. Hirst
Durkheim, Bernard and Epistemology
   Routledge & Kegan Paul 1975
Social Evolution and Sociological Categories
   Allen & Unwin 1976

B. Hindess and P. Q. Hirst
Pre-Capitalist Modes of Production
   Routledge & Kegan Paul 1975, 1977
Mode of Production and Social Formation
   Macmillan 1977

Marx's 'Capital' and Capitalism Today

Volume Two

Antony Cutler
Department of Sociology, Middlesex Polytechnic

Barry Hindess
Department of Sociology, University of Liverpool

Paul Hirst
Department of Politics and Sociology, Birkbeck College, University of London

Athar Hussain
Department of Economics, University of Keele

Routledge & Kegan Paul
London, Henley and Boston

First published in 1978
by Routledge & Kegan Paul Ltd
39 Store Street,
London WC1E 7DD,
Broadway House,
Newtown Road,
Henley-on-Thames,
Oxon RG9 1EN and
9 Park Street,
Boston, Mass. 02108, USA
Photoset in 10 on 12 Times by
Kelly and Wright, Bradford-on-Avon, Wiltshire
and printed in Great Britain by
Redwood Burn Ltd
Trowbridge and Esher
© A. J. Cutler, Barry Hindess, Paul Q. Hirst and
A. Hussain, 1978
No part of this book may be reproduced in
any form without permission from the
publisher, except for the quotation of brief
passages in criticism

British Library Cataloguing in Publication Data

Marx's 'Capital' and capitalism today.
Vol. 2
1. Marxian economics
I. Cutler, A J
335.4'12'0924   HB97.5   77-30216

ISBN 0-7100-8855-8
ISBN 0-7100-8856-6 Pbk

Contents

Prefatory Note — vii

Part I Money and Financial Institutions — 1

1. Money: Its Definition and Functions — 5
2. The Status of Different Functions of Money — 16
3. Forms of Money — 28
4. Barter and Monetary Exchange — 56
5. The Circulation of Money — 77
6. Credit, Financial Markets, and Financial Institutions — 89

Part II Enterprises and Capitalist Calculation — 109

7. Calculation as Ideology — 111
8. Problems of a General Theory of Capitalist Calculation — 128
9. Enterprise Calculation and Production Methods — 163
10. A Critique of the Enterprise as a Universal Calculating Subject — 189
11. Enterprise Calculation and Sources of Finance — 202
12. The Sraffa Model as a Theory of Reproduction Prices — 215

Conclusion — 233

Bibliography — 294

Index to both volumes — 297

Prefatory Note

This volume continues the argument that was introduced and whose general bearing on Marxist theory was explained in the first volume.

One point should be noted here, Tony Cutler has differences with the form of the conclusion. These differences are confined to the appropriateness of a political conclusion to a work of this kind and do not affect the substantive theoretical positions in the body of the text. These differences also do not concern the discussion of national economies or enterprises as concepts in the conclusion. The conclusion represents the view of the other three authors.

Part I

Money and Financial Institutions

Marx's analysis of money is neglected. By and large, the exegeses of *Capital* and commentaries on it concentrate on value, reproduction, and prices of production, and they seem to neglect the fact that a fair proportion of *Capital* is actually devoted to either the analysis of money or of financial institutions. In recent years the only exception to this is de Brunhoff's book *Marx on Money*. The neglect of the analysis of money and financial institutions is even more paradoxical in view of the fact that according to the analyses of Lenin and Hilferding we are in the era of the dominance of finance capital.

The analysis in this part of the book is an attempt to remedy this deficiency. What follows in the next six chapters is neither a commentary nor an exegesis of Marx's analysis of money. Some of the issues raised here are not discussed by Marx or by Marxists. It is no exaggeration to say that Marxists have practically nothing systematic to say about the functioning of financial institutions. There are serious weaknesses in Marx's analysis, so one of the aims here is to point out those weaknesses and argue that the analysis of money in *Capital* as it stands cannot be sustained. One has to reject not only the notion that money is the measure of value but also all those arguments which rely on the theme that money represents something, e.g. the socialness of exchange, etc. Money neither hides anything nor reveals anything. This, however, is not to suggest that there is nothing valuable in Marx's analysis of money. Indeed there is. But it is not a philosophical or an epistemological reading which is required to isolate what is valuable and what is not valuable in Marx's analysis. Instead what is needed is a systematic analysis of money, monetary exchange, and financial institutions. And this is what we attempt to do in this part of the book.

Chapter 1

Money: Its Definition and Functions

Most discussions on money start with what seems like a sterile ritual, namely, the enumeration of the functions of money, which are supposedly obvious to everyone who uses money but are none the less worth repeating. In monetary theory, though the functions of money are regarded as obvious and uncontroversial, the relative importance of those functions is a matter of dispute and controversy. Every undergraduate in economics learns by rote that, while pre-Keynesian economists (not a temporal category) emphasised the means-of-payment function, Keynes emphasised the store-of-value function of money. Still, in what may seem like a gratuitous concession to a sterile tradition, we start with Marx's discussion of the functions of money. The discussion of the functions of money is not interesting but for the fact that Marx's discussion of it is at some points theoretically suspect and that the obviousness accorded to the functions of money is illusory and it masks as uncontroversial what is, in fact, open to question.

'The commodity that functions as the measure of value and either in its own person or by a representative as the medium of circulation is money. Gold and silver is therefore money.' (*Capital*, vol. 1, p. 130) This is how Marx defines money on the assumption that money takes the form of commodity money. There is nothing new in defining money in this manner. That money is what functions as money is accepted both by Marxists and bourgeois economists. There are certain implications which follow from defining money in terms of its functions and it is those which are important and often neglected. Leaving aside the measure-of-value function of money for later discussion, from Marx's definition it is clear that money as the medium of circulation need not take any particular form—or at least it need not take the form of commodity money—and that money can be distinguished from non-money only on the basis of the function it performs in the process of circulation. The argument, in other words, is that the status of money *qua* medium of circulation is not affected by whether money is commodity money, or fiduciary money, or credit money. Money as the medium of circulation can take a variety of forms and the functions it performs in the process of circulation are not sufficient, except in a very general sense, to determine the form it takes. The correlate of the definition of money in terms of its functions is the assumption that money can take a variety of forms and shapes. Thus the usual definition of money is always coupled with the question: what determines the form of money?

The fact that money can take a variety of forms is usually taken to imply that the form of money is arbitrary: it takes the form which its users decide to give it. Hume, for example, starts his essay *Of Money* with the statement that 'Money is not properly speaking one of the subjects of commerce; but only an instrument which men have agreed upon to facilitate the exchange of one commodity for another.' To say that the form of money is agreed upon by men who use money is, in fact, to say nothing more than that money takes a particular form because it has that form. This kind of argument not only dispenses with the analysis of the determinants of the form of money but makes it impossible to explain a change in the form of money of the kind which has taken place in capitalist countries during the last hundred years or so. For Marx money has a social reality and thus the form it takes is socially determined. Marx mentions different forms of money but neither in *Capital* nor in the *Contribution to the Critique of Political Economy* does he systematically analyse the determinants of the different forms of money. The analysis does not go beyond tangential remarks of the following kind: 'But we may affirm this much, that just as true paper money takes its rise in the functions of money as the circulating medium, so money based upon credit takes root spontaneously in the functions of money as the means of payment.' (*Capital,* vol. 1, p. 127) The problem is that the argument that the form of money is socially determined and that different forms of money take root in different functions of money does not necessarily dispel the assumption that the form of money is arbitrary. Hilferding in his *Finance Capital,* for example, does start by saying that the form of money is not arbitrary but socially determined; but later on he ends up explaining the change in the form of money, from gold money to paper money, in terms of the realisation by the state that paper money is as good a medium of circulation as gold money. The point is that the thesis of the arbitrariness of the form of money is not affected by arguing that it is not individuals but the society or the state which chooses the form of money. The thesis leads to the belief that the form of money is chosen on the basis of personal convenience or preference; and this belief is not affected if society or the state is substituted for the individual. The form of money has nothing to do with personal preference and convenience; particular forms of money presuppose particular conditions of existence. For example, credit money cannot exist without the existence of a network of credit wide enough to encompass a wide variety of economic agents. Further, the form of money is of economic significance, contrary to what is implied by the belief that the form of money is arbitrary. True, the status of money *qua* medium of circulation is not affected by the form it takes; but this implies nothing more than that the economic significance of the form of money cannot be deduced from the role money performs in the process of circulation of commodities. The medium-of-circulation function of money, though the defining function of money, does not envelop all the pertinent aspects of the effects and the functions of money. The form of money is of significance from the point of view of the relations of the distribution of the social product and from the point of view of the power of financial institutions to create credit. These connections will be developed later. For the present purposes the main point is that the definition of money in terms of its functions, on the one hand, gives rise to the problem of the determination of the form of money, and on the other hand, it eliminates the problem because the form of money is not relevant to what is taken as the defining function of money. We turn now to the other implication of the definition of money in terms of its functions.

It is obvious that particular functions can serve as the criteria of identification of money only if those functions are performed by money only and not by non-money. Otherwise, there is no way in which money can be distinguished from non-money. Conversely, if an analysis of money proceeds on the assumption, either explicit or implicit, that the functions of money are not really specific to money then that analysis, despite its claim to the contrary, is not based on the definition of money in terms of its functions. The significance of this proviso will become clear later on when we come to discuss the difference between barter and monetary exchange. By way of a general argument at this stage the main point is that the functions which money performs should affect the process of exchange in some definite way and that monetary exchange should be treated as qualitatively different from barter. Alternatively, the question of whether or not money exists should be treated in the same way as the question of what specific form the process of circulation takes. Unless the form of circulation and the existence of money are tethered together, it has to be argued that the existence or the non-existence of money makes no difference to the process of circulation. But then the implication is either that the functions of money are not specific to money or that they have no effect on the process of circulation of commodities. In either case there is no rationale for the analysis of money and the role it plays in the process of circulation. These remarks at this stage may seem too general to have any significant bearing on the analysis of money. Later on in the section on barter and monetary exchange it will be argued that the distinctiveness of Marx's analysis of money rests on the assumption that the existence of money cannot be divorced from the form of exchange of commodities. Two requirements are clear, namely, that the definition of money and the discussion of its functions should be coupled both with an analysis of the forms of money and their determinants and with an analysis of the difference between barter and monetary exchange.

Before analysing the issues mentioned above it is necessary to raise a basic problem concerning the analysis of money in *Capital*, vol. 1. There the analysis is based on the assumption that money takes the form of commodity money, in particular gold and silver. (See the quote from *Capital* above.) The question is why is it necessary to assume this? The analysis of money in *Capital*, it should be noted, is not the analysis of commodity money but the analysis of money in general regardless of the form it takes. There is a discrepancy between the scope of the analysis of money in *Capital*, vol. 1 and the assumption on which that analysis is based and it is that discrepancy which needs explaining. De Brunhoff in her book *Marx on Money* does realise that Marx's assumption casts doubt on the generality of his analysis; but she disposes of the problem with the mere comment that the assumption represents a good abstraction and that commodity money is privileged among forms of money because it is the original or the primordial form of money. In fact, the goodness of Marx's assumption is not at all evident. Some parts of Marx's analysis are valid only if money takes the form of commodity money, while some other parts remain valid regardless of the form which money takes. We have already pointed out that money *qua* medium of circulation can take a variety of forms; so Marx's assumption does not affect the argument which exclusively refers to the medium of circulation function of money. But Marx's discussion of money *qua* measure of value does rest on the assumption that money is commodity money. The fact that the assumption is necessary in some cases while not in others means that it cannot be justified on the grounds that it simplifies the analysis without affecting its generality. Moreover, the assumption cannot be justified by reference to the fact that commodity money is the original form because that fact by itself is of no importance except in the context of the discourse which assigns the origin an epistemological privilege by assumption.

The assumption that money is commodity money is tied to the assumption that money is also the measure of value. The connection between the two is made clear by the following passage from *Capital*.

> The truth of the proposition that 'although gold and silver are not by nature money, money is by nature gold and silver' is shown by the fitness of the physical properties of these metals for the functions of money. Up to this point, however, we are acquainted only with one function of money, namely, to serve as the form of manifestation of the value of commodities, or as the material in which the magnitudes of their values are socially expressed. An adequate form of manifestation of value, a fit embodiment of abstract, undifferentiated, and therefore equal, human labour, that material alone can be whose every sample exhibits the same uniform qualities. On the other hand, since the difference between the magnitudes of value is purely quantitative, the money commodity must be susceptible of merely quantitative differences, must therefore be divisible at will, and equally capable of being reunited. Gold and silver possess these properties by nature. (*Capital*, vol. 1, p. 89)

The argument, in other words, is that a measure has to have the same properties as what it measures; the measure of value should thus be homogeneous and divisible like the socially necessary labour which constitutes the value of commodities. Marx, in effect, treats measurement as pictorial representation. The identity between the properties of money and human labour is elsewhere expressed by Marx by calling money the social incarnation of human labour. The attributes which money has to have in order to function as the measure of value, it should be noted, are only pertinent when money takes the form of commodity money. Qualities like divisibility, homogeneity, etc. are not pertinent at all when money does not take the form of commodity money, i.e. it is either fiduciary money or credit money. What this passage points to is that the two defining functions of money are not at par with each other. While the measure-of-value function of money necessitates that it take a particular form the medium-of-circulation function does not. This passage raises the following problems, namely, if money has to be commodity money in order to function as the measure of value then what is the status of that function *qua* defining function of money regardless of the form it takes; and if the function is not specific to commodity money then how does non-commodity money—paper money, for example—express the value of commodities?

For Marx the value of a commodity means something definite, namely, the 'socially necessary labour' required directly or indirectly to produce it. Here we are not concerned with the status of value as a measure of economic magnitudes; that has been discussed in Volume One of this work. Instead we are merely concerned with the technical problem of the expression of value. Values are measured in terms of the standardised labour-time or in the units of unskilled labour. Thus, money when it measures and expresses value only expresses relative values. In other words, money measures values of commodities relative to its own value. This is discussed in a general context in detail in *Capital* (vol. 1, ch. 1) under the heading of 'relative and equivalent form of value'. The main point is that money can express relative values only if it itself has a value. Commodity money can express values because it does have a value which is equal to the value of the money commodity. But what is the value of non-commodity money? The non-commodity money, for present purposes, signifies a money whose quantity does not bear any specific relation to the quantity of any commodity. Alternatively, there is no specific relation between the denomination of money and the quantity of any particular commodity. Thus, in the case of non-commodity money there exists, by definition, no commodity which can, so to say, legitimately lend money its value. The implication is that non-commodity money cannot measure and express values like commodity money; as a result, the measurement of value cannot be regarded as a defining function of money.

Marx discusses the non-commodity forms of money in *Capital,* but he does not indicate what determines the value of non-commodity money and how non-commodity money measures values. Most Marxists do not realise that the claim that money measures value is problematic; Hilferding is one of the few who does. Hilferding argues that while the value of commodity money is determined by the value of the money commodity, the value of non-commodity money is measured by the values of commodities exchanged for it. The implication of the argument is that there are two different ways of assigning value to money each applicable to a different form of money. Hilferding has solved the problem of assigning value to non-commodity money purely in formal terms. The difficulty with his solution is that it has nothing to do with value as it is defined in *Capital*. In fact, the procedure for assigning value adopted by Hilferding is more in line with the one used by Adam Smith rather than the one used by Marx and Ricardo. For Adam Smith the value of a commodity is equal either to the amount of labour embodied in it or to the amount of labour embodied in the commodities given in exchange for the commodity in question. The two are not identical for Marx; for him the former represents value and the latter the exchange-value. And, as it is well known, Marx criticised Adam Smith for conflating the two. The result is that Hilferding, in his attempt to sustain the claim that money is the measure of value, ends up subverting the concept of value as it is defined in *Capital.*

The main point in discussing Hilferding is not that his arguments have been accepted by Marxists. The procedure for assigning value to non-commodity money adopted by Hilferding was criticised by Kautsky soon after the appearance of *Finance Capital*; and, more recently, the procedure has come in for criticism from Mandel. The point in discussing Hilferding is to point out that there is no way in which non-commodity money can be assigned value without undermining the concept of value as it is defined in *Capital.* Hilferding's analysis of money cannot be simply rejected on the grounds that in the realm of politics he was an opportunist and a revisionist in the realm of theory. Hilferding's analysis is based on the analysis of *Capital,* and a lot of the problems associated with his analysis are, in fact, the problems carried over from *Capital.* True, Hilferding's analysis of money was criticised by Lenin; but the criticism—summary though it is—can be equally well applied to Marx's analysis.

The problem in general terms is clear, namely, that non-commodity money has no value and any attempt to find a value for it so that it can function as the measure of value cannot be anything other than an attempt which consists in finding a commodity whose value, it can be claimed, is equal to the value of non-commodity money. The main point is that this way of assigning value is tantamount to changing the concept of value. The problem does not lie in the commodity which is chosen but in the very procedure itself; and what is more important, it is not specific to Hilferding. Mandel, who is very critical of Hilferding, proposes to assign value to non-commodity money by reference to the amount of gold for which it can be exchanged. There is very little difference between Mandel and Hilferding; the latter wants to use all the commodities for which non-commodity money can be exchanged as the point of reference for assigning value to it, while the former wants to use just gold and nothing else. The fact that gold is monetary metal does not affect the status of Mandel's proposal and make it different from Hilferding's, because the problem is how to assign value to non-commodity money and from that point of view there is no difference between gold and other commodities.

It is clear now that the measurement of value cannot be regarded as the defining function of money. The argument so far only applies to non-commodity money; as a result, it may be argued that commodity money, unlike non-commodity money, does measure values. What we show now is that even this restricted proposition is not without problems. Money, regardless of the form it takes, is, according to Marx, both the measure of value and the standard of prices. The latter simply means that prices are expressed in monetary units. A divergence between values and prices is, as Marx points out, to be expected; and this divergence, one may add, is autonomous of the form of money. The question is how can commodity money express both prices and values at the same time when they are not equal to each other? Money necessarily expresses prices because it is the medium of circulation. (We will come back to this point later.) But, how does money express values in that situation? In fact, in that case there is no expression of values. It may be argued that, nonetheless, values can be expressed in terms of the value of the money commodity. But that expression does not have the social significance which the expression of values by money is supposed to have in *Capital*.

The measurement and the expression of value is of epistemological rather than of economic importance in *Capital*. In vol. 1 and part 1 of *Capital* the process of exchange of commodities has a dual significance, namely, on the one hand, it is the process of redistribution of means of consumption and production in the economy based on the production of commodities and, on the other hand, it is the process of socialisation of private producers. It is the latter which is important in the present context; it implies the conception of the social as interpersonal relations between producers. This may not be the conception of the social in other parts of *Capital*; but it is this particular conception which underlies the discussion of money in *Capital*. The argument is that, in a commodity-producing economy, relations between men—social relations in other words—appear as relations between things in the sense that relations between men take the form of the sale and purchase of commodities. The relations between commodities are in actual fact, according to the argument, relations between men in disguise. However, it is important that relations between things are recognised as relations between men or as social relations; the importance of the disguise consists in the fact that it is not total. The misrecognition of the nature and the significance of the process of circulation in turn raises the problem of recognition. It is here that money becomes important. Money is a sign in that it signifies the socialness of exchange; and it does so by functioning as the measure of value. 'It (money) is the measure of value inasmuch it is the socially recognised incarnation of human labour.' (*Capital*, vol. 1, p. 97) The point is that money *qua* socially recognised incarnation of human labour has no significance other than in the context where social relations are conceived as interpersonal relations and disguised as relations between things. Further, money *qua* measure of value has no relation to it in its capacity as the medium of circulation. The dual character attributed to money in *Capital*, i.e. the measure of value, on the one hand, and the medium of circulation, on the other, rests on the dual character attributed to the process of circulation in *Capital*, i.e. the process of socialisation and the process of the distribution of commodities. What one needs to discard is the conception of the social as interpersonal relations and with it the conception of the process of circulation as the agency for the socialisation of private producers. Once this is done the notion that money is the measure of value disappears automatically.

To reject the idea of money as a sign and thus money as the measure of value, it will be said, is to reject something which is original to Marx and lacking in the analysis of money by bourgeois economists. The dual character attributed to the process of circulation, it is true, is specific to Marx and it is that which forms the basis for the theory of fetishism—a theory which is not to be found in Ricardo and bourgeois economists. That may be so; but one cannot argue in favour of saving something just because it is specific to Marx on any grounds other than of dogmatism. The weaknesses of the theory of fetishism have been dealt with in great detail elsewhere; and it would be a diversion to repeat those arguments here. However, it is worth pointing out that the notion of money as a sign is not specific to Marx. That money is the sign or the representative of wealth forms the basis of the analysis of wealth in the seventeenth century. Not only that, the notion of the value of money as it is used in monetary theory, i.e. the volume of goods for which money can be exchanged, is based on the idea of money as sign. Money signifies commodities—the commodities which it signifies depend on the preferences of the individual in question—and that is the reason, or at least one of the reasons, why it is an object of demand. In contrast, for Marx money does not signify commodities as such but labour embodied in commodities. The point, very briefly, is that both in Marx and in monetary theory, despite the differences between them money is treated as a sign.

Once the notion of money as sign is rejected a whole series of problems connected with what money actually represents disappear too, and then the way is open for the analysis of the concrete conditions under which money exists, the form it takes, and the role it performs under particular conditions. The rejection, in particular, implies that one cannot read off the character of the social relations from the mere fact of the existence of money. An example of such a reading is provided by the widespread belief among Marxists that the existence of money is incompatible with socialism. This belief follows from the idea of money as the sign of the socialness of exchange. The argument as to why money will disappear under socialism is briefly as follows: the replacement of capitalism by socialism means that relations between men no longer appear as relations between things and as a consequence there is no need for a sign to help recognise that the latter is actually the former in disguise. This—it is true—is not the only way in which the argument can be put; the disappearance of money under socialism can be explained in terms of the disappearance of commodities, and thus the disappearance of money. There is not much difference between the two arguments; the former treats money and the latter commodities as the sign of social relations. The point is that the arguments against using money as a sign apply equally well to using commodities as signs. The aim here, however, is not to provide an analysis of the reasons for the existence of money under socialism; the argument here is directed against a particular type of argument which consists in assigning pregiven significances to entities like commodities, money, etc. What we have done so far is to argue that the discussion of the functions of money should be complemented by an analysis of the forms of money and differences between barter and monetary exchange and that the measure of value function of money should be discarded.

Chapter 2

The Status of Different Functions of Money

Qua medium of circulation, money is the substitute in exchange for all commodities and also for financial assets in the case where claims are bought and sold like commodities. Marx expresses this relation in the language of representation by calling money 'the metamorphosed form of commodities'; the terminology, however, is not important. Marx's analysis, as will become clearer later, is not completely enveloped by the theme of representation. Obviously, as all the textbooks on money tell us, money has many functions other than that of the medium of circulation. Apart from the two defining functions, namely, that of the measure of value and the medium of circulation, Marx attributes to money the function of the standard of price and the means of deferred payment (the means of payment in the terminology of Marx).

Leaving aside what these functions actually denote, the questions are why money performs functions other than those of the medium of circulation, and what is the status of those functions. Unless these questions are answered, the discussion of the functions of money cannot be anything more than a descriptive listing of those functions—an exercise which is of little theoretical consequence. The aims in this section are, first, to show what the relation between the different functions of money is and, second, to analyse the connection between the functions money performs and the conditions under which it exists.

Leaving aside the measure-of-value function which will not be discussed again, the three functions of money which Marx mentions, namely, those of the medium of circulation, the standard of prices, and the means of deferred payment, are not at par with each other. The first function is primary in the sense that it is the defining function of money, while the other two, it could be argued, are derivative or secondary functions in that they follow from the former. The hierarchical relationship between different functions of money does not imply that they are separable; i.e. the primary function can be separated as a function specific to money from the other, so to say, contingent functions. It is here that there is an important difference between Marx and monetary theorists. The latter, after listing the functions of money—their list differs in some important respects from that of Marx—classify them into what is specific to money and what is not. It is often pointed out that while money *qua* means of payment (medium of circulation in the terminology of Marx) is unique, money *qua* store of value, the standard of prices, or the unit of account, etc. is not—the latter in the sense that commodities, financial assets, and even imaginary entities can function as the store of value and the unit of account. The fact that different things perform either the same or similar functions is, as such, not of great interest. What needs to be explained is why money performs the functions which, as it is claimed, can as well be performed by non-money. Marx, on the other hand, is not interested in the classification of the functions; instead his discussion takes the form of explaining how and under what conditions money *qua* medium of circulation performs other functions. The argument in general terms is that it is the means-of-payment function which leads money to perform other functions.

We need to explain why money *qua* means of payment or the medium of circulation is necessarily the unit of account or the standard of prices. The exchange of commodities is, by definition, the exchange of equivalents. The notion of unequal exchange is a contradiction in terms; and it presupposes the existence of a standard which can be used to judge either the equity or the inequity of the terms on which exchange takes place. There exists no such general standard of evaluation. Equivalence in exchange implies that whatever a commodity is exchanged for is necessarily a measure of its price. This relation follows from the simple fact that the process of measurement is in actual fact always a process of establishing equivalences; and the latter is the same as indicating the possibility for substituting one thing for the other.

The conceptualisation of exchange suggested here is, one may note, very different from that in *Capital*. Marx treats the relation of exchange as the relation of identity and not as the relation of equivalence. This is clear in the following well-known passage from the opening chapter of *Capital*. 'Let us take two commodities, e.g. corn and iron. The proportion in which they are exchangeable . . . can always be represented by an equation in which a given quantity of corn is equated with some quantity of iron: e.g. 1 quarter corn = x cwt iron.' (*Capital*, vol. 1, p. 37) The point is that exchange of corn for iron does not imply that a particular quantum of the former is equal to a particular quantum of the latter; instead, it simply implies a relation of equivalence, i.e. 1 quarter of corn has the same price as x cwt of iron rather than, as Marx has it, 1 quarter of corn is the same as x cwt of iron. There is an important difference between the two: if the relation of exchange is interpreted in the first way then one cannot infer from the relation of exchange that 1 quarter of corn and 1 cwt of iron contain an equal quantity of something—that something is what Marx terms the socially necessary labour. Briefly, the point is that Marx interprets the relation of exchange as the relation of identity; and that interpretation is crucial for the way in which Marx deduces the concept of value, or the fact that labour is the substance of value, from the obvious fact that one commodity exchanges for another. Marx, in other words, treats the relationship of exchange as an ontological relationship, a relationship which can be used to infer the nature and the attributes of the commodities which form the terms of the relationship, e.g. they are products of labour, they are endowed with utility, etc. This point was discussed in detail in the previous volume. In fact, the relationship of exchange, one should insist in order to avoid false problems, does not imply anything other than what the relationship says, namely, that the two commodities in question are substituted in exchange for each other.

The interpretation of the relation of exchange as the relation of equivalence implies (which is crucial for the argument here) that measurement and the expression of prices of commodities are a necessary correlate of the exchange of commodities. In a monetary economy, the expression of prices in monetary units is thus a necessary correlate of the fact that in such an economy goods are not exchanged for goods but for money. Alternatively, money has to be the measure of prices or the unit of account in its capacity as the medium of circulation. Money as the measure of prices has no epistemological significance, while money as measure of value does have in the argument of *Capital*.

In an economy based on the production of commodities—a

The Status of Different Functions of Money 19

category which includes both capitalist and some non-capitalist economies—monetary units occupy a privileged position *qua* units of account, in the sense that calculations in such economies are for the most part based on the magnitudes which are determined in the process of circulation and thus necessarily expressed in monetary units. The fact that calculations can be carried out in non-monetary units does not imply that those units are interchangeable with monetary units. Here, it is necessary to distinguish between formal possibilities and the possibilities which are actually available under given conditions. The fact that calculations can be carried out, say, in terms of tons of wheat—or more exactly, the price of a ton of wheat—rather than monetary units does not indicate anything more than a formal possibility on the grounds that there are no natural units of measurement. But that formal possibility does not imply that calculations carried out in terms of non-monetary units have the same social validity and relevance as those carried out in monetary units. To bring out the pertinence of the point at issue here we take the case of the determination and expression of wages. In *Capital* wages are either expressed in terms of commodities necessary for the reproduction of labour or in terms of value: the value of labour-power. And wages, even when they are expressed in terms of monetary units, e.g. so many shillings per day, as they often are in *Capital,* actually refer to the value of labour-power; because the assumption in the first two volumes of *Capital* is that values are equal to prices. The procedure adopted in *Capital*, treating monetary magnitudes as if they are value magnitudes expressed in monetary units, has the effect of glossing over the important fact that payment for labour-power under capitalism is in the form of money and, what is important, that bargaining for wages is always bargaining for money wages and not for either the commodities necessary (however that necessity may be defined) for the reproduction of labour-power, or the value of labour-power, or the rate of exploitation. The contract between labourers and capitalist firms is always a contract in terms of money and that contract from the economic point of view is not the same as a contract drawn in terms of commodities. Marx, by assuming that wages are just sufficient to enable labourers to buy commodities necessary for their reproduction—an assumption which amounts to assuming that wages are fixed in terms of commodities and then paid out in terms of money—neglects what is in fact a central feature of the determination of wages in a capitalist economy, namely, that bargaining between a group of workers and the capitalist firm which employs them is by itself never sufficient to enable those workers to procure what is necessary for their reproduction. We leave aside the problem associated with the specification of the commodities necessary for the reproduction of labour-power. The reason—this is not just specific to Marx—for expressing wages in terms of commodities rather than money is that it is consumption in which one is interested and from that point of view it is the former rather than the latter which is relevant. The point is that the real wage (wage in terms of commodities) and the money wage do not have the same economic status in that their respective loci of determination are different. The latter is determined in the labour market while the former is determined both in the labour market and the market for commodities. In fact, the real wage is never determined directly as the result of bargaining between workers and capitalist firms.

There is a paradoxical aspect to calculations in terms of monetary units which is crucial. Under capitalism calculations are carried out and contracts drawn up in monetary units but the relevance of those calculations and contracts consists in what they imply either about consumption or production—activities which are based on the use of specific commodities rather than money. Money, by itself, is neither a means of consumption nor of production; but the possibilities of consumption or production open to economic agents in a monetary economy are determined by calculation carried out in monetary units. Calculations in terms of monetary units are characterised by a form of opaqueness in the sense that they have to be retranslated in terms of commodities— the list of commodities varying from one economic agent to another—to see what they imply about the possibilities of consumption or production. Marx calls money the metamorphosed form of commodities; the imagery is useful in conveying what is at issue here. Precisely because money is the metamorphosed form of all and not just a group of commodities it is not immediately apparent what the relationship between money and a group of commodities is. Economic agents buy and sell specific groups of commodities, and thus they are each interested in a restricted range of commodities only; but they carry out calculations in terms of something which is the metamorphosed form of *all* commodities. It is this discrepancy which makes monetary calculations opaque. The discrepancy's effects and implications are of particular importance in the times of inflation—which for present purposes means a change in the scale of measurement of commodities in monetary units—for in that case monetary magnitudes have to be constantly retranslated in terms of commodities in order to ascertain what the possibilities of consumption or production actually are. This discrepancy is inherent in a capitalist economy and economic agents have no option but to use money as the unit of account because money is the medium of circulation. Associated with this discrepancy is a whole set of measures and procedures for the 'correct' interpretation of the meaning of monetary calculations. The cost-of-living index, for example, is a formula for translating a selected group of commodities into a sum of money. Similarly, what is known as inflation accounting is a set of procedures for the 'correct' interpretation of the figures which monetary calculations yield. In both cases the implication is that monetary figures do not convey the specific information required by a group of economic agents, hence the need for specific measures like the cost-of-living index, the rate of profit adjusted for the rate of inflation, etc. The point is that these measures do not have any rationale for their existence but the discrepancy between the medium of calculation: money, and the things which are eventually of interest to economic agents: specific groups of commodities.

Before leaving the subject of the unit of account and the unit of measurement it is necessary to point out the wider implication of the way in which economic magnitudes are expressed in *Capital*. The analysis in the first two volumes, as indicated above, is based on the assumption that values are equal to prices. The problem is that the two magnitudes are not measured according to the same units; values are measured in terms of labour-time, prices in terms of money. This difference is, however, neglected in *Capital* on the grounds that money is the socially recognised incarnation of value and as a result values can only be expressed in terms of monetary units rather than in labour-time. This, by the way, is the reason why Marx is so hostile to the notion of 'labour money'. We have already pointed out the questionable theoretical basis on which the argument rests; what we want to do here is to point out some of the implications of the assumption. Both prices and values are expressed in terms of monetary units in *Capital*; but money *qua* measure of value does not have the same status as money *qua* measure of prices. Money in its former capacity, as explained earlier, has to be commodity money and it expresses something which is determined in the process of production, i.e. values, for reasons which are not economic but epistemological. Money in its latter capacity, in contrast, measures something which can never be determined independently of the process of circulation, i.e. prices; it does not have to take the form of commodity money and it expresses prices because it is the medium of circulation. And that expression has no epistemological importance. These differences are not, however, taken into account and money is treated as the measure of both value and prices simultaneously. The result is that values and value-based measures, e.g. the rate of exploitation, the organic composition of capital, etc., appear more relevant than they actually are to the analysis of capitalist economies. Further, the procedure masks the problems which arise in establishing the relationship between prices and values. At places in *Capital* Marx uses the observed data about money wages, the composition of costs, the price of commodities, etc. to deduce the rate of exploitation and the organic composition of capital. That deduction is invalid because the observed data is based on prices and there is no reason to suppose that values are equal to prices. But given Marx's habit of expressing values in monetary units (so many shillings), it is difficult to see what is actually involved in the deduction and what its status is.

Apart from being the measure of price, money is also the means of deferred payment—the means of payment in the terminology of Marx. The existence of money *qua* means of deferred payment is tied to the existence of credit; and the credit which Marx considers is of a particular form, namely, trade credit. Trade credit implies that money flows are separated in time from commodity flows; more specifically, the latter precede the former. This temporal separation for Marx represents a change in the status of money from the medium of circulation to the means of deferred payment. The point is that the temporal separation is a result of an economic relationship which is distinct from the sale and purchase of commodities, namely, credit. However, trade credit is not a good example to take to illustrate the distinctive nature of the two relationships, because it represents a special case of credit whereby lending and borrowing is tethered to the sale and purchase of commodities. And the validity of Marx's argument is not restricted to trade credit.

Credit, in purely formal terms, is the payment and the repayment

The Status of Different Functions of Money   23

of money separated in time. Time is central to the relations of credit and it is this which distinguishes them from other economic relations. The important point is that money is both the medium of circulation of commodities and, so to say, the medium in which lending and borrowing is conducted. And the reason for this identity is that the relations of credit are ultimately tethered to the sale and purchase of commodities. The argument, in general terms, is that money *qua* medium of circulation more or less automatically assumes the functions arising out of the activities related to the circulation of commodities. An alternative and a useful way of expressing the fact that money is both the medium of circulation and the means of deferred payment is that money circulates among economic agents in two different capacities. We can, then, distinguish between the two circuits, distinct but related, which money traverses, namely, the financial circuit (that associated with lending and borrowing), and what we may term the commodities circuit. This alternative formulation enables us to point out that the fact that money performs a number of different functions simultaneously is not just of formal significance, but has an economic significance. The two circuits mentioned earlier are necessarily related and the nature of the interrelations between them is of importance in understanding particular economic phenomena in monetary economies. For Marx there is a two-way, not a one-way, relationship between the two circuits. First, the rate of circulation of commodities and thus the circulation of money *qua* medium of circulation depends on the volume of credit which is extended. Second, the volume of credit which is extended itself depends on the rate of circulation of commodities for the reason that financial circulation is constituted of the extension of new credit, on the one hand, and the repayment of loans granted earlier, on the other. The latter depends on the rate of circulation of commodities and the former on the rate at which previously granted loans are repaid. In short, the argument is that expansion of credit fuels its own further expansion. It is this relationship which Marx and others have used to explain how an expansion of credit can first lead to a boom and then eventually to a recession. The argument, in simple terms, is that the expansion of credit leads to an acceleration in the rate of circulation of commodities and thus an increase in the rate of production of commodities, which in turn leads to a further increase in the rate of circulation and thus a further expansion of credit. The process comes to an end sooner or later because the supply of commodities overtakes the demand for them as a result of increase in production. This results in a reduction in the rate of production and consequently the circulation of commodities which in turn leads to a reduction in the volume of credit and so on. The process sketched here depends on the two-way relationship between credit and the circulation of commodities; and the argument is centred around the following corollary of the relationship, namely, the volume of credit which a given rate of circulation of commodities gives rise to is not, except in rare cases, equal to the volume of credit required to sustain that rate of circulation. Marx uses the same dual relationship to explain what seems paradoxical at first sight, namely, interest rates are low and the availability of credit easy during boom periods when the demand for loans is high; and, conversely, interest rates are high and credit difficult to come by during the periods of depression when the demand for credit is low. The explanation rests on the argument that the factors which lead the demand for credit to increase (increase in the demand for commodities) at the same time also leads the supply of credit to increase even further. The aim here, however, is not to assess and discuss the dual relationship and its effect, but instead to point out that associated with the different functions money performs is the problem of establishing the relationship between the circulation of money *qua* medium of circulation and that *qua* means of deferred payment.

Besides this, there is an important link between money *qua* means of deferred payment and the form of money, credit money in particular. Briefly, money takes the form of credit money when payment from one economic agent to another takes the form of the transfer of deposit in a financial institution, and those deposits are created by financial institutions themselves. There is a two-way link between credit money and lending and borrowing, i.e. the circulation of money *qua* means of deferred payment. On the one hand, the development of credit money presupposes a network of credit wide enough to envelop all categories of economic agents. The reason is that deposits are a particular effect of lending and borrowing, and payment among economic agents can take the form of the transfer of deposits, as is the case when money takes the form of credit money, only if all or a large majority of economic agents hold deposits in financial institutions and are, therefore, part of the network of credit. On the other hand, though the practice of lending and borrowing is not dependent on money taking the form of credit money, its volume and the power of financial institutions, as will be shown later in detail, do depend on this. Briefly the reason is that in the case where money is credit money financial institutions lend what they themselves create; and thus any limitation on their power to create credit or deposits must have its basis either in the criteria they use to assess creditworthiness of economic agents or in the requirement that liabilities of financial institutions should be settled in a particular medium. The point, in general terms, is that the limitation is due to the way in which financial institutions are organised and their functioning regulated. On the contrary, when money does not take the form of credit money but, say, takes the form of commodity money, financial institutions lend what they themselves do not create; and thus the amount of the money commodity in existence, gold, etc, in that case imposes an external limit on the power of financial institutions to create credit. The difference between the two cases consists in the nature of the limit on the power to create credit. Besides this, the development of credit money implies the disappearance of separation between the circulation of money *qua* medium of circulation and that *qua* means of deferred payment; because, in that case, every payment is overlaid with credit relations in that it takes the form of the transfer of deposits in financial institutions—things which are products of credit relations. The development of credit money, in effect, means a generalisation of credit relations; this, in particular, implies that money cannot be a medium of circulation without at the same time being the means of deferred payment.

The development and the extension of credit in capitalist countries has been associated with the development of the market in financial assets—the market in financial liabilities and claims arising out of the operation of lending and borrowing. Marketable financial assets are of particular importance in the analysis of the functions of money because they are similar to money in some important respects. One of the features which distinguishes money from commodities, especially in the case where money is not commodity money, is that the latter is an object of use either in consumption or production but the former is not. There are two points which are important here: first, money *qua* medium of circulation is a substitute in exchange for commodities and also for financial assets and, second, like money financial assets are not objects of use. The latter implies that financial assets are sold and purchased just by reference to the financial return they yield; so, in effect, trading in financial assets is synonymous with speculation. Though speculation is not specific to financial assets, it is, in most cases, of secondary importance in trading in commodities. Trading in financial assets, on the other hand, implies that the holding of money balances is always an alternative to holding of financial assets. In other words, a substitute is always an alternative. What the two points together imply is that, given the existence of the market in financial assets, money itself assumes some of the characteristics of a financial asset in the sense that calculations concerning the holding of money become part of calculations which concern the holding of financial assets. Further, money when it takes the form of credit money is necessarily a financial asset, because then it is nothing more than an acknowledgment of a credit transaction between a financial institution and an economic agent. The theoretical discovery that money is not only a means of payment but also a financial asset is attributed to Keynes. But this discovery, as the discussion here points out, is nothing more than a reiteration of the fact that in an economy with an extensive network of credit, money buys not only commodities but also financial assets, and thus that magnitudes relating to both commodities and financial assets are measured in monetary units.

It is necessary now to map out the relevance and the limits of the discussion of different functions and, so to say, *personae* of money. In the argument here the medium-of-circulation function plays a dual role: it is what defines money and it is what explains why money performs functions other than this defining one. However, it is necessary to point out that the functions and the status of money cannot be determined by means of a purely formal discussion. The actual functions which money performs are determined by the conditions under which money functions as the medium of circulation. Money, for example, can only appear as a financial asset or take the form of credit money when the network of credit is extensive and envelops a wide variety of economic agents; but neither the development nor the extension of the network of credit can be deduced from the fact that money is the medium of circulation. The discussion here takes for granted a financially developed capitalist economy, because it is the analysis of the role of credit and money in which we are interested. However, the discussion of the functions of money here is by way of a clearance operation; it does nothing more than to point out and indicate how to avoid the false problems which arise in the analysis of money. The main argument in this and the previous section can be summarised in the form of the following three propositions:

1 the functions which money performs are not a random or accidental collection, on the contrary, they form an interrelated and structured combination;

2 the functions which money performs are associated with definite economic effects; as a consequence the analysis of functions must be coupled with the analysis of particular economic effects; and

3 neither the role nor the functions of money can be discussed in isolation from the characteristics of the economy in which money functions as such.

Chapter 3

Forms of Money

It was argued earlier that since the status of money *qua* medium of circulation is not affected whether it takes the form of commodity money, fiduciary money, or credit money, etc., the form of money cannot be determined or explained by reference to the function it performs in the process of circulation of commodities. Further, though the form of money does not affect the medium-of-circulation function, it does affect the power of financial institutions to create credit. The implication is that the form of money is not devoid of economic significance. Here the main aims, in general terms, are, first, to formulate criteria for distinguishing between different forms of money and, second, to indicate the pertinence and the economic significance of different forms of money.

The grounds on which one can distinguish one form of money from another are not systematically discussed and spelt out in the literature. The distinction, when it is made, is usually based on the physical form which money takes; it is on this basis that gold-and-silver money, or commodity money, is distinguished from paper money. The physical attributes of money may have a heuristic value, but they are as such not of great economic significance. What they indicate—if they do indicate anything—is that different forms of money may have different costs of production depending on the material of which they are made. But they are of no use in the case where money does not take any tangible form; credit money, for example, does not have any tangible form, it is simply an entry in the ledgers of a financial institution or a bank.

Marx and following him Hilferding do refer to and discuss different forms of money, but they do not indicate the criteria for

Forms of Money 29

distinguishing between different forms of money. At places Marx seems to establish a kind of correspondence between the forms and the functions of money. To quote once again a passage which was quoted earlier:

> But we may affirm this much, that just as true [presumably inconvertible or fiduciary money] paper money takes its rise in the function of money as the circulating medium, so money based upon credit takes its root spontaneously in the functions of money as the means of payment [the means of deferred payment in the terminology employed here]. (*Capital*, vol. 1, p. 127)

To this passage one may for completeness add that commodity money is grounded in the measure-of-value function of money. The argument, to put it in general terms, is that to each function there corresponds a particular form of money suited to it, and as a result money takes different forms as it assumes different functions. Convincing though the argument may seem, the forms of money cannot be deduced from the functions of money without a surreptitious reliance on some sort of mythical choice among the forms of money. To explain: paper money, according to the argument, arises out of the medium-of-circulation function of money; but the status of 'arising out of' is not clear. Commodity money can function as the medium of circulation just as well as paper money; so it cannot be argued that the function itself indicates that money takes the latter rather than the former form. It can, however, be argued that paper money arises out of the medium-of-circulation function in the sense that, though both paper and commodity money can perform the same function, the former is cheaper to produce than the latter; as a result, the former is preferable to the latter. The argument may seem far-fetched but this is, more or less, how Hilferding accounts for the substitution of paper money for commodity money. The argument after the amendment, it may be noted, is no longer based on the suitability of paper money *qua* medium of circulation but on economy in the cost of producing money or performing the function in question. The argument may account for paper money but it cannot explain why commodity money ever existed *qua* medium of circulation except in terms of the ignorance and irrationality of men. Further, the choice to which the argument refers is mythical, for there exists nobody who can make that kind of choice because particular forms of money presuppose particular conditions of existence, and their economic significance, as will become clear during the course of argument in this section, extends well beyond the cost of production of money. The argument is tested here by reference to paper money; it becomes even more untenable when applied to credit money.

It is not to the functions of money that one should turn to find a basis for distinguishing between different forms of money, but to the process by which money is created, or, better, the stock of money altered. In general, the creation of money involves two distinct operations, namely, the manufacture of money in the case where it takes a tangible form and the way in which newly created money is put into circulation. It is the former with which we are for the most part concerned and we leave aside the latter for discussion later.

Money, for example, takes the form of commodity money when the creation of money entails the production of a particular commodity, i.e. money commodity (e.g. gold and silver); and there is a one-to-one correspondence between the quantity of money, measured in terms of monetary units, and the quantity of money commodity, measured in physical units. The main distinguishing feature of commodity money, e.g., money based on gold, is that its quantity is restricted by the amount of money commodity in existence, and the process of its manufacture is the same as the process of production of commodities. The definition of commodity money given here covers a number of cases. It obviously covers the case where there is no difference between the amount of commodity money, say, a coin of a given denomination can buy, and the amount of money commodity it contains; but it also covers the case where the two differ—in particular, where the value of money in terms of money commodity exceeds the bullion value of the coin. The reason is that the divergence between the two does not affect the principle which governs the creation of money. The divergence is, however, not devoid of economic significance; it implies that the creation of money is a monopoly of a particular institution and that institution appropriates a part of the social product by virtue of its power to create money. Historically, the monopoly of the creation of money has rested with the state, and seigniorage and debasement have been the ways in which the state has appropriated a part of the social product—they are, that is, a particular form of taxation. The divergence between the value of money and its bullion value has, in other words, been coupled with money's being legal tender. Commodity money, say gold money, need not take the form of coins; it can as well take the form of paper money. A paper money based on gold, as Hilferding points out, is commodity money and not paper money or fiduciary money. What makes the paper money, in that case, commodity money is that its creation is limited by the quantity of gold in existence. What this case points out is that the identification of the forms of money on the basis of the substance of which money is constituted can lead to a spurious distinction between the form of money. According to the argument here, for example, gold coins and paper money, despite their physical differences, may well represent the same form of money.

It is, however, necessary to qualify the argument here. Just the fact that paper money is convertible on demand into a money commodity, say gold, is not sufficient to characterise the paper money as a form of commodity money. The gold standard provides a relevant example. When capitalist countries were on the gold standard, money usually took the form of paper money and that paper money was convertible into gold at a fixed rate—the conditions governing the convertibility varied from one country to another. But that convertibility, though a constraint on the creation of paper money, did not imply a one-to-one correspondence between the stock of paper money and the quantity of gold in the country in question. For the effectivity of the convertibility varied from one economy to another and its relevance depended on the category of transaction. The convertibility of paper money into gold was of no great importance so far as domestic transactions were concerned because then the paper money itself rather than gold was the legal tender and the customary medium of circulation. None the less, the convertibility was necessary in the context of international transactions because then it was gold rather than paper money which was the medium of circulation. The implication is that the constraint which the convertibility imposed on the creation of paper money crucially depended on whether or not international accounts were in balance. Strictly speaking, money under the gold standard was neither commodity money, nor fiduciary or paper money, but a combination of both. As we will point out later, it represented a system of creation of money which was heavily dependent on the international flow of capital.

In contrast to commodity money, fiduciary money, or what Marx calls true paper money, is not tied to any particular commodity. More specifically, the creation of fiduciary money is not constrained by the quantity of any particular commodity. The fact that fiduciary money takes the physical form of paper money is of no economic significance because there is no specific relation between the denomination of the currency note and the size of the paper of which it consists. Moreover, fiduciary money need not take the form of paper money; it can as well take the form of coins so long as there is no systematic connection between the denomination of the coin and, so to say, the bullion or the metal value of the coin. These points by themselves are not important, but their implication is. The implication is that the process of creation of fiduciary money is completely separated from the process of production of commodities; as a result, it is not constrained by the availability of labour or means of production as is the case when commodity money is created. Commodity money, when it is based on a rare metal, e.g. gold and silver, is further subject to either an absolute limit on its quantity or a limit on the rate at which it can be created. These constraints implied by the availability of money commodity may be temporarily removed by altering the relation between the quantity of money commodity and monetary denomination, that is, by a debasement of commodity money. But the important point is that the constraint is not removable for ever because the constraint ultimately rests on the nature of money as commodity money.

An illustration of this constraint is provided by the problems arising out of the use of gold as one of the means of payment in international transactions. The quantity of new gold which comes on the market is limited by the rate at which it is mined. And the rate of production of gold is predominantly determined by geological conditions: the richness of the mine, the depth at which gold is found, etc.; it is, in other words, not geared to the rate at which international trade increases. What has been the case is that the rate of production of gold has not kept pace with the increase in international trade which has taken place since the Second World War. The problem it gives rise to is that if gold is to be either the sole (which it has not been since the war) or the main means of payment in international transactions then its quantity is not sufficient to sustain the existing volume of international transactions. A solution to this problem in the form of debasement of national currencies—alternatively, a rise in the price of gold in terms of national currencies—was proposed by those who wanted international payments to be completely based on gold. The problem is that this solution cannot be anything more than temporary because the initial problem was caused by the production of gold not keeping pace with the increase in international trade, a problem which cannot be eliminated by the debasement of national currencies. The dilemma posed by the use of gold as the means of international payment is as follows: a once-for-all debasement does nothing more than to postpone the problem of the shortage of international means of payment, and a continual debasement, on the other hand, effectively means a subversion of the sought-for gold standard. The main point is that the creation of commodity money, given the relation between it and the money commodity, is autonomous of the rate of circulation of commodities and thus the use of commodity money *qua* medium of circulation; and it is this autonomy which is responsible for the problem associated with the use of commodity money.

The creation of fiduciary money, on the other hand, is not subject to any such constraint; more specifically, it is not constrained by conditions governing the production of any particular commodity. There is, thus, in general terms, no constraint either on the quantity or the rate of growth of fiduciary money. The result of the lack of constraint is that there can never be a general problem of the shortage of fiduciary money, as can be the case when money takes the form of commodity money. This is, however, not to suggest that there are no restrictions of any kind on the creation of fiduciary money. Indeed there is such a restriction and, moreover, it is necessary if fiduciary money is to be acceptable as the means of payment. Rarity is a condition of existence of all forms of money, a thing cannot be money unless it is scarce. The pertinence of this remark will become clear when we come to discuss the distributive implications of the creation of money. Rarity, in the case of commodity money, is ensured by the conditions which govern and constrain the production of the money commodity. The limitation on the issue of fiduciary money is generally secured by legal means. The issue of fiduciary money has, for the most part, been a legally protected monopoly of a public institution or the central bank; and the obverse of the legal monopoly of issue is the legally enforced circulation of fiduciary money *qua* legal tender. In the case where fiduciary money is issued by the central bank, the restrictions on the issue of fiduciary money arise out of the rules and regulations which govern the functioning of the central bank. Given the differences in the way in which central banks are organised and regulated, one cannot lay down general rules which govern the issue of fiduciary money. There is, however, a feature common to central banks in advanced capitalist countries which is relevant here. Central banks in advanced capitalist countries, though public institutions, are not treated as a department of government; they are autonomous of day-to-day changes in the policies of governments. The significance of this autonomy consists in the fact that the functioning of central banks and thus the issue of the legal tender is not under immediate political control. Central banks are run as financial institutions in the sense that they observe established financial criteria when they issue fiduciary money and they jealously guard their autonomy in the name of sound finance. So that the issue of fiduciary money in advanced capitalist countries is subject to the rules and regulations which govern the functioning of financial institutions. In some countries, e.g. some countries of the third world, central banks do not have the same institutional autonomy as they do in advanced capitalist countries. The result is that restrictions on the issue of fiduciary money in the former are not the same and in many cases are a lot less strict than those in the latter. Even if there are no financial controls on it the issue of fiduciary money is still subject to restrictions arising out of the fact that it has economic effects which may not be acceptable, e.g. inflation, the balance-of-payment problem, etc. An extreme case of this is provided by the German inflation of the 1920s which arose out of the massive creation of fiduciary money by the government.

The discussion of restrictions on the issue of fiduciary money more or less immediately brings in juridico-political relations, while the same in the case of commodity money does not. What we want to do is briefly to consider the juridico-political aspects of the two forms of money. The legal tender need not take any particular form; it can be either commodity money or fiduciary money or credit money. However, the exercise of political power which makes money legal tender does not have the same significance in each case. In the case where money is commodity money, the legal backing of the money means the certification of its value in terms of money commodity. This certification—which amounts to laying down a relationship of representation between the denomination of money and a given weight of money commodity—may or may not be coupled with a redistributive relation whereby the state appropriates a part of the proceeds in the form of seigniorage. The important point is that commodity money need not be legal tender at all; the implication is that it can exist and circulate without any political and legal backing. Gold, for example, circulates as a means of payment in international transactions without being legal tender or having any specific political backing. A legally enforced circulation of commodity money is, however, necessary when the value of the coin exceeds its bullion value; otherwise the divergence between the two cannot be maintained. There is, on the other hand, no problem of the ascertainment of the value of fiduciary money; fiduciary money does not refer to anything beyond itself. Political and legal backing is much more central to fiduciary money than it is to commodity money. It is, to be more specific, necessary to secure the conditions required for the existence of fiduciary money, namely, to ensure that it is accepted as the means of payment within an area and to ensure its rarity through the legal control on its issue. On the other hand, the acceptance of commodity money as the means of payment does not depend on the fact that it is legal tender; instead it depends on the fact that it represents the money commodity. And, as pointed out above, the rarity of commodity money is ensured by the conditions of its production rather than by legal control on its issue. The importance of political and legal backing to its existence is shown by the fact that fiduciary money is always identified with a particular geographical area or a particular nation-state. Fiduciary money is, at least in the first instance, national money in the sense that the limits of its general acceptibility as the medium of circulation are determined by the domain of exercise of the political power on which the fiduciary money is based. This need not be the case with commodity money; for example, money based on gold was in the first instance an international rather than a national money. The main point, in general terms, is that change in the form of money from commodity money, in particular gold money, to fiduciary money involves a change in the pertinence of juridico-political relations to the issue and the circulation of money. This change is of special importance in the analysis of the rise of national monetary systems and the effects associated with them. Before we discuss the constitution and the implication of national monetary systems it is necessary to indicate the features of credit money.

As we said earlier, money takes the form of credit money when payments associated with the sale and purchase of commodities or lending or borrowing take the form of transfer of financial deposits. To start with, the distinguishing feature of credit money is that it does not take any tangible form. A deposit, which is identified with credit money here, is nothing more than an entry in a ledger. Credit money is similar to fiduciary money in that there is no general restriction either on its quantity or the rate of growth. Deposits are products of lending and borrowing operations; as a result, restrictions on the issue of credit money are, in effect, the same as those on lending and borrowing. The latter may either consist of statutory limits on lending by financial institutions or they arise from the way in which financial institutions are organised and are related to each other. It is the financial institutions which are of primary importance in the sense that not only are they important in their own right but they also determine, at least in a general way, the form taken by statutory controls.

One important difference between fiduciary legal tender and credit money is that while the former is unique and universally accepted as the medium of payment in a country this is not necessarily true of the latter. To elaborate and to point to the implications of this difference: in capitalist countries the issue of fiduciary money is the monopoly of the central bank, while lending and borrowing and thus the creation of deposits are not a monopoly of any financial institution, the central bank or otherwise. The correlate of a number of financial institutions accepting and creating deposits is the multiplicity of credit money. The importance of the multiplicity consists in the fact that deposits of none of the financial institutions—except that of the central bank because of its statutory position—are universally accepted in payment for financial liabilities arising out of the sale and purchase of commodities and lending and borrowing. Strictly speaking, a deposit in a financial institution or a bank is only a medium of payment among economic agents who hold accounts in that financial institution. Alternatively, the deposit of a financial institution is transferable only within its own boundaries. However, economic agents who hold deposits in a bank are not restricted to using their deposit to make payments only to those economic agents who hold deposits in that bank; they are free to use their deposits as if they are universally accepted as the means of payment. This is only possible if the bank is able to convert its deposits into something which is universally acceptable as the medium of payment, e.g. deposit in the central bank. This requirement on banks is, in effect, a restriction on their power to create credit because they do not manufacture what is generally acceptable as the means of payment. The necessity of conversion of deposits into something which is universally—i.e. within national boundaries—acceptable as the medium of payment rests on the fact that there is not one but a number of financial institutions. The implication is that the limit on the power of financial institution to create deposits or credit money is rooted in what may seem an insignificant fact, namely, that no financial institution has a monopoly of lending and borrowing. The statutory control of the creation of credit rests on the fact that it is only the deposits of the central bank which are universally accepted as the means of payment, and financial institutions need to keep deposits in the central bank if their own deposits are to be used by economic agents as if they are universally acceptable in payment for financial liabilities. The control of the creation of credit by the central bank, for the most part, consists in influencing the quantity of what financial institution and banks keep, e.g. deposits in the central bank, financial assets of one kind or the other, to ensure the convertibility of their deposits.

In the argument above, it is indirectly implied that the existence of legal tender is necessary for credit money to exist. Legal tender, when it coexists with credit money, need not take the form of currency notes; it can as well take the form of deposits in the central bank, i.e. the institution which has the monopoly of the issue of the legal tender. The important point about legal tender in advanced capitalist countries is that, though it is universally acceptable within the national boundaries, it is for the most part not used in transactions. Most of the payments in those countries take the form of the transfer of deposits in private financial institutions; in other words, the universally acceptable means of payment is in fact not universally used. The legal tender is used for specific categories of transactions, some of which are important while others are not. So far as Britain is concerned the legal tender—currency notes and coins and deposits in the Bank of England—is used for the following three categories of transactions, namely, retail or small transactions, transactions among banks, and transactions between private economic agents and public state apparatuses. The first is not important, and the second and the third can be subsumed under the same category, because, for the most part, transactions between private economic agents and public state apparatuses are through the intermediary of financial institutions.

The importance of transactions between financial institutions can be seen from the fact that payments among economic agents in a financially developed economy are more or less always through the intermediary of financial institutions in the sense that they take the form of the transfer of deposits. Thus, correlated with transactions among economic agents other than financial institutions—households, firms, etc.—is a network of transactions among financial institutions in which those economic agents maintain accounts or keep deposits. The two, so to say, form a dual. To every transaction between economic agents who keep their deposits in different financial institutions there corresponds a correlated transaction between the two financial institutions in question. A deposit is, as pointed out earlier, nothing more than an entry in a ledger, and the transfer of deposit the subtraction of a number from one account and its addition to another. Entries and numbers are freely transferable within a financial institution in that their transfer is not contingent on any financial transaction. However, deposits or entries cannot be transferred from one financial institution to another without a financial transaction. A deposit, or better a transferable deposit, is essentially a power to make payments and the exercise of that power by the possessor of the deposit can impose a financial liability on the financial institution. This broadly speaking is the reason why a financial institution will not credit an account unless it receives something in return. That something need not be anything tangible; in fact, it is not because it takes the form of a deposit either in the central bank or in some other financial institution.

The financial structure in advanced capitalist countries is essentially a hierarchical and interlocking system of accounts and entries. To take the example of the British financial system for illustration: clearing banks—the banks whose deposits are predominantly used as the means of payment within the British economy—can for present purposes be regarded as a set of separate accounts at the Bank of England; and each of these accounts is, in turn, composed of the accounts of private economic agents and financial institutions which do not maintain accounts at the Bank of England. The Bank of England, so to say, is the account of accounts. All transactions between the Bank of England accounts and between them and the Bank are conducted in terms of the Bank of England's deposits or the legal tender. Private economic agents are grouped under particular clearing bank accounts in the Bank of England and transactions between them are, in effect, also financial transaction between their respective banks. The privileged position of the Bank of England deposit is due the fact that the Bank has the monopoly possession of the deposits of public state apparatuses, the foreign exchange reserves of the country, and is also the seller of government securities. What this means is that all transactions between private economic agents and public state apparatuses, international transactions, and the purchase of newly issued government securities eventually involves transaction between financial institutions and the Bank of England, and that these transactions are conducted in terms of the Bank of England's deposits. Practices and the organisation of financial institutions are not the same in all capitalist countries; but despite these differences the privileged position of the legal tender as the means of payment ultimately rests on the requirement, either legal or customary, that certain categories of transactions can only be conducted in terms of the legal tender. The legal tender has two aspects to it, namely, it combines together a group of financial institutions into a monetary system by functioning as the medium of financial settlement among them, and its exclusive use as the medium of payment in certain transactions provides the basis for the functioning of monetary policy—the control by the central bank of the creation of credit by private financial institutions.

Credit money is, thus, based on the multiplicity of financial institutions whose deposits are partial means of payment and which are bound together into a national monetary system by a central bank. The limit on the power of financial institutions to create credit essentially arises from the fact that their deposits are not universally accepted as the medium of payment. The implication, obviously, is that there is no limit on the power to create credit of a financial institution which has the monopoly of all lending and borrowing or alternatively has the monopoly possession of all deposits. The lack of the monopoly of deposits is maintained by a form of division of labour between the central bank and other financial institutions. Though the deposits of central banks are universally acceptable as the medium of payment in their respective countries, they do not exercise their power to create credit to the full because they restrict themselves to keeping only a limited range of deposits, e.g. those from financial institutions and public state apparatuses. Central banks restrict themselves to a supervisory role and to complementing the functioning of other financial institutions; but in order to retain this position they have to have monopoly possession of a certain category of deposits and the right to undertake certain categories of transactions.

The national monetary system in the sense taken here has not always existed, in the sense that a central bank with a supervisory role and with a power to lay down the functioning of financial institutions has not always existed. Two factors have played a crucial role in the rise of the central bank and managed monetary system in advanced capitalist countries, namely, the instability of the banking system which accompanied the development and extension of credit in capitalist countries, on the one hand, and extension in the scale of activities and expenditure undertaken by public state apparatuses, on the other. The former because it ultimately led to the regulation of the functioning of financial institutions by means of laws, and the latter because the control of the monetary system by the central bank and public state apparatuses, for the most part, rests on the importance of government securities among financial assets. The control, in other words, rests in large part on the leverage of public state apparatuses in their capacity as debtor to financial institutions.

The extension in the volume of public expenditure which has taken place in capitalist countries has a double significance in the present context. First, it has meant an increase in the relative importance of transactions between private economic agents and public state apparatuses and hence an increase in the significance of the requirement that such transactions should be conducted in terms of the legal tender. Second, the increase in public expenditure has been accompanied with an increase in borrowing by public state apparatuses. For example, the British public debt was negligible before the First World War and it increased to enormous proportions during the war and after it as a result of a massive increase in government expenditure, a large part of which was financed out of borrowing. So the managed monetary system as it exists in capitalist countries today did not emerge because politicians and public at large, enlightened by Keynesian arguments, decided one day that the problem of unemployment is endemic to capitalism and, thus, it is necessary to manage the creation of credit and have what is called today a monetary policy in order to influence the level of employment. Unemployment did not emerge as a problem for public policy because economic theorists finally discovered the true causes of unemployment under capitalism. The argument here is that the rise of the managed monetary system and the possibility of conducting a monetary policy was premised on specific factors like the increase in government expenditure and the resultant increase in the holding of financial securities in the hands of financial institutions. The British government did not start selling securities because it wanted to conduct a monetary policy by buying and selling securities; instead, it had to have such a policy because it was earlier forced to sell securities in order to finance its expenditure. What this means is that the intervention of the government in the monetary system is conditioned by the fact that public state apparatuses are debtors to financial institutions and they are subject to financial constraints. The emergence of the managed monetary system in advanced capitalist countries is a result of a number of different factors and it cannot be analysed in terms of discretionary choices by a government assumed to be above the economy and unencumbered by financial constraints.

The discussion of a national monetary system based on fiduciary money, or organised around a central bank empowered to issue the legal tender, immediately raises the problem of relations between national monetary systems. The domain of the mandatory acceptance of the legal tender does not extend beyond the relevant national boundaries. A legal tender may be accepted beyond its boundaries; but its status then is different. Within its legal boundaries a legal tender has no substitutes; but outside those boundaries it has no such privilege and it can be substituted by other currencies. The problem of the relation between national monetary systems, though not peculiar to fiduciary money, is central to it. Given its legal condition of existence, fiduciary money is in the first instance national money. This need not be so with commodity money; for example, gold was and still is an internationally accepted money commodity. The same was true for silver until it stopped serving as a money commodity. In fact, the rise of international monetary problems in the sense of the problem of conversion of one national money into another is a problem connected with the rise of national fiduciary money.

The problem of the relation between national monetary systems arises because the domain of the division of labour which is international extends beyond the domain of the national monetary system. Within a national economy there is no general problem concerning what is to serve as the means of payment. Deposits of banks may only be partial means of payment; but within the national economy in question they can be used as if they are universally accepted because they can be converted into the legal tender. But in international transactions there is a problem as to what is to serve as the means of payment. We go on now to explain how this problem arises in the case where international payments are made through the intermediary of financial institutions. Earlier, we pointed out that banks or financial institutions whose deposits are used as the means of payment can be treated as a set of accounts in the central bank and that payment from one economic agent to another is in effect a financial transaction between the financial institutions in which they maintain their accounts. And, transactions between those financial institutions are settled by means of the deposits of the central bank, hence the reason for treating them as accounts in the central bank. Thus, all national transactions can be treated from the financial point of view as transactions between accounts in the central bank. By the same reasoning international transactions between economic agents are from the financial point of view transactions between accounts not in the same but in different national central banks; and, thus, in effect, all international transactions are in the last resort transactions between different central banks. The problem of the relation between national monetary systems is, therefore, a problem of what is to serve as the means of settling the mutual claims of national central banks. The implication is that the problem does not concern what economic agents want to accept and what they do not, and the problem is not in an immediate sense political. Political factors do matter but only in so far as they affect the financial relations between central banks.

Central banks are not at par with ordinary banks in the sense that they are not part of a monetary mechanism as banks and financial institutions in a national economy are. There is no counterpart of the legal tender in international transactions; as a result, international means of payment are not given once and for all and they are liable to change. This is a corollary of the coexistence of autonomous and semi-autonomous national economies with each other. The means of payment which are accepted internationally are accepted as a result of the mutual agreement and economic interests of the central banks involved. Gold, for example, is accepted as an international means of payment not because central bankers are enamoured of gold but because at least some of them have a vested interest in retaining gold as the medium of payment. The source of the vested interest is either a gold hoard in the vaults of the central bank or a gold mine within the national boundaries. National fiduciary money, when it is accepted as an international means of payment, is accepted because of the economic importance of the economy in question. The dollar is a case in point. The central bank whose deposits circulate as an international means of payment is, in some respects, in the same relationship to other central banks as those central banks are to the banks under their respective domains. The relevant consideration in drawing this parallel is that a central bank never faces the problem of the lack or the shortage of the means of payment to settle the financial claims of its member banks against itself; because it itself creates the means for settling those financial claims. Most central banks are, however, subject to a financial constraint when it comes to settling the claims of other central banks, because each of them by itself does not produce the means for settling mutual claims of central banks against each other. The nature of the constraint depends on whether gold or some national or international fiduciary money is used. The total quantity of gold and the possibilities of changes in it, as pointed out earlier, depend not on economic but on geographical and geological conditions. Given the fact that the additions of newly mined gold to the stock of existing gold are small, it follows that a central bank can acquire a sizeable hoard of gold only at the expense of other central banks. The implication is that an effort by all central banks to ease the financial constraint they face by acquiring more gold cannot succeed. On the other hand, all central banks can simultaneously increase their reserves of international means of payment when it consists of fiduciary money. In the case of fiduciary money, though each central bank faces the financial constraint imposed by the fact that it does not manufacture the means for the settlement of financial claims, central banks taken together do not face any financial constraints because they can then create international means of payment. The financial constraints mentioned here do not apply to the central bank whose deposits or notes circulate as an international means of payment. However, this freedom from the financial constraint is only partial because the international use of a national money is neither universal nor guaranteed. The argument, in general terms, is that the consequence of international economic relations is a restriction on the national monetary system.

Both the effectivity and the exact consequence of the restriction depend on the nature of international economic relations and the status of those relations within the national economy in question. We examine these issues by reference to the policy of free trade under the gold standard and to the post-Second World War trading and monetary arrangements among advanced capitalist countries.

The principle of free trade is a negative rather than a positive principle; in isolation it does nothing more than to rule out the trade policies which discriminate among commodities according to the place of their production. The exact economic significance of a free trade policy depends on the specific conditions under which that policy is followed. What is relevant for the argument here is that the free trade policy as it existed in Britain was coupled with the gold standard. Though there is no necessary connection between them—the former concerns transactions in commodities and the latter money—their respective significance depends on the fact that together they in large part determined the relationship of the British economy to the rest of the world. The gold standard, purely in formal terms, was nothing more than a set of rules concerning the sale and purchase of gold with a view to keeping its prices in terms of pound sterling constant. Just the fact of the sale and purchase of gold does not indicate anything more than that the value of the pound sterling in terms of gold was constant. Its importance consists in the fact that fluctuation in the price of gold depended on the inflow and outflow of capital out of London and the stabilisation of the gold value of the pound sterling was a part of the policy geared to the regulation of the flow of international capital. The free trade policy rested on the international flow of capital in the sense that Britain ran a balance-of-payments deficit from the end of the nineteenth century onwards and that deficit was covered by the inflow of short-term capital. This is exactly how Britain has, for the most part, financed her post-Second World War deficits; but the significance of the balance of payments, and trade in commodities, was not the same as it is now. Under the gold standard, trade in commodities was secondary in importance to the international flow of capital in and out of London. It is the latter rather than the former which influenced the policies that the Bank of England followed. Britain's economic links with the rest of the world were dominated by financial relations and the repercussions of the policies followed by the Bank of England on the British economy in the forms of their effects on employment and incomes—the factors whose importance we take for granted these days—were not regarded as important. The commitment on the part of the Bank of England to exchange the pound sterling at a fixed rate was a constraint on it in the sense that it was, as a result, forced to vary the rate of interest and the conditions affecting the availability of credit in order to conserve its not-too-large gold reserves. The important point is that it was only the international financial implications which were relevant to the Bank of England (which then was a commercial bank and very much behaved as one). And there had to be a fundamental change in the nature of economic policy within Britain itself before there could be a monetary policy geared to the functioning of the British economy.

The change in the nature of monetary management came during the inter-war period. Harrod rightly calls the tenth report of the American Federal Reserve Bank (1923) a revolutionary document in monetary history in that it signalled the demise, at least in the US, of the gold standard. The significance of the demise consists in the fact that it meant a change in the principle which governed the creation and the supply of money; the money supply was no longer to be fixed by reference to inflows and outflows of gold, but was to be regulated in such a way as to iron out the fluctuations in economic activity in the American economy. The establishment of the Exchange Equalisation Account in the Bank of England marked a similar event. For the existence of the account implied the insulation of the supply of money and the availability and the terms of credit from the influence of inflow and outflow of capital and the regulation of these by reference to economic conditions in Britain. These events are a part of a series of events which brought about a change in the nature of monetary management and which finally led to the kinds of public policies which are now so familiar to us. The two events meant, on the one hand, a complete break from commodity money and, on the other hand, a denigration of the international flow of capital as the basis for the formulation of monetary policy. The flow of international finance capital continued during the inter-war period but its scale was smaller and its pattern very different from that in the pre-war (1914) period.

Though not directly relevant to the argument here it is interesting to note the implication that the Leninist characterisation of capitalism cannot be applied to the inter-war period and, thus, also to the post-Second World War period. Lenin's characterisation of capitalism in its imperialist stage is premised on the dominance of international financial relations in the structuration of international relations. This may have been so in the pre-war (1914) period, but the international movement of capital lost its importance after the war due to a number of factors—the most important of which was monetary management geared to the functioning of the national economy. The point, in general terms, is that policies concerned with management of national economies—leaving aside the question of what exactly they are and what their effectivity is—affect the nature of international economic relations by affecting the basis on which a national economy is delineated from the rest.

Central to the change in the nature of monetary management is the emergence of unemployment as an economic problem. The implication is that there are different modalities of the problem of unemployment. The problem of unemployment did not always exist as an economic problem. The unemployed have always existed under capitalism; but they have not always been registered as economic agents who have failed to sell their labour either due to the lack of offers for employment or due to their not having the skills in demand by employers or due to ignorance about the possibilities of employment. In the nineteenth century the problem of unemployment was perceived in relation to the problems of poverty, homelessness, crime, vagrancy, etc. These problems are not directly economic; they are in the first instance moral or social problems or problems connected with the exercise of political power. Keynes starts his General Theory with the accusation that classical economists—a category which does not include Marx—do not have an answer to the question: what determines the level of employment. The force of this accusation and the popularity of the General Theory beyond the restricted circle of economic theorists, despite the fact that the book is primarily a work of economic theory with nothing to say about practical problems of employment policy, is due to the fact that the book appeared when unemployment had already started existing as an economic problem. Keynes did not discover the problem of unemployment as is argued by the history of economic ideas and theories with varying degrees of sophistication; what he did was to create within an economic theory dominated by the problems of distribution a space for the problem of unemployment. The problem of unemployment can only be posed in the context of an analysis of the functioning of the national economy and this is the main reason why the problem could not be grafted on to the marginalist or the neo-classical theory.

The marginalist theory is essentially a theory of distribution and this is the reason why it is, for the most part, concerned with the determination of the relative prices of commodities. There are in the theory factors of production, commodities, and individuals but no units of production(firms) and no national economy. The latter two are not pertinent to the distribution of commodities and incomes which individuals derive from their sale. There is, however, a conception of the national economy in the neo-classical monetary theory; in fact, no monetary theory is possible without such a conception. The point is that the supply or the stock of money—a variable which is central to the neo-classical and to the Keynesian theory as well—cannot be defined without reference to the national economy. Money, when it is fiduciary money, has to be defined as such with reference to a particular national economy. And even when money is commodity money or a fiduciary money tethered to a money commodity—as was the case in Britain and the US when they were on the gold standard—the supply of money cannot be defined without reference to the geographical contours of the national economy in question. Gold, which has been the main money commodity, is not found evenly dispersed over the globe, and, as a result, the production of it is and was restricted to a few countries. The geographical localisation of the production of gold implies that its quantity in those countries which do not produce it can only be altered by means of international transactions: sale and purchase of commodities and flow of capital. What this means is that the supply of money—if it takes the two forms indicated—cannot be defined without delineating the boundaries of the national economy and this is the reason why the discussion of the supply of money under the gold standard becomes nothing more than a discussion of international flow of capital. This detour into the necessity of a conception of national economy to monetary theory enables us to explain why the problems and the functioning of the national economy were first discussed in monetary theory. It is said that the Keynesian revolution consists in the transformation of monetary theory from a theory of the level of prices to the theory of employment. The locus of the Keynesian revolution had to be monetary theory because it is only there that the problem of the determinants of the level of employment could be raised. Both money and employment share the same theoretical terrain in that their analysis is an analysis at the level of the national economy.

Both the policies and the discussions concerned with unemployment—including under the latter rubric not only those in economic theory but also more mundane and popular discussions of unemployment—bring to light and emphasise particular features of the economy which may not be pertinent otherwise. It is these features with which we are briefly concerned here. To start with, an unemployment policy is essentially a national policy in the sense that the rate of employment which the policy sets out to reduce is defined and measured with respect to the boundaries of the national economy, and the incidence of the policy measure is, for the most part, restricted to the national economy. Given the way in which unemployment is defined, then coupled with any discussion of unemployment is the emphasis on the locus of production of commodities and discrimination among commodities according to whether they are produced within national boundaries or not. Commodities are, in effect, divided into two categories, namely, those whose production creates employment and those whose production does not. A large variety of employment policies are possible and followed in capitalist countries; they range from direct measures like investment in public-works programmes to indirect measures in the form of fiscal and monetary policies to influence the output and thus the employment decisions of firms. But, in general, all employment policies are concerned with influencing the scale of production of commodities and other economic activities which generate employment. The interest in production, in turn, implies an interest in the forms of organisation of firms and their economic effects. Capitalist governments have not always been interested in industrial organisation; industrial policies are relatively recent innovations and they have emerged in the wake of employment policies. Further, economic relations and policies acquire a different significance in a context where unemployment becomes the main economic problem. Taxes, for example, change in significance from being just sources of revenue to instruments for influencing and deflecting decisions of economic agents in a particular direction. Similarly, the sale and purchase of government securities instead of just being the particular form in which public state apparatuses borrow and repay funds becomes also a means for influencing the availability and the terms of credit to private economic agents.

The status and the significance of international trade in commodities too undergoes a change. There is always a certain inconsistency between the principle of free trade and the concern for unemployment. The former is opposed to any discrimination between commodities according to their place of production, while the latter implies and favours such a discrimination. The principle of free trade came under attack in Britain in the 1920s and it was abandoned in the 1930s. Free trade and protection have both been subjects of dispute and controversy at different times and in different national economies; but the nature of the arguments for and against protection have not always been the same. Free trade was opposed in Britain in the inter-war period out of concern over unemployment, and the argument for protection was, in effect, nothing more than an argument in favour of the substitution of domestic labour, i.e. the labour registered in national employment statistics, for foreign labour, i.e. the labour which does not count. This argument is very different from the one put forward by Ricardo against protection which concerned the distribution of income between different classes in the economy and the way in which protection affected the distribution of income. The difference in the two kinds of arguments consists in the status assigned to international trade in commodities. Concern for unemployment not only affects the status and the significance of international trade in commodities, but it also implies a change in the hierarchy of importance of different forms of international transactions. Capitalist national economies are tethered to each other by the ties of trade, finance, and investment; the relation between them, as a result, consists of a number of different kinds of transactions. We have already argued that under the gold standard, at least so far as Britain was concerned, international transactions connected with flow of capital dominated over other forms of transactions. Concern over unemployment shifted the importance to international trade in commodities and away from the international flow of capital. The balance-of-payment accounts, as they are divided, arranged, and used for purposes of public policy in capitalist countries today, assign international trade in commodities the central place. The argument here, it may be noted, is exactly the opposite of what is put forward by Lenin in his *Imperialism: The Highest Stage of Capitalism*. An index of the change in the hierarchy of international transactions can be seen from the fact that balance-of-payment accounts as they are compiled today have only existed in the post-Second World War period.

The point, in general terms, is that the emergence of unemployment as the main economic problem in capitalist countries was among the things which changed the significance of international economic relations and the constraints which they imply on the functioning of the national economy. International economic relations started to be judged in terms of their implications for the level of employment. This change took place in a number of different domains, e.g. analysis of international economic relations and public policies. Pre-Keynesian analysis of international economic relations consisted of the effect of outflow and inflow of capital from an economy on the price level of that economy. The Keynesian theory changed the emphasis of the analysis from the price level to the level of employment. In the domain of public policy governments started using the rate of exchange of their currencies against others with a view to influencing the level of exports and imports and thus the level of employment in the economy. Capitalist economies have a perpetual problem of fitting their employment policies together with their international economic relations. They cannot opt out of international economic relations, e.g. trade in commodities, in the interest of maintaining employment, because they are part of the international division of labour and the level of employment in each of them depends on the export of commodities. On the other hand, international economic relations imply constraint on the employment policies that particular capitalist countries can follow. For example advanced capitalist countries are committed by treaties and agreements not to follow certain types of policies which discriminate against foreign-produced and in favour of home-produced commodities. Further, they are committed to maintaining the convertibility of their respective currencies into the currencies of other countries. The former means that, for the most part, capitalist countries are prevented from protecting the home industry as a way of reducing unemployment in the economy. The latter is a monetary restriction and is complementary to the former in the sense that the lack of restriction on international trade in commodities has to be coupled to the free convertibility of one currency into another at least for purposes of trade. Free convertibility of one currency into another is a restriction on the creation of credit or money in the sense that there may be a demand to convert a part of the credit which is granted into a foreign currency whose quantity depends on international rather than on national factors. This convertibility is not peculiar to the post-Second World War arrangements; it existed under the gold standard in the form of free convertibility of a national currency into gold and freedom to export and import gold. But the economic significance of the convertibility and the constraint it implies on the national economy is not the same in the two cases. As pointed out earlier, the supply of money or the creation of credit under the gold standard was tied to the international flow of capital; but this tie had no wider economic significance because the monetary system was not then, in contrast to now, managed so as to influence the functioning of the economy. Under the present monetary system convertibility is essentially a restriction on the extent to which the availability of credit and the rate of interest can be used to influence the functioning of the national economy or the rate of employment.

To tie together the loose ends of the argument: there is a problem concerning the relationship between different monetary systems (coterminous with national economies) because while the means of payment are national, transactions connected with the circulation of commodities and flow of capital are not only national but also international. This discrepancy between the domain of circulation of the means of payment and the span of economic transactions when coupled with freedom of international trade and movement of capital implies a restriction on the creation and issue of means of payment. The specific form which this restriction takes and the economic significance it has depends on the way in which the national monetary system is regulated. The importance of the pre-First World War gold standard consists in the fact that under it the international flow of capital dominated the policy pursued by monetary authorities and that it represented a case where the issue of fiduciary money was still subject to the national reserves of particular money commodity, gold. The emergence of unemployment as an economic problem and other factors eventually led to a change in the nature of monetary management. This change, so far as the form of money is concerned, meant the end of the link between the issue of fiduciary money and the gold reserves. The implication is that a monetary management geared to the functioning of the economy presupposes the existence of fiduciary money and that such a monetary management is ruled out so long as the issue of money is tethered to gold or for that matter any other money commodity. The change in the nature of monetary management did not take place suddenly and, as indicated above, it was not a result of one particular factor. The main purpose behind the lengthy and not directly relevant discussion of unemployment is to point out the part which the problem of unemployment played in the birth of public policies geared to the functioning of the national economy and hence the change in the nature of monetary management. At a general level the argument is that the significance of international economic relations, of which international monetary relations are a part, crucially depends on the way in which policies within a national economy delineate it from other economies.

We have so far neglected the distributive implications of different forms of money and it is to these relations that we now turn. The basic argument is that the creation of money regardless of the form it takes is a distributive relation. The nature of the relation is clear when money takes the form of commodity money, say, gold. The producers of gold appropriate a part of the social product simply by virtue of the fact that the commodity they produce is the means of circulation. The newly produced gold can be put into circulation either by using it to purchase commodities or by lending it. The social product is appropriated in the first case in the form of commodities and in the second in the form of interest. The economic effects of the creation of money in the two cases are not the same: it is the production and prices of commodities which are immediately affected in the first case and the rate of interest and the availability of credit in the second. When gold circulates as money in the form of gold coins and a coin buys more gold than it itself contains then both the producer of gold and the authority issuing the coin share, so to say, in the proceeds from the creation of money. In a general sense the same distributive relation holds in the case of fiduciary money, with the difference that then there is no commodity whose producer shares in the proceeds. In the case of credit money it is financial institutions who appropriate a part of the social product in the form of interest on the loans that they extend by virtue of the simple fact that their deposits circulate as the means of payment. The use of deposits as the means of payment by economic agents grants financial institutions power to earn interest. The implication is that the power does not arise from the possession of what is called money capital. It was argued earlier that credit money does not exist on its own but it is coupled with fiduciary money. The implication is that both financial institutions and the governments share in the proceeds from the creation of money or seigniorage.

It was pointed out earlier that the power of governments to issue the legal tender is subject to limitations; what we want to do now is to point out the distributive implications of those limitations. In keeping with the precepts of 'sound finance' governments in advanced capitalist countries finance the excess of their expenditure over revenue not by printing money but by borrowing. This in institutional terms takes the form that government departments do not finance their expenditure by borrowing directly from the central bank (the financial institution which has the power to issue the legal tender) but, instead, by borrowing from other financial institutions and, to a lesser degree, from households and firms, etc. Governments generally borrow by selling marketable securities through the intermediary of the central bank. Given the fact that transactions between the central bank and other financial institutions are conducted in terms of the legal tender or, what is the same thing, the deposits of the former, the central bank on behalf of the government borrows what it itself creates, namely, its own deposits. This peculiar feature of government borrowing is what distinguishes it from borrowing by other economic agents. In general economic agents borrow because they themselves do not create the means of payment; but public state apparatuses (the central bank included) borrow despite the fact that they can and do themselves create the means of payment universally acceptable within the economy. Public state apparatuses do not form a unitary organisation and the main reason why they do not exercise the power to issue legal tender is that the way in which central banks are organised and the financial and accounting rules which govern their functioning rule out the exercise of that power except in emergencies. Among accounting rules the one which is of particular importance here is that central banks regard the legal tender or their deposits as their liabilities—they are, one may add, liabilities in a purely fictitious sense. What this means is that central banks, in view of their accounting rules, cannot create deposits without at the same time acquiring assets in return for those deposits. Central banks regard government securities as assets because they are not their liabilities but the government's. The important point is that, in general, central banks do not buy securities directly from government departments, for that would amount to printing money or creating deposits by fiat. But central banks are perfectly willing to buy back government securities from other financial institutions as part of their management of the monetary system—which, for the most part, operates through the sale and purchase of government securities. So, in effect, central banks are willing to create deposits and thus the legal tender in return for government securities provided they have been sold once. The distributive implications of the procedure followed by central banks are as follows: if a central bank buys securities from a government department then that is tantamount to the government's appropriating the whole seigniorage by itself. On the other hand, the creation of a deposit by the central bank in return for an already issued security amounts to the creation of money and thus the legal tender as in the previous case, with the difference that in this case the government shares the seigniorage with financial institutions, the main buyers of government securities, by paying them interest. From a distributive point of view, the doctrine of 'sound finance' is in its effect a defence of the right of financial institutions to share in the seigniorage.

We can draw certain general conclusions from the fact that coupled with the creation of money there is a distributive relationship, a relationship which changes with a change in the form of money. Given this fact, one cannot deduce the form of money either from the functions of money or from the consent or agreement of men who use money. This, in a general sense, also indicates why a change in the form of money can be a subject of political dispute and struggle. The political struggle centred around the reinstitution of silver as a monetary metal at the turn of this century in the US provides a striking example of such a dispute. Furthermore, the distributive relationship sheds light on the reasons for the present-day use of gold as an international means of payment. It may seem particularly irrational to dig gold from great depths to store it in the vaults of some central bank; this is what, in fact, happens when gold is used as an international means of payment. But it is only irrational if one tries to assess the appropriateness of a form of money by reference to the functions of money—an assessment which does not shed any light on the conditions of existence of gold as money. Associated with the use of gold as an international means of payment is a network of vested interest on the part of producers and hoarders of gold which accounts for this use.

Chapter 4

Barter and Monetary Exchange

Now we come to what is the most important part of Marx's analysis of money, namely, the properties of monetary exchange. We have already pointed out that the discussion of the functions of money is not interesting unless those functions are associated with definite effects. The discussion in this section is based on the contention that the fact that money is the means of payment and, thus, the definition of money in terms of its functions, is not significant unless monetary exchange is, at the same time, regarded as different from non-monetary exchange or barter. The effects associated with the existence of money are in the first instance restricted to the process of circulation and if they do extend beyond the process of circulation it is because that process precedes and follows both production and consumption of commodities. The point is that analysis of money should be primarily concerned with the process of circulation. This is, in effect, what this section sets out to do.

There is an important difference between Marx and monetary theorists. When Marx discusses the medium-of-circulation as opposed to the measure-of-value function, what he discusses, in fact, is the circuit of circulation of commodities—a schematic representation of the path which commodities traverse from when they leave the process of production to when they are bought for consumption or their utilisation as the means of production. Monetary theorists, in contrast, do not start with the circulation of commodities and the form that takes, but instead with why an individual—that individual is meant to be representative and is thus mythical—would rather keep money than spend it immediately on commodities. The point of departure of monetary theorists is money as an object of demand. Thus for them money is something which is at par with commodities. The analysis of money in monetary theory is seen as an extension of the analysis of demand and supply of commodities; it is complementary to what in bourgeois economic theory is termed the value theory. For Marx, though both commodities and money enter and participate in the process of circulation they do so in different capacities. The former and the latter are just not at par with each other. The fact that commodities are objects of use in their capacity either as means of consumption or means of production and that money is neither implies that money and commodities do not occupy symmetric positions in the process of circulation of commodities.

The asymmetry of the respective positions of money and commodities is evident in the way in which Marx writes the circuit of circulation of commodities for a monetary economy, namely, C–M–C. (C denotes commodities and M money). The asymmetry is central to the distinction between monetary exchange and barter. The circuit of circulation of commodities treats the process of circulation as the transformation of commodities into other commodities—a formulation which is valid for both monetary exchange and barter and which expresses the simple, though not inconsequential, fact that eventually the whole purpose of selling commodities is to buy commodities. The difference between monetary exchange and barter, for Marx, consists in the difference in the circuits of circulation of commodities in the two cases. While the process of transformation of commodities into commodities takes an indirect form under monetary exchange it takes a direct form under barter (expressed by the circuit of circulation C–C). If we leave the argument at that it does nothing more than to repeat what is common currency; under barter commodities are exchanged for commodities but under monetary exchange commodities are first exchanged for money and then many for commodities. The difference between the two circuits is not something which is of purely formal significance, i.e. the number of steps required to complete the circulation of commodities. The difference does have economic effects, as we will explain later. But for present purposes what is important is that the difference in the two circuits of circulations and, thus, effects associated with those circuits are tethered to the existence of money.

Since money is defined in terms of the function it performs in the process of circulation it is necessary to establish clearly the relationship between the means-of-payment function of money and the form which the circulation of commodities takes. Starting with the circuit C–M–C, it may be asked how we identify what is to be included under C and under M. The identification of what C represents presents no difficulty since it represents things which by virtue of their physical properties serve as means either of consumption or of production. But what does M represent? It is the attempts to answer this question which indicate that the original question is not as simple as it seems on first sight. At first, it may be said that M represents money, but how does one identify money? Money cannot be identified on the basis of its physical properties, because, as we pointed out earlier, money does not require a particular physical form to be money. The answer, as one would have guessed by now, is that money is defined by reference to its defining function. But the problem is that the answer is not sufficient to identify money. For, how does one tell whether or not something is actually performing the function of the medium of circulation (the defining function of money)? There is no way in which the question can be satisfactorily answered except by reference to the specific form which the process of circulation takes in the presence of money or, what is the same thing, by associating with money an effect which can serve to identify it. It is here that the place which money occupies in the circuit of circulation of commodities becomes pertinent; it is that place which indicates the way in which money enters the process of circulation and differentiates money from commodities. M is what figures as intermediary in the circuits of circulation of commodities; it is what is acquired in order to be ultimately exchanged for something else. It may be noted that the common observation that money is acquired not for its own sake but for the sake of buying commodities is turned on its head here, i.e. money is whatever is generally acquired not for its own sake but for the sake of acquiring other commodities. This criterion, one may note, is blurred; it lumps together money with financial assets and commodities bought for purposes of speculation. However, the inclusion of these things with money is not accidental, for—as we pointed out earlier with respect to financial assets—they do share some of the characteristics of money. We leave the criterion as it is since the aim is to point out the effect of the existence of money on the circulation of commodities and neither financial assets nor speculative trading can exist without money.

The presence of an intermediary in the circuits of circulation is essential to specifying the form which the circulation of commodities takes. The circuit C–C, which characterises non-monetary exchange, in actual fact represents a bilateral exchange. The reason is that the only way in which commodities can be directly transformed into commodities is when each seller of commodities at the same time buys the commodities of the buyer to whom he sells his own commodities. There is no place for an intermediary in bilateral transactions; it is redundant. Here, one has to remember that a commodity acquired not for use but for the sake of exchange later is an intermediary.

The presence of an intermediary makes an essential difference to the form which the circulation of commodities takes. The absence of an intermediary in the circuit C–C implies that nothing is bought for the sake of future sale; in other words, everything is bought *qua* object of use. The circuit C–C is thus compatible only with a specific category of transactions, i.e. transactions where each seller of commodities buys the commodities of the person to whom he sells his own—bilateral transactions. On the other hand, the circuit C–M–C represents a multilateral exchange. The intermediary is the link between two transactions in the sense that it is acquired through one transaction and disposed of through another. The presence of two transactions rather than one within the circuit of circulation means that an economic agent buys commodities from and sells commodities to different persons. The two transactions together thus form a multilateral transaction. What the discussion here points to is that barter is not just the exchange of commodities for commodities but, instead, the direct exchange of commodities for commodities. This qualification, though it may seem pedantic, is necessary, because the formulation, exchange of commodities for commodities, includes both bilateral and multilateral transactions and thus does not distinguish between forms of transaction. An important point in this connection is that a commodity which is acquired not for consumption or use but for sale in future effectively functions like money rather than an object of use. Money is defined by its functions, and anything, so long as it functions like money, assumes the characteristics of money. The claim that the distinction between monetary and non-monetary exchange is the same as the distinction between bilateral and multilateral transactions and the discussion here may seem obvious, but the existence of money is not always associated with a particular form of exchange.

To bring out the significance of what is argued here it is useful to point out the procedure followed by monetary theorists when analysing money. Neo-classical monetary theorists first construct an elaborate system of exchange and this system is regarded as and termed barter exchange on the grounds that nothing called money enters into the process of exchange. The construction of the so-called monetary model of exchange consists of nothing more than introducing a thing called money into what is regarded as the system of barter exchange. The exact procedure varies from one theorist to another but all of them keep within the general outline sketched here. There are two important implications which underlie the general procedure. First, the construction of what is regarded as the model of barter is based on the assumption that the non-existence of money does not in any way affect the possibilities of exchange. The barter of economic theory does not, so to say, represent a rude and primitive state of the economy; instead, it represents a state in which there is no restriction on the possibilities of exchange. Second, given the way in which barter is conceived, the existence of money is completely divorced from the possibilities of exchange and as a result, money is not defined by reference to its functions in the process of circulation. We have already pointed out that the definition of money in terms of its functions is of no theoretical significance unless we associate particular effects, e.g. the possibility of multilateral exchange, with the function which is supposed to define money. Monetary theorists adopt a nominalist definition of money: a thing is money because it is called money. They regard money as something which is at par with commodities in the sense that the former, like the latter, is treated as an object of demand. Money is different from commodities because the factors which determine the demand for the former are different from those which determine the demand for the latter. Money is demanded for the sake of commodities it buys and commodities, on the other hand, are demanded for their own sake. The whole point of calling something money is to indicate that the determinants of its demand are different from those of the rest.

The way in which monetary theorists conceive of money and monetary exchange gives rise to some peculiar problems. Monetary theorists are constantly faced with the problem of justifying the existence of money. The need for justification arises because, first, the possibilities of exchange are regarded, at least to begin with, as independent of the existence of money and, second, money is treated as an object of demand. The former implies that the existence of money cannot be deduced from a particular form of transaction, e.g. multilateral transactions; the result is that monetary theorists are forced to postulate *ad hoc* restrictions on what they consider barter in order to justify the existence of money, e.g. the high cost of transactions in the absence of money, etc. On the other hand, the latter, in conjunction with the assumption that money is not demanded for its own sake but as a surrogate for commodities, means that there is no guarantee that money always remains an object of demand. And the problem is that an economy in which no economic agent wants to keep money cannot be a monetary economy. There is a strange inconsistency between monetary history and monetary theory. Historians of money point to the virtues and the beneficial effects of money and regard money as one of the greatest innovations of humanity while, on the other hand, monetary theorists find it difficult to account for the existence of money and, thus, of the monetary economy and the continuance of that economy. The problems which monetary theory faces and the way in which it tries to answer those problems by constantly revising the list of the determinants of the demand for money are direct products of the way in which money and monetary economy are conceived in monetary theory.

For Marx money and monetary economy require no justification. The existence of money is identified with a particular type of transaction, the multilateral transaction, and such transactions are necessary for the existence of most types of the division of labour and specialisation based on the production of commodities. For example, a capitalist economy cannot exist without multilateral transaction and thus the existence of money. Further, for Marx there exists no problem of accounting for why money is demanded by economic agents because—as will become clear during the course of the later discussion in this section—the way in which he writes the circuit of circulation implies that money and commodities are not at par with each other and the former, unlike the latter, is not an object of demand.

These are nothing more than general indications of the differences which separate Marx's analysis of money from that of monetary theorists. And to say that multilateral exchange is essentially monetary exchange is to do no more than to indicate the path on which the analysis of money and monetary economy has to proceed. What we want to do now is to specify the properties of monetary exchange in greater detail. A lot of what follows may seem trite and commonplace, but the main aim here is to bring out the problems which are hidden behind the cloak of obviousness.

Every exchange of a commodity is a dual process: it is a sale and purchase at the same time. 'The apparently single process is in reality a double one. From the pole of the commodity owner it is a sale, and from the pole of the money owner it is a purchase. In other words, a sale is a purchase, C–M (sale) is also M–C (purchase).' (*Capital*, vol. 1, p. 108) The fact that sales are dual to purchases is expressed by the relation that the total volume of sales is identical to the total volume of purchases. This identity, one may note, does not involve money; Marx's reference to money is for purposes of indication only. The identity is valid for both barter and monetary exchange. The identity by itself is trivial, but one must specify its significance carefully because in the usual discussions of the so-called quantity equation it is often misrepresented. Not only is it the case that the identity does not refer to money, but also it does not say anything about the balance between demand and supply.

> Nothing can be more childish than the dogma that because every sale is a purchase and every purchase a sale, therefore the circulation of commodities necessarily implies an equilibrium of sales and purchases. If this means that the number of actual sales is equal to the number of purchases, it is mere tautology. But its real purport is to prove that every seller brings his buyer to the market. Nothing of the kind. (*Capital*, vol. 1, p. 113)

Marx is attacking here what is generally termed 'Say's Law' and the main point is that the balance between demand and supply cannot be deduced from the fact of exchange itself. None the less, the identity is not devoid of significance; it is of help in specifying the relationship between participants in exchange and the form of circulation.

Although the process of circulation is composed of individual sales or purchases, Marx does not analyse the process of circulation in terms of them but in terms of the circuits of circulation, specific combinations of sales and purchases. Circuits of circulation are based on the assumption that economic agents sell commodities in order to purchase commodities, hence the notion of transformation of commodities into commodities through exchange. Since what economic agents sell and what they purchase depends on their respective economic positions, households, units of production specialising in the production of particular commodities, etc., the circuits of circulation emphasise the fact that the process of circulation is hemmed in by production and consumption on either side. It is not that Marx regards production as being more important than circulation, as quite a few Marxists believe, but that he regards circulation as an intermediary stage between the production of commodities and their subsequent utilisation or consumption. For present purposes the main importance of the description of the process of circulation in terms of circuits of circulation is that it makes clear the special position of money with respect to commodities in the process of exchange. If the process of circulation is merely seen as a conglomeration of individual sales and purchases, the transformation of commodities into money (C–M) or vice versa (M–C), then commodities and money are seen to occupy symmetric, and thus interchangeable, positions in the process. So far as the process of circulation is concerned, money and commodities, as a result, appear at par with each other. The position of money only becomes different from that of commodities when sales and purchases are paired to form circuits of circulation. It is only then that money appears as an intermediary in transactions, i.e. something which is acquired in order to be exchanged later, and, thus, as the medium of circulation. In the case of barter it does not matter whether the process of circulation is analysed in terms of circuits or in terms of sales or purchases, because then all commodities are by the definition of barter sold or purchased only once and thus there is no intermediary in transactions.

Since the notion of circuits plays such an important part in Marx's analysis, it is necessary to discuss the notion in greater detail. Circuits are meant to describe movements whether of industrial capital, commercial capital, commodities, etc., and the components-of-circuits stages of the movement. Capital, for Marx, does not denote a collection of things as it does in economic theory and accounting, but a particular form of movement consisting of particular components, hence the detailed discussion of the circuits of capital in volume 2 of *Capital*. What circuits do is to emphasise the interrelations between different economic activities, e.g. consumption, production, and circulation; this is true not only for circuits of circulation but also for circuits of industrial capital. The movement which circuits of circulation describe is in the form of the transformation of commodities into commodities and this movement always refers to a particular economic agent. And that agent is specified by the commodities he sells, represented by C at the beginning of the circuit, and buys, represented by C at the end. Once again, such a specification of economic agents is not peculiar to circuits of circulation; capitalists too are specified by the commodities they buy and sell. The point, in general terms, is that coupled with all the circuits which Marx uses there is a particular conceptualisation of the economic agent to which the circuit refers.

But the problem is that it is not always clear in *Capital* that although the circuit is not attributed to anyone in particular, the movement which a circuit describes actually refers to a particular economic agent. The main reason is that Marx often, but not always, conducts analysis at the level of social capital and specifies the tendencies of capitalism as if social capital is a unitary entity. The movement of social capital, one may note, does not have the same status as the movement of individual capital. Individual capital refers to an economic agent, namely, a capitalist firm; and one can talk about the movement of individual capital in the sense that capitalist production is organised in firms, and the calculations which govern the production of commodities are carried out at the level of the firm. But there is no economic agent which corresponds to social capital and there are no calculations which envelop the whole of social capital. Therefore, the movement of social capital, when it is treated as a unitary entity, is based neither on the organisation of production nor on economic calculations as they are actually carried out under capitalism. The implication is that social capital as a unitary entity refers to a mythical economic agent which one may term the society.

To get back to the circuits of circulation: the notion of transformation of commodities into commodities through exchange is only valid with reference to a particular economic agent. For in the aggregate, taking all economic agents together, the process of exchange is not a process of transformation but a process of redistribution of commodities, hence the name the process of circulation. Further, not all transformation of commodities into commodities through exchange describes a circuit in the sense in which it is taken in *Capital*. Commodities at the beginning of the circuit denote the end products of the process of production which by virtue of their pattern of distribution cannot serve as objects of use, while commodities at the end of the circuit are distributed in such a way that they can serve either as means of consumption or of production. Thus, the sale of commodities with a view to a speculative purchase of commodities—the purchase of commodities not for use but for sale later—does not constitute a circuit. Circuits are schematic representations of the phases of the circulation, and, unlike the budget constraints of economic theory, they refer neither to prices of commodities nor to the composition or the time pattern of an individual economic agent's sales and purchases.

However, it is the schematic representation which is needed when distinguishing barter from monetary exchange. All circuits are constituted of two phases (Marx's term), namely, sale and purchase. The characteristic of barter is that the two constituent phases are contemporaneous in the sense that they are traversed by the same transaction. The two constituent phases of the circuit C–M–C are, in contrast, not contemporaneous; they may be both spatially and temporally separated from each other. The differences between barter and monetary exchange become even clearer if we examine circuits pertaining to the two forms of exchanges in conjunction with what may be termed their dual. Just as every sale has a dual to it, purchase, every circuit has also a dual attached to it. The dual of a circuit is composed of the duals to its constituent phases. The dual to the barter circuit C–C is itself a circuit namely, C–C; but, in contrast, the dual to the monetary circuit C–M:M–C (writing the circuit so as to distinguish between its constituent phases clearly) is M–C:C–M, which does not constitute a circuit of any kind. The dual consists of a purchase M–C and a sale C–M, but purchase and sale of different commodities. Hence, they cannot be linked together to form a circuit. In fact, M–C and C–M, the two constituents of the dual, are each a constituent phase of a different circuit of circulation. In other words, each circuit C–M–C partially overlaps with two other circuits; and this partial overlap is the effect of the existence of money.

The significance of these differences is as follows: the completion of a circuit means the completion of the process of circulation from the point of view of the economic agent in question. So the fact that barter consists of circuits each of which is paired with another (its dual) means that it can be analysed as a series of unconnected transactions between pairs of economic agents. Monetary exchange, on the other hand, cannot be analysed as if it consists of a collection of pairs of isolated transactions, because then every circuit partially overlaps with two other circuits and is, thus, directly or indirectly related to all other circuits. Monetary exchange consists of an interconnected web of transactions. What is clear, therefore, is that the difference between bilateral and multilateral transactions does not simply consist in the number of economic agents involved in a transaction.

It is the separation of sales from purchases in an individual circuit and thus the presence of an intermediary which creates an interdependence between transactions under monetary exchange. This separation is at the same time tantamount to an enlargement in the possibilities of exchange. Barter, consisting of bilateral transactions, as it does, is restricted to the transactions where each seller at the same time buys the commodities of the economic agent to whom he sells his own. The introduction of money and thus the possibility of conducting multilateral transactions implies the removal of this restriction. Marx expresses this concept in the following terms:

> The circulation of commodities [i.e. monetary exchange] differs from the direct exchange of products [barter] not only in form but in substance. . . . We see here, on the one hand, how the exchange of commodities breaks through all local and personal bounds inseparable from barter, and develops the circulation of the products of social labour; and, on the other hand, how it develops a whole network of social relations spontaneous in their growth and entirely beyond the control of actors.(*Capital*, vol 1, p. 112)

In fact, Marx does not regard barter as the exchange of commodities because he sees it as an extension of personal relations and as a relationship which does not make relations between men appear as relations between things—contrary to what, according to Marx, happens under monetary exchange. However, it is not the respective epistemological significance of barter and monetary exchange but the economic significance of the enlargement of the possibilities of exchange as an effect of the existence which is of interest here. The importance of money cannot be deduced from its effects; instead, it depends on the social relations of production. Multilateral transactions are necessary for there to be a general division of labour and specialisation based on the exchange of products. Capitalist division of labour involves multilateral transactions; as a result, it cannot exist without the existence of money. Two features of capitalist economies are relevant here, namely, the purchase of labour for its employment in the production of commodities, and specialisation of firms (units of production) in the production of particular commodities. The implication is that a labourer either does not consume the product he produces (this is necessarily the case if the product happens to be a means of production) or that the product which he produces accounts for a very small part of his consumption. Both the cases rule out the possibility of a bilateral transaction between firms and labourers and, as a result, transactions between firms and labourers are multilateral transactions. They, thus, presuppose the existence of money. Money is praised by monetary historians as one of the greatest inventions of humanity which has helped the development of commerce and industry, etc. The pertinence of the enlargement of the possibilities of exchange depends on the social relations of production. Money is necessary for the existence of capitalist relations of production. Specialisation in production necessitates the redistribution of products so that products can be consumed or used in production. In the case of means of production the redistribution can take the form of an allocation through a production plan and thus, they need not take the form of commodities. But the redistribution of consumption goods may well take the form of their sale to consumers, as it does in socialist economies. The reason is that the direct allocation of consumption goods, with the exception of necessities, is not feasible because, first, the consumption patterns of households, given differences in their composition, are different and, second, the amount of information which is required to formulate a plan for the direct allocation of consumption goods is massive due to the simple fact that the number of units of consumption far exceeds the number of units of production. There is, therefore, a space—a very restricted space one may add—for the existence of money and commodities in socialist economies.

The separation of the sales of an economic agent from his purchases which implies the enlargement of possibilities of exchange has two distinct but related aspects: spatial and temporal. Spatial separation means that an economic agent sells his commodities to and buys commodities from different economic agents and that he is not restricted to selling his commodity to a particular economic agent, contrary to the case under barter. The correlate of the spatial separation is the existence of a separate market for each commodity. In a general sense, there is a market for a commodity when its sales and purchases among different economic agents are interdependent in the sense that the terms of one transaction affect those of the others. It is only in a monetary economy that one can speak of the market for a commodity because it is then that an economic agent is free to sell his commodity to anyone who wants to purchase that commodity. Under barter, as pointed out above, economic agents do not have that freedom because each of them is restricted to selling his commodity to someone whose commodities he himself wants to purchase. Under monetary exchange transactions are grouped into transactions in particular commodities, while under barter they are grouped into transactions among pairs of economic agents. There is, as a result, no necessary connection between different transactions in the same commodity under barter.

Temporal separation, on the other hand, means that the sales of an economic agent are not contemporaneous with his purchases. Temporal separation is usually correlated with spatial separation with a few exceptions. For example, speculation (the purchase of commodities with a view to their sale later in the same market) implies a temporal separation but no spatial separation, in the sense that commodities are sold and purchased from the same market. The most important effect of the temporal separation is that the process of circulation acquires a time dimension in the sense that associated with each circuit there is a period of time which it takes for commodities to be transformed into commodities.

The lack of synchronisation between sales and purchases of an economic agent is a necessary feature of monetary exchange. Money occupies the time gap which separates sales from purchases and it is not always realised by monetary theorists that the elimination of that gap means the elimination of the space for the existence of money. For the present purposes, the main point is that the time gap between the sales and purchases of economic agents is filled by money balances in their possession. The implication is that it is the very form which monetary exchange takes rather than, as monetary theory would have it, the desires and wishes of economic agents which explains why they hold money balances. We pointed out earlier that monetary theory treats money as an object of demand; it, as a result, accounts for money balances held by economic agents in terms of their demand for money. Economic agents, according to monetary theory, demand money because though money itself is not an object of use it, being a medium of circulation, can be readily exchanged for things which are of use either in consumption or production. The demand for money, in other words, is a derived demand, and money balances are held for the sake of convenience. One may note here that to monetary theory the fact that money is the medium of circulation is relevant only in so far as it explains why economic agents hold money. In terms of the discussion here the question, why do economic agents hold money, is in effect, the same as why does monetary exchange exist. Once economic agents are granted the discretion to hold money they also have to be at the same time granted the discretion not to hold money. The latter in conjunction with the fact that the demand for money is only a derived demand gives rise to the possibility that none of the economic agents actually want to hold money. But this possibility means the abolition of money. What is clear now, however, is that coupled with the notion that money is an object of demand is the possibility of the abolition of monetary economy.

The existence or non-existence of money has nothing to do with the choices which economic agents make; instead, it depends on the organisation of production and the nature of division of labour and specialisation. The existence of money is necessary when units of production produce commodities and specialise in their production and is of no relevance when products do not assume the form of commodities. Economic agents have no more right or power to introduce or abolish money than they have to introduce forms of organisation of production. A necessary condition for the existence and continuation of monetary exchange is that the existing stock of money is held by economic agents and this condition is satisfied when economic agents do not buy and sell commodities at the same time.

Since the lack of synchronisation of sales and purchases of economic agents or alternatively the holding of money balances plays such an important part it is necessary to indicate the reasons for the lack of synchronisation under capitalism. To start with one has to emphasise the differences between participants in exchange. They consist of, on the one hand, households (units of consumption) who, for the most part, sell labour and buy consumption goods, and on the other hand, firms. Given their income, the pattern of purchases of households is by and large governed by their day-to-day needs of consumption goods. And their ability to distance the pattern of their purchases from the pattern of their consumption is limited by the fact that they have a meagre capacity to hold inventories. As to the pattern of their income, that is governed in the case of households which depend on the sale of labour by the institutional practices concerning the payment of wages, and in the case of rentier households by the frequency of payment of rent, interest, and dividends. The argument is that the frequency of payment of incomes to households is, generally speaking, an institutional datum. Given the differences between the factors which respectively govern the patterns of income and purchases of households, there is no reason why the two patterns should coincide. In general, the frequency of receipt of income by households is lower than the frequency of their expenditure. The case of firms is different; they, as compared to households, have a greater capacity to hold inventories and, as a result, they are in a better position to separate the pattern of their purchases from the pattern of their utilisation of commodities in production. However, there are limits on the extent to which firms can vary the pattern of their expenditure. First, there are the costs of holding inventories and, second, labour has to be bought and paid at regular intervals because it cannot be stored. As for the pattern of receipts of firms they are determined by the pattern of their sales to either households or firms. Once again the main point is that the factors which respectively govern the patterns of expenditure and of receipts are different and firms have a limited power to vary those patterns. The implication is that the two patterns are likely to diverge. What we have done is to point out that the lack of synchronisation of the sales and purchases of an economic agent and thus the holding of money balances by economic agents can be deduced from the differences in the factors which respectively govern the patterns of sales and of purchases and without any recourse to the notion that money is an object of demand.

The possession of money balances by economic agents does not signify their desire for money but rather that they have yet to go through the second phase of their circuits of circulation. Money not being either a consumption or a production good is restricted to the process of circulation and, as a result, whatever stock of money exists is held as the repository of purchasing power by economic agents. The fact that there are always some economic agents who hold money balances—a state of affairs which is necessary, as indicated above, for the continuation of a monetary economy—means that the process of circulation under monetary exchange always remains incomplete in the sense that there are always some circuits which remain to be traversed. Under barter, consisting as it does of disjoint pairs of transactions, one can always isolate any number of related pairs of transactions and treat them as if they constitute an autonomous entity unrelated to the rest. One can, thus, take an arbitrary starting point and talk about the end of the process of circulation. But, in contrast, under monetary exchange one cannot separate a number of circuits of circulation and treat them as if they are not related to the rest, because then, as explained earlier, all circuits of circulation are either directly or indirectly related to each other. Monetary exchange, unlike barter, has no beginning and no end. Marx expresses the difference in the following terms:

> The process of circulation [monetary exchange], therefore does not like the direct barter of products become extinguished upon the use-values changing places and hands. The money does not vanish on dropping out of the circuit of metamorphosis of a given commodity. It is constantly being precipitated into new places in the area of circulation vacated by other commodities. (*Capital*, vol. 1, p. 112–113)

The main point is that use-values, objects of social use, when they change places and hands, complete the full circuit under barter but only half a circuit under monetary exchange. Further, since every circuit under monetary exchange partially overlaps with two other circuits the beginning of every circuit implies the completion of another circuit started before it and its completion the beginning of another circuit which extends into the future. In general terms, the argument is that under monetary exchange circuits of circulation are not only interlinked with each other in space but also in time.

The implication is that monetary exchange has to be treated as a continuous and an interlinked process in time. More specifically, what this means is that one cannot treat the circulation of commodities within a period of time as if it has no relation to what happens before and after that period. It is relevant here to raise the issue of the status of the partition of time into periods. It is a common practice in economics to conceive of time in terms of periods and locate—and thus define—present, past, and future with respect to a period rather than an instant of time. Once time is divided in this way the fact that money constantly stays in the process of circulation appears in the form of money being a link between past, present, and future time-periods. Keynes said that money is the link between present and future; he could equally well have said that money is the link between present and past. The appearance of money as the link between time-periods has, by itself, nothing to do with the functions of money, it is simply a result of the fact that economic theorists for analytical convenience partition time into periods. But economists use the fact that money is the link between present and future to attribute to money the function of store of value—a function which is meant to be different from the means-of-payment function of money. Roughly, the distinction between the two functions, as it is made in monetary theory, is as follows: money functions as the means of payment when it is acquired and exchanged for some commodity within the same time-period and it functions as the store of value when it is kept in the form of a hoard for more than a time-period. This is not how the distinction is described but that is what, in effect, it amounts to. Money, alternatively, functions as the store of value when expenditure and receipts of economic agents within the time-period in question do not balance. In view of the earlier discussion on the lack of synchronisation between receipts and expenditure, such an imbalance is to be expected and is essential for the continuation of a monetary economy. Furthermore, the imbalance is a necessary effect of money performing the function of the means of payment. The argument is that the means of payment appears as the store of value when time is partitioned into periods and dated; as a result, one cannot treat the two functions of money as if they represent two different *personae* of money. One may note that the argument is not directed against the division and dating of time but rather against not recognising its effect. Time is important and it figures in the calculations concerning the holding of money balances; but we may leave this aspect of time aside for later discussion.

The way in which monetary exchange is conceptualised here puts into question the theoretical models, the Walrasian model in

Barter and Monetary Exchange 73

particular, which economists use to analyse monetary economy and money. What we want to do now is briefly to indicate why this is so. It is commonly assumed that the Walrasian model—and other models of general equilibrium as well—are models of a barter economy. This assumption is valid only if by barter one means the absence of a thing called money. There are no restrictions on the possibilities of exchange in these models which supposedly represent barter. This may in the light of previous discussion suggest that it is a misnomer to call the Walrasian model a model of a barter economy; it should, instead, be termed a model of a monetary economy, on the grounds that the multilateral exchange which is admissible in the model implies the existence of things which function like money. But the problem is that there are some features of the Walrasian model which are similar to those of barter rather than monetary exchange. This is particularly so in relation to the way in which the process of exchange as a whole and the temporal dimension is conceptualised in the model. There is no explicit conception of temporality in the Walrasian model. To start with, there is no past in the model in the sense that bygones are regarded as irrelevant and the starting point arbitrary. If there is no past there is in the model no future either in the sense that the process of circulation starts and finishes within the period in question. The whole object of the exercise is to make participants in exchange dispose of their commodities and acquire in return whatever they want; and all this is accomplished within the period in question. So, in effect, the Walrasian model treats the process of exchange as a self-contained process with a definite end and a beginning—a treatment which is more in line with barter than monetary exchange.

There are circuits of circulation in the Walrasian model in the sense that the assumption is that participants in exchange sell commodities in order to buy them. But these circuits are written as budget constraints: the requirement that for each individual his receipts equal his expenditure. Prices within the Walrasian model are assigned the function of equating the demand for commodities to their supply. The equation of demand to supply, it is interesting to note, means the completion of the circuits of circulation pertaining to participants in the Walrasian exchange. Money, when it exists in the Walrasian model, is regarded like any other commodity in the sense that a demand and a supply function are attributed to it. Money, as a result, does not appear as an intermediary, to employ the terminology used in our discussion, but instead at the beginning and the end of circuits of circulation. In the model, money in possession of economic agents at the beginning of the period is at par with the commodities they bring to the market to sell, and similarly money in the hands of economic agents at the end of the period is at par with the commodities they have acquired by virtue of their utility to them. So the existence of money does not mean in the model what it does in the discussion here, namely, that there are always some circuits which remain yet to be completed. The main point, therefore, is that the Walrasian model is based on the assumption that all circuits start and finish during the period in question—an assumption which equates exchange to barter. The result is that the Walrasian model represents neither barter nor monetary exchange. The former because the possibilities of exchange open to economic agents in the model are the same as, if not greater than, those available to them in a monetary economy.

Now we turn to the fact that the completion of a circuit takes time and time for which money balances are held figures in economic calculations. Money as the link between the sales and purchases of an economic agent appears as what one may term the repository of purchasing power. It may, however, be argued that purchasing power need not be held in the form of money and it can as well be held in the form of either commodities or financial assets. Since a thing functions as a repository of purchasing power when it is acquired for its exchange later it is clear that anything which is bought and sold on a regular basis, or is convertible into money, can function as a repository of purchasing power. We have already pointed out that financial assets (including non-marketable financial claims) and some commodities as well can function as intermediaries in circuits of circulation. The argument in general terms is that the existence of organised markets in commodities and financial assets, on the one hand, and the existence of financial institutions issuing a variety of financial claims on the other, leads to the substitution of other things for money as repositories of purchasing power. However, money being the means of payment is privileged among intermediaries in the sense that it, being the means of payment, can never be completely substituted by another intermediary and if something else is a perfect substitute for it then that, obviously, is money. Furthermore, there are differences among repositories of purchasing power in the sense that each of them may imply a different restriction on the exercise of the purchasing power which they hold in store. The source of the restriction consists in the fact that purchasing power can only be exercised provided it is in the form of the means of payment, and the terms on which a repository or store of purchasing power can be converted into money are subject to particular conditions and restrictions. And the nature of restriction varies from one thing to another; in the case of commodities and marketable financial assets restrictions are based on the conditions which govern their sale and purchase, while in the case of financial liabilities restrictions are in fact those which are imposed by the financial institutions issuing those liabilities.

Among repositories of purchasing power it is financial assets, financial claims issued by financial institutions, and the real estate which are of particular importance in capitalist countries. The proliferation of financial assets and financial claims issued by financial institutions in capitalist economies is linked with extension of the network of credit and thus with credit money. What this means is that both credit money and financial 'substitutes' for money are products of the same network of credit. Given the multiplicity of financial substitutes for money, there is a problem of demarcating money from non-money. This problem is of particular importance to monetary theory because if money is treated as an object of demand then it is necessary to specify what is actually demanded. But in the context of the discussion here the problem is of no great significance because here it is the form of transactions rather than what money designates which is of importance. Financial substitutes of money, like money, appear as intermediaries in circuits of circulation and their presence, as a result, does not affect the form of transaction. For the purposes of the present discussion one can define money as a repository of purchasing power whose possession does not imply any restriction on the exercise of that power. And one may add that an important characteristic of a financially developed economy is that things which satisfy this criterion are not given once and for all.

The presence of intermediaries other than money changes the character of the process of circulation. Thus far the process of circulation is treated as if it is solely composed of circuits implying the transformation of commodities into commodities. The presence of intermediaries other than money means that the process of circulation cannot be treated just as a process concerned with the redistribution of commodities so that they can serve as objects of social use. However, this qualification, though it has implications for the factors which govern trading in commodities, does not affect the discussion here which is principally concerned with the distinction between barter and monetary exchange.

The discussion of the repositories of purchasing power may seem very similar to the Keynesian discussion of money. This is true but there are some important differences. First, money is not treated here as an object of demand and the substitution of money by other things is explained here in terms of the development of the financial network and speculative trading in commodities rather than in terms of psychological propensities. The Keynesian theory leads to a general theory of choices among money and its substitutes, but such a theory is impossible in the context of the discussion here. Differences among economic agents are of crucial importance here, which undermine to start with the basis of any general theory of choice. Here, economic agents do not just denote individuals as they do in Keynesian theory, they also include specific types of institutions, e.g. firms, financial institutions, etc. Briefly, the range of choices regarding the form in which purchasing power is to be held and the calculations which govern those choices depend on the economic agent in question. For example, the methods of calculation employed by households are just not the same as those employed by firms, nor for that matter are the choices available to them the same.

Chapter 5

The Circulation of Money

The previous chapter was by and large restricted to the examination of the differences between barter and monetary exchange. What we want to do now is to analyse the relationship between the circulation of commodities and the circulation of money and to discuss the nature of the problem which is unique to monetary economy, namely the problem of financing.

For Marx the circulation of money is not at par with the circulation of commodities. Throughout *The Critique of Political Economy and Capital* he accords primacy to the circulation of commodities over the circulation of money and insists that the former is responsible for the latter. 'Hence although the movement of the money is merely an expression of the circulation of commodities, yet the contrary appears to be the actual fact, and the circulation of commodities seems to be the result of the movement of money.' (*Capital,* vol. 1, p. 116) This argument is based on a distinction which is employed throughout *Capital* and it takes the familiar form of the real movement appearing as the apparent movement. The distinction between real and apparent movement is epistemological, but we are not concerned with that aspect of the distinction. For present purposes what is important is the fact that the circulation of commodities is not regarded as symmetric to the circulation of money. The asymmetry rests on the assumption that the principal—if not the only—function of the process of circulation is the redistribution of commodities so that they can serve as objects of social use and the circulation of money is subservient to that purpose. This asymmetry, we may note, is a straightforward corollary of the differential position assigned to money and commodities in circuits of circulation.

What is said here apropos of the process of circulation and differences between the respective positions of money and commodities in that process may appear obvious and even banal. That may be so but the point is that the implications of the argument here are not always taken into account and the argument is indirectly contradicted by the way monetary theorists analyse money. To elaborate; once it is accepted that it is the circulation of commodities which is primary, and that the circulation of money is subsidiary to it, the process of circulation cannot be analysed in terms of the demand and supply of money. The neo-classical monetary theory distinguishes between, so to say, the composition of demand and the absolute level of demand for commodities. The former is determined by relative prices, and money does not enter into it; thus, the determination of the composition of demand forms the subject of what is termed value theory rather than monetary theory. The absolute level of demand, on the other hand, is determined by the demand and supply of money. The absolute level of demand for commodities is the same thing as the level of national income and, given the assumption that the supply of money is fixed, it is determined by the demand for money. What this means is that it is the circulation of money, linked to the demand for money, which determines the circulation of commodities, linked to national income. For neo-classical economists it is money which makes commodities circulate rather than the other way around.

For Marx money is not an object of demand while for neo-classical monetary theorists it is. It is this difference which ultimately explains the difference in the status of the circulation of money in Marx and neo-classical economists. For Marx, given the manner in which he writes the circuit of circulation, the analysis of the process of circulation can never start with money. Leaving aside lending and borrowing of money, the fact that money appears as the intermediary in the circuit of circulation means that all money balances in the possession of an economic agent are the end result of prior sales by him, and all changes in those balances have to be accounted for in terms of sales and purchases of commodities. In contrast, the analysis of the process of circulation can start with money rather than commodities in the neo-classical monetary theory. There, as pointed out above, money and commodities occupy symmetric positions and the analysis of the process of circulation can start with either. In fact, money is more important than an individual commodity because the demand for it determines the scale of demand for all commodities. Neo-classical monetary theorists often start their analysis with the assumption that money balances in the possession of an economic agent undergo a proportional change and then they set out to analyse the effect of that change. Such an assumption is impossible in the context of Marx's analysis, because there every change in money balances has to be accounted for in terms of transactions in commodities. The only case where the kind of change postulated by neo-classical economists is possible is when the monetary unit is changed—as, for example, it was in France in the 1950s. But a change in the monetary unit does not warrant any economic analysis, because by itself it is of no economic significance. The aim here is not to discuss the neo-classical monetary theory in detail but to point out that seemingly trivial disputes concerning whether or not money is an object of demand or whether or not the circulation of money is subsidiary to the circulation of commodities do have implications for the kind of questions which are asked and the nature of the problems which are posed in the analysis of money and monetary economies.

The fact that commodities are objects of demand while money is not implies that the circulation of commodities does not take the same form as that taken by the circulation of money. 'Circulation is a perpetual movement of commodities though always of different commodities, and each commodity makes but one move.' (*Contribution to the Critique of Political Economy*, p. 98). Here, Marx implicitly assumes that there is no speculative trading, because otherwise commodities may well make more than one move. But the point still remains that the circulation of commodities means a continual exit of commodities from the process of circulation and their replacement by new commodities. In contrast to commodities, 'The currency of money is the constant and monotonous repetition of the same process. The commodity is always in the hands of the seller; the money, as the means of purchase always in the hands of the buyer.' (*Capital*, vol. 1, p. 115) The difference is that whereas commodities enter the process of circulation ultimately to leave it money constantly stays in the process of circulation. The circulation of money, as a result, is in effect the redistribution of the existing stock of money.

The circulation of money is, therefore, the redistribution of purchasing power. This is especially clear in the case when money takes the form of credit money. We have already pointed out that money takes the form of credit money when payments among economic agents take the form of the transfer of deposits in financial institutions—these deposits are nothing more than entitlements to make payment up to a certain amount. The circulation of commodities in that case means a redistribution of deposits held by economic agents in financial institutions and their total volume is not affected by payments which economic agents make to each other. So the circulation of commodities in a financially developed capitalist economy is mirrored by changes in the entries in the ledgers of financial institutions—entries which represent purchasing power held by economic agents.

That there is a relation between the circulation of money and commodities is commonly accepted, and the relation is generally expressed in terms of the velocity of circulation of money. The velocity of circulation of money is nothing more than an average of the number of times units of money change hands during a given period. It is necessary to be clear what its significance is; it is nothing more than a general index of the redistribution of the existing stock of money or the volume of commodities sold and purchased during a given period. If it is accepted that it is the circulation of commodities which is primary and that the circulation of money is subsidiary to it, then the velocity of circulation cannot be regarded as an autonomous factor because its magnitude depends on the rate of circulation of commodities. In particular, one cannot assume as some monetary theorists do, that the velocity of circulation of money remains constant or takes some preassigned value, because such an assumption implies a restriction on the rate of circulation of commodities—a restriction which, in effect, means that it is money which makes commodities circulate rather than the other way around. Marx, too, in places assumes that the velocity of circulation of money is constant; this assumption is, on the face of it, inconsistent with Marx's constant emphasis that the circulation of money is but a reflex of the circulation of commodities. We will discuss this assumption in detail later on.

The point is that in general terms one cannot say anything more than that the velocity of circulation of money depends on the rate of circulation of commodities, and one cannot be any more specific than this without inverting the postulated hierarchy between the circulation of money and commodities. This can be explained in the following way. Commodities, unlike money, do not form a homogeneous entity; differences between commodities do matter from the point of view of circulation. Given the fact of the division of labour and specialisation, on the one hand, and the double separation of the labourers from the means of production, on the other, an economic agent purchases only a restricted range of commodities rather than commodities in general. The implication is that the rate at which commodities circulate depends on their composition, and thus the velocity of circulation of money also depends on the composition of commodities. For a given composition of commodities offered for sale, the rate of expenditure depends on the stock of money, on the one hand, and the distribution of the stock of money among economic agents, on the other. The pertinence of the former is generally accepted, but the importance of the latter is not acknowledged. In fact, the importance of the latter follows from the differentiation of commodities and the fact that each economic agent is interested in a restricted range of commodities only. In monetary theory, in contrast to what is argued here, the demand for commodities, i.e. the rate of circulation of commodities, depends on the demand and supply of money. So, in general terms, what we have done is to replace the notions of the demand and supply of money by those of the stock of money and the distribution of the stock of money. But the discussion here is not completely parallel to the discussion in monetary theory; unlike in monetary theory, here there is no general problem of the determination of the scale of the demand for commodities separate from the problem of the composition of the demand for commodities. We pointed out earlier that the distinction between the two problems corresponds to the distinction between what is called in economic theory the value theory and monetary theory—a distinction which is not pertinent to the discussion here.

The discussion of the relation between the circulation of money and the circulation of commodities points to a problem which is peculiar to a monetary economy, namely the problem of financing. One can in a general sense argue that the circulation of commodities leads to the circulation of money because all purchases in a monetary economy have to be financed. Naturally, there is no problem of financing in barter. Marx points out that 'In the direct barter of products, each commodity is directly a means of exchange to its owner, to all other persons an equivalent, but that only in so far as it has use-value for them.' (*Capital,* vol. 1, p. 88) However, the problem of financing is not the same as the problem of realisation, i.e. the problem concerning the sale of commodities supplied on the market. The fact that each commodity is the means of purchase to its owner does not mean, as Marx makes clear, that it is actually accepted as such. It may be noted that to say that there is a problem of financing in a monetary economy is to repeat the essential properties of monetary exchange; sales of an economic agent are separated from his purchases, and money is the link between the two. However, under the guise of the problem of finance we do not want to repeat the discussion of the previous chapter in different terms. Instead, what we want to do here is to discuss what is termed the quantity equation, and the way in which Marx uses that equation to answer the question of how much money is required to finance the sale of a given volume of commodities.

The fact that money is the medium of circulation means that to each flow of commodities from one economic agent to another there corresponds an equal flow of money in the reverse direction. In a financially developed economy not all flows of money are associated with the circulation of commodities; earlier we pointed out that a part of the circulation of money in such economies is associated with the operation of lending and borrowing. However, in the discussion in this chapter we neglect the financial circulation of money because it is of no direct importance here. The equality between the two flows, i.e. the flow of commodities—in reality the exit of commodities from the process of circulation and their replacement by new commodities—and the flow of money—in fact, the redistribution of the existing stock of money—is universally expressed by the familiar quantity equation:

$$P \cdot Q = M \cdot V$$

Tedious though it may be it is necessary to specify in greater detail what this equation does signify and what it does not. P is the price of commodities, Q the quantity of commodities, M the stock of money and V the velocity of circulation of money. $P \cdot Q$ denotes the flow of commodities during the period in question and similarly, $M \cdot V$ the flow of money. As it stands, the equation is based on the requirement that all purchases in a monetary economy have to be paid for in money. Further, the equation expresses this requirement *post festum* in the sense that Q refers to commodities actually sold rather than those offered for sale—the two, as one is well aware, need not be the same. V in the equation has to be regarded as a balancing item, in the sense that it makes the two sides of the equation equal. One may also note here that the value of V, the velocity of circulation of money, apart from the factors mentioned above, also depends on what is included under the rubric of M. Those who are familiar with monetary theory are well aware that the definition of M differs from one monetary theorist to another; the aim behind the qualification is to point out that the equation is not neutral to the definition of money. One can briefly specify the status of the equation in the following terms: the equation expresses the relationship of equality between the flow of money and the flow of commodities and as such it is neither about the determination of prices nor about the relationship between the stock of money and prices or commodities. All this may seem unduly pedantic but it is necessary if one is to register the differences in the interpretations of this equation.

Marx uses the quantity equation to answer the question:

> Every commodity, when it first steps into circulation, and undergoes its first change of form, does so only to fall out of circulation again and to be replaced by other commodities. Money, on the contrary, as the medium of circulation, keeps continually within the sphere of circulation, and moves about in it. The question therefore arises, *how much money this sphere constantly absorbs*. (Our emphasis) (*Capital*, vol. 1, p. 117)

For Marx the answer to the question is that 'the amount of means of circulation is determined beforehand by the sum of prices of these commodities (i.e. commodities offered for sale).' The important point is that Marx equates the problem of financing with that of representation of commodities in terms of money. The relevance of the theme of representation to the discussion of the problem becomes clear when Marx argues that 'the money in reality represents the quantity or sum of gold ideally expressed beforehand by the sum of prices of commodities.' (*ibid.*)

However, the problem of financing has nothing to do with the representation of commodities in terms of money. From the point of view of representation it is the sum of prices of commodities rather than the composition of commodities which matters. A sum of money is capable of representing any collection of commodities so long as its value is equal to the sum of money. However, as we pointed out earlier, the composition of commodities from the point of view of financing does matter because, given the fact of specialisation and the separation of the labourer from the means of production, the rate of expenditure depends, on the one hand, on the distribution of the stock of money and, on the other, on the composition of commodities which are offered for sale.

In our interpretation of the quantity equation we emphasised that commodities in the equation refer to commodities actually sold rather than commodities offered for sale, for the reason that then the equality of the flow of commodities (P . Q) with the flow of money (M . V) follows from the fact that money is the means of payment. However, one cannot from this fact deduce the amount of money required to finance the collection of commodities offered for sale for the reasons indicated above. But an attempt to do so transforms the problem of financing into the problem of representation.

The treatment of money as the representative of wealth or for that matter commodities is not specific to Marx. Foucault points out that the analysis of wealth in the seventeenth century, i.e. before Adam Smith, is dominated by the theme that money represents commodities. So far as the analysis of money is concerned the theme of representation is retained even after the displacement of the analysis of wealth by what Marx termed the classical political economy. For example, though Ricardo has little in common with the analysts of wealth in the seventeenth century his analysis of money is still dominated by the notion that money represents commodities—a notion which can be found also in neo-classical monetary theorists like Pigou and Marshall. Marx does not discard the theme of representation; what he does is to change the status of representation. We pointed out earlier that for Marx money performs the function because it represents the socialness of exchange. Marx is different from Ricardo in that, unlike him, he analyses in detail the medium-of-circulation function of money and the relation between the circulation of money and commodities. Though Marx uses the theme of representation, he is not indifferent to the way in which it is used.

For example, Marx is very hostile to the use of the fact that the flow of commodities is equal to the flow of money or the equation $M . V = P . Q$ for explaining the determination of the level of prices—a use to which the equation has been commonly put.

The law that the quantity of the circulating medium is determined by the sum of the prices of commodities circulating, and the average velocity of currency (V in the equation) may also be stated as follows. . . . The erroneous opinion that it is, on the contrary, prices that are determined by the quantity of the circulating medium, and the latter depends on the quantity of the precious metals in a country; this opinion was based by those who first held it, on the absurd hypothesis that commodities are without a price, and money without a value . . . and that . . . an aliquot part of the medley of commodities is exchanged for an aliquot part of the heap of precious metals. (*Capital*, vol. 1, pp. 123–4)

To start with one may note that the determination of prices to which Marx refers is tied with representation; money determines prices of commodities in that it represents them and any discrepancy between the quantity of money and the sum of prices of commodities is corrected by an appropriate movement of the latter. What Marx does is to reverse the axis of representation in that he argues that it is not the quantity of money which determines the sum of the prices of commodities but the other way around. The result is that the theme of representation is retained but primacy is accorded to commodities rather than money. It is the quantity of commodities, measured in terms of their prices, which determines the quantity of money in the sphere of circulation. The velocity of circulation of money comes into the argument because over a period of time each unit of money on average makes more than one move. The result is that when commodities are to be circulated over a period of time they require a quantity of money which is only a fraction of their value (measured in terms of prices). At times Marx assumes that the velocity of circulation of money is variable, and at other times—especially when laying down the relationship between the quantity of commodities and the quantity of money—he assumes it be constant. Throughout the discussion of how much money is absorbed by the sphere of circulation Marx assumes that the quantity of money is variable, and it is for this reason that the velocity of circulation of money does not occupy an important place in his analysis. The velocity of circulation of money and thus whether it is a constant or a variable are of importance only when the quantity of money is assumed to be constant—as in monetary theory.

That the quantity of money is determined by the quantity of commodities is nothing more than a general claim. Marx does not indicate the mechanism through which commodities determine the quantity of money. In fact, no such mechanism can be indicated. The creation of money, as we pointed out in Chapter 3, depends on specific factors and those factors change with change in the form of money. One cannot, as a result, posit a general relation between the quantity of commodities and the quantity of money. The reason why Marx does not try to specify such a mechanism is because the relationship between money and commodities is one of representation rather than determination. In this respect, Marx is no different from some of the neo-classical monetary theorists who also do not specify the relation between money and what, for them, it is supposed to be linked to, namely, prices of commodities.

Though Marx remains within the confines of representation and there is no need for us to retain the theme of representation, the inversion is not without its effects. In inverting the hierarchy of representation Marx assumes something which neo-classical economists will find very hard to accept, namely, that prices are already attached to commodities when they step into the process of circulation. Obviously, Marx assumes this because for him it is values of commodities which directly or indirectly determine their prices. However, this is not the only justification for the assumption. The point is that the neo-classical contention that it is the market which determines price is, as some neo-classical economists themselves point out, meaningless. Except for particular types of trading, e.g. auctions, most sales and purchases in a capitalist economy take place on the basis of prices given by either the buyer or the seller of the commodity. Those prices may well be revised on the basis of the behaviour of sales and purchases of commodities but the point still remains that prices are determined by particular economic agents on the basis of calculations they carry out. The form of calculation and thus the way in which the behaviour of the market is taken into account vary from one economic agent to another. Therefore, the formula that it is the market which determines the price obscures the important fact that prices depend upon the forms of calculations employed by a restricted category of economic agents. In fact, just the claim that it is the quantity of money which determines the level of prices says nothing about the determination of prices because, as Marx points out, there is not a wholesale exchange of commodities for money. The quantity of money by itself is not pertinent to the determination of prices no matter how they may be determined. Patinkin realises this and he sets out to remedy the deficiency in the neo-classical account of the determination of prices by marrying the principle of representation with a theory of demand for money.

Further, as indicated in the earlier discussion, the inversion of the hierarchy and thus the attribution of primacy to the circulation of commodities avoids the problem which afflicts monetary theory. Once again it is not necessary to assume that the circulation of money is the phenomenal form of the circulation of commodities in order to retain Marx's analysis of money *qua* medium of circulation.

The rejection of any link of representation between money and commodities and thus the treatment of the circulation of money as a phenomenal form means that there cannot be a simple answer to the question of how much money is required to circulate a given sum of commodities. The amount of money required will depend, on the one hand, on the composition of commodities and, on the other, on the distribution of the stock of money or purchasing power among economic agents. In other words, there is no precise answer to this question and any attempt to give a precise answer transforms the problem of financing to the problem of representation. For it is only in the context of representation that the composition of commodities and the distribution of money does not matter.

However, the fact that one cannot give a precise answer to the question does not imply that the problem of financing is non-existent. The problem of financing not only exists but is also important. The problem, however, has a specific locus. There is no general problem of financing in the sense that the economy as a whole or capital as a whole does not face the problem of financing. The problem of financing exists for individual economic agents in the sense that they have to finance their purchases by either selling commodities or borrowing or using money balances in their possession. So, in general, the discussion of financing more or less immediately leads to the discussion of credit—a topic which will be discussed in the next chapter. However, Marxists have generally posed the problem of financing not by reference to a particular economic agent but by reference to the social capital as a whole. For example, Marx in volume 2 of *Capital* (ch. XVII) asks how the realisation of surplus value is financed. For Marx the conditions for financing the realisation of surplus value are the same as that for financing the circulation of a given volume of commodities under simple commodity production—the form of production with which Marx is exclusively concerned when he discusses money in volume 1 of *Capital*. Marx is right in arguing that there is no special problem of the realisation of surplus value separate from the circulation of commodities. The point is that financial conditions governing the circulation of commodities are not altered by the mere fact that commodities to be circulated are products of a capitalist rather than a non-capitalist unit of production.

Nevertheless, the point remains that there is no general problem of the realisation of surplus value. It is important to note that the question of how capitalists manage to realise surplus value does not arise out of the discussion of circulation of commodities. Instead it arises out of the belief that capitalism is an anarchic system of production and it is only by chance or accident or special circumstances that it manages to realise surplus value and thus survive. This belief does not play an important part in Marx's analysis of circulation in that the realisation of surplus value is not regarded as a general problem in volume 2 of *Capital*. But it does, for example, dominate Rosa Luxemburg's analysis of reproduction and the realisation of surplus value, and the analyses of other Marxists. This is the reason why Rosa Luxemburg so violently objects to Marx's statement that the problem of the realisation of surplus value is the same as the problem of circulation of commodities under simple commodity production. What one needs to reject is the conception of capitalism as an anarchic system of production. The notion of anarchy is coupled with what is generally termed the conscious organisation of production—a form of organisation of production which supposedly represents socialism but does nothing of the sort; in fact, it represents a mythical state of affairs whereby the workings of the economy are reduced to the calculations of a conscious and all-embracing subject. The anarchy of a capitalist economy is established and the conditions for the survival of capitalism deduced by reference to the mythical economy. Briefly, the argument is that there is no general problem of the survival and reproduction of capitalism and the fact that capitalist economies manage to survive does not justify surprise and bewilderment. Once this position is adopted one can analyse the specific problems which arise under capitalism and their financial implications—if they have such implications.

Chapter 6

Credit, Financial Markets, and Financial Institutions

So far we have either neglected credit or discussed it only tangentially. What we want to do in this chapter is first, to indicate the relations between credit and the circulation of commodities, second, to point out the specific features of financial markets, and third, to analyse the relationship between the forms and the volume of credit and the way in which financial institutions are organised and run. Marx has very little to say about credit in his analysis of money and when he talks about credit in volume 1 of *Capital* he restricts himself to trade credit. Though there is a lot more on credit in volume 3 than in the earlier volumes, most of the discussion is descriptive and the analysis of credit does not go beyond schematic indication of its effects. It is these schematic indications which Hilferding uses in his *Finance Capital*. Despite the fact that we are meant to be in the era of the dominance of finance capital there is very little by way of an analysis of financial institutions in Marxism. One, though not the sole, reason for this is that the Marxist analysis operates at the level of different forms of capital rather than at the level of economic institutions like industrial companies and financial institutions. It may be said that there is no difference between the two levels because an industrial company represents an industrial capital and similarly a financial institution an interest-bearing capital. The point is that an industrial company remains an industrial capital regardless of whether that company is a small private concern, or a partnership or a joint-stock company. *Mutatis mutandis* the same is true for a financial institution. The result is that analysis in terms of different types of capital specified in terms of their respective circuits either neglects or regards as secondary the organisational forms of industrial companies and financial institutions.

To turn now to the relation between the circulation of commodities and lending and borrowing. Carrying on from the discussion in previous chapters the relation can be specified by reference to money balances in the possession of economic agents, on the one hand, and the necessity of financing transactions in a monetary economy, on the other. It was argued earlier, in Chapter 4, that the gap between sales and purchases of an economic agent is filled by money balances. These money balances constitute the basis for a link between the circulation of commodities and credit in the sense that they may either take the form of a deposit in a financial institution—as they necessarily do when money takes the form of credit money—or be substituted by a financial asset. In a financially developed capitalist economy, as pointed out earlier, there is a whole spectrum of financial claims and assets which fills the gap between sales and purchases of economic agents. The actual form in which purchasing power is held depends on the characteristics and attributes of the economic agents. The implication is that in such an economy the relations of credit are not restricted to particular economic agents or transactions; instead, they envelop all economic agents and transactions. In terms of the functions of money what this means is that the distinction between the means of payment and the means of deferred payment disappears in an advanced capitalist economy. The fact that economic agents hold their purchasing power in the form of financial claims and assets means that they lend, but, as is obvious, economic agents not only lend but they also borrow. Apart from financial institutions, economic agents borrow and lend because their expenditure and receipt patterns do not coincide.

In a financially developed capitalist economy, for the most part, lending and borrowing by economic agents (financial institutions are not, for expositional reasons, included in the category economic agents) is through the intermediary of financial institutions in that when they borrow they borrow from a financial institution and when they lend they lend to a financial institution. Lending by economic agents does not affect the circulation of commodities in that it is simply a result of the decision concerning the form in which purchasing power is to be held. In a financially developed economy economic agents cannot but lend to financial institutions because by and large they have to hold purchasing power in the form of claims on financial institutions. The fact that economic agents lend is of importance mainly from the point of view of distribution in that it may mean that they receive income in the form of interest. It is borrowing by economic agents which is important from the point of view of circulation of commodities.

The main effect of credit is to increase the rate of circulation of commodities in the sense that it makes possible purchases which would not otherwise be possible. When there is no lending and borrowing of the medium of circulation all purchases have to be financed by the proceeds of previous sales. This restriction applies to all economic agents except those who have power to create money. The effect of this restriction is to make the pattern of purchases of an economic agent subservient to the pattern of his income. The availability of credit implies the removal of the constraint on the rate of circulation of commodities in that it enables an economic agent to purchase commodities without first selling commodities. Thus its effect is to make the pattern of expenditure of an economic agent relatively autonomous of his receipts. The qualification, relatively, is necessary because the pattern of expenditure of economic agents cannot be completely autonomous of the pattern of their receipts, since loans have to be ultimately repaid. Lending and borrowing, on the one hand, and the repayment of loans, on the other, mean that the redistribution of the stock of money does not just depend on the circulation of commodities. Alternatively, as described in Chapter 2, in a financially developed economy money traverses two different circuits, namely, the commodities circuit and the financial circuit and these two circuits are interdependent in the sense that the sale and purchase of commodities affect lending and borrowing and vice versa.

In general terms credit enlarges the possibilities of exchange open to economic agents. But the exact effect and the significance of this enlargement depends on who these economic agents are and the forms which credit takes. In volume 3 of *Capital* Marx assumes that the provision of credit under capitalism is restricted to capital, in particular industrial capital. And the analysis of the effects of credit under capitalism by Marx and Marxists, in particular Hilferding and Lenin, is by and large centred around its effect on the boundaries of the units of production under capitalism. Their analyses raise two separate questions: first, what is the nature of the link between credit and the organisation of the capitalist unit of production and, second, is it legitimate to restrict the analysis of the effects of credit to its effect on the units of production, especially in so far as present day capitalism is concerned?

Capitalist units of production can be conceptualised in a number of different ways. They are at the same time sites of production, loci of economic calculations and measurements, economic agents which buy and sell commodities and pay taxes, and organisations which have a specific legal status. Marx regards capitalist units of production as both the means of production and money capital, which are continually being used and replaced. The boundaries of a capitalist firm are delineated by the commodities it buys and sells and other economic transactions which it conducts, e.g. lending and borrowing; the scale of production carried out within the confines of a firm depends on the volume of money capital at its disposal. For present purposes what is important is that both the scale and the composition of production carried out within a firm and thus its boundaries depend on the calculations of that firm. The argument is that neither the methods of calculation which capitalist firms employ nor the forms of their organisation impose any general restriction on their boundaries. There are some forms of organisation of capitalist firms which lend themselves to change more easily than others but for the purposes of the present argument we may neglect such differences. Once the possibility of changes in the boundaries of firms exists, the provision of credit becomes relevant. The argument is that credit is unevenly distributed because some firms, for one reason or the other, are more creditworthy than others, and what this uneven distribution implies is that some firms grow faster than others. One of the causes of concentration in capitalist economies is the uneven distribution of credit. It is this effect of credit which Marx emphasises in his schematic outline in *Capital*, volume 3.

But for Lenin and Hilferding it is not so much unequal access to credit but instead what Hilferding calls the intimate relationship between banks and industrial firms which is the cause of concentration under capitalism. The problem is that the organisational link between banks and industrial firms which forms the basis of Lenin's and Hilferding's periodisations of capitalism is specific to only a few capitalist economies. For Hilferding finance capital signifies, on the one hand, the suppression of free competition by means of cartels, trusts, price and quantity agreements among firms and, on the other hand, the existence of close organisational links between firms and banks. Hilferding's characterisation would pose no special problem but for the fact that financial capital is assumed to be dominant not just in Germany—the country where banks did have close relationships with industrial firms—but in all capitalist countries. If we adopt Hilferding's characterisation absolutely to the letter then we have to argue that neither Britain nor the USA was ever under the dominance of finance capital. It is not only that the American and the British banks did not have the kind of links with industrial firms to which Hilferding refers but their organisation and the rules which govern their functioning ruled out such a link. For example, British banks and financial institutions did not—and still do not—provide anything more than short-term loans to industrial firms.

There are a large number of similarities between capitalist national economies, e.g. the existence of a network of credit which embraces the whole economy, restrictive agreements among firms, and concentration and centralisation of industrial firms. But that is not the point at issue. What we are concerned with here is the propriety of using a relationship which is specific to particular economies as a basis of periodising capitalism in general. It is clear that Hilferding's and Lenin's characterisations of twentieth-century capitalism cannot be sustained as they stand. For the present analysis what is important about Hilferding's and Lenin's analyses is that they seem to rest on the assumption that the effect of credit is independent of the organisation of the financial structure. It is this assumption which is at issue when Lenin and Hilferding generalise about capitalism from specific cases, and apart from that both of them have very little to say about the structure and organisation of financial institutions. The neglect of organisational forms and the lack of attention to differences in the organisational forms which economic institutions can assume is not peculiar to the analysis of financial institutions. It is also characteristic of the analysis of industrial firms; for the most part, it is the size and whether or not they are international, rather than organisational and institutional peculiarities of firms in capitalist countries which have been subjects of analysis. However, just the facts that a firm is large and that the production of a particular commodity is concentrated in the hands of a few firms tell us very little. Briefly, what we want to argue is that credit does have an effect on the organisation of the units of production under capitalism but the nature of that effect crucially depends on the organisation and the structure of financial institutions, on the one hand, and of industrial firms, on the other.

Even if all the above qualifications are accepted it still remains the case that the analysis of the effects of credit under capitalism in Marxism is centred around the effect of lending and borrowing by industrial firms on their organisational boundaries. Lending and borrowing in capitalist economies is not just between industrial firms and financial institutions; the network of credit in such economies spans all categories of economic agents. It is not only that credit to consumers and credit to public state apparatuses from financial institutions in advanced capitalist countries is as large in volume as credit extended to industrial firms, if not larger. There has been an important shift in the composition of credit since Hilferding and Lenin wrote on financial institutions. Both consumer credit (including mortgages) and public credit (to public institutions) have increased faster than industrial credit. The implication is that the analysis of the financial structure in terms of the relationships between financial institutions and industrial firms remains incomplete and rests on a neglect of the fact that the economic interests of finance capital extend well beyond industrial capital. As a result, it is necessary to discard the privilege implicitly given to the effect of credit on the organisation of industrial firms in Marxism. Credit in advanced capitalist countries, to put it generally, not only leads to concentration and centralisation of industrial capital but also forms the basis of public expenditure, and housing and transportation policies which rely on private ownership of houses and cars and the mass ownership of consumer durables.

The development of the network of credit in capitalist economies has been associated with the development of the market in financial assets. Financial assets, as we pointed out earlier, share some of the characteristics of money in that, like money, they are not objects of use and thus are acquired for the sake of their exchange later and further, like money, they are repositories of purchasing power. From the point of view of credit the main importance of marketable financial assets is that they enable a creditor to recover his capital before the maturity of the loan. What marketability of financial assets does is to make the terms on which the capital is borrowed relatively independent of the terms on which it is actually lent by those who keep the financial asset till it matures. What we want to do here is to analyse, first, the particular form of trading associated with financial assets, namely speculation and, second, the role and place of the stock market in advanced capitalist countries.

Credit, Financial Markets, and Financial Institutions 95

Speculation is a particular form of trading whereby a commodity is bought just for the sake of its sale later in the same market. It may seem that this definition subsumes the activity of merchants under the category of speculation. But the point is that though the activity of merchants involves the purchase of commodities for the sake of their sale later, that sale and purchase are not in the same market. For example, commercial firms purchase commodities in the wholesale market in order to sell them in the retail market; and the two markets are not the same in the sense that the participants in those markets are different. Further, the activity of merchants is a specialised activity while speculation is not in the sense that economic institutions do not specialise in speculation as they may do in buying and selling commodities. Speculation is of particular importance in the case of financial assets because trading in them cannot but be speculation. Speculation, however, is not restricted to financial assets; commodities too can form the subject of speculation. Commodities *qua* subject of speculative trading assume the characteristics of financial assets. Here the obvious example is real estate, which is bought and sold like financial assets.

The condition of existence of speculation is fluctuation in prices; as a result, things whose prices remain constant cannot form the subject of speculative trading. If speculation thrives on fluctuation in prices it gives rise itself to fluctuations. Speculation involves a particular form of calculation different from those forms which govern ordinary trade in commodities. Speculative trading, unlike ordinary trading, is not so much based on the absolute level of prices as it is on the difference between current and expected future price. If the level of prices matters in speculation it is because it is thought to be related to changes in prices. In the case where a commodity forms the subject of speculation the fact that it is an object of use is of no direct relevance and it is only the expected change in its price which is important. Briefly, the argument is that associated with speculative trading is a special form of calculation, and the replacement of ordinary trading by speculative trading implies a change in the form of calculation. The change is particularly obvious in the case where firms and companies are acquired by financial institutions not for the purposes of production but for the purposes of speculation. In that case the means of production and other assets in the possession of the company, e.g. land and buildings, are not valued so much for what they will contribute to the production of the commodity in question but for how much they will fetch in the market. In advanced capitalist countries it is not only commodities but also agricultural farms, industrial firms, etc, which can assume the characteristics of financial assets.

Both in Marx and in Hilferding speculation is regarded as a form of trading which performs no useful social function and as something which keeps financiers busy but does not affect the workings of industrial capital. Both of them overlook the fact that speculation is a necessary concomitant of the market in financial assets and financial institutions. The argument is that speculation can only be regarded as irrelevant to the functioning of capitalism in general, and industrial capital in particular, if the same is considered true for the market in financial assets. Hilferding regards the sale and purchase of commodities as necessary to the survival of the society. On the other hand, he regards the sale and purchase of financial assets as unnecessary to the production of commodities and the realisation of profits. The sale of new financial assets is actually a form of borrowing, and in a general sense it has the same status as any other form of borrowing. Though the sale and purchase of already issued financial assets does not add to the volume of credit, none the less the terms of their sale and purchase are important, for they determine the terms on which new financial assets can be floated. What this means is that speculation in financial assets determines the terms on which firms can borrow by selling marketable securities and thus it cannot be regarded as something which is irrelevant to the functioning of industrial firms. Further, financial assets which are traded on financial markets in capitalist economies include not only bonds, bills, and debentures, i.e. instruments for raising money capital, but also equities. Equities have a dual character, namely, on the one hand, they are means for raising capital and like other financial assets they represent an entitlement to receive a certain category of income, while, on the other hand, they represent the fact that the firm which issues them is organised in a particular way. The control of a public company is transferable through trading in its shares. Thus trading in equities of a firm not only determines the terms on which it can issue new shares and bonds but also whether or not it can survive as an independent economic organisation. So speculation in financial assets has not only a financial implication but also an implication for the structure of the organisation of the industrial capital. It is clear that neither of the two implications can be regarded as irrelevant for the functioning of industrial capital and the form of reproduction in capitalist economies.

We have already referred to the fact that there two forms of trading on the market for financial assets, namely trading in new financial assets and trading in already issued financial assets. The economic significance of the two forms of trading are not the same. It is only the former which adds to the total volume of credit in the economy. The latter, on the other hand, means a transfer of funds between the participants on the market and it is a form of realising the capital represented by the financial asset in question. But it is the latter which is important from the point of view of the determination of the rate of interest on marketable financial assets, because in general the volume of already issued financial assets far exceeds the new issue.

The respective economic significance of trading in new financial assets and already issued ones and the link between the two forms of trading indicated here has an important implication for Marx's discussion of the determination of the rate of interest. In *Capital*, vol. 3 Marx discusses the determination of the rate of interest in terms of the demand and supply of loanable funds. Just for the purposes of the present argument we assume that all borrowings take the form of the sale of marketable financial assets. Given this assumption, the demand for loanable funds is represented by the new financial assets which are on offer for sale, while the supply of loanable funds is in turn represented by the demand for new securities. It is only the demand and supply of new securities which is relevant so far as the demand and supply of loanable funds is concerned. But the problem is that from the point of view of a purchaser an already issued financial asset—an asset whose purchase does not add to the volume of credit—is a substitute for the one which is newly issued. The implication is that there is no way in which one can distinguish the supply of loanable funds from trading in already issued securities. Further, as pointed out earlier, the terms on which newly issued securities are issued are determined by the terms on which already issued securities are traded. The basic issue concerns the significance and the status of the rate of interest. In the context of the theory of the determination of the rate of interest put forward in *Capital* the rate of interest is assumed to represent just the cost of borrowing funds. But the prices of financial assets which determine the rate of interest not only represent the cost of borrowing but also the return from placing funds in financial assets whether newly issued or already issued. Thus the argument is that both the former and the latter are determined jointly in the financial market, and the determination of the rate of interest cannot be equated with the demand and supply of loanable funds.

The aim here is not simply to assess and criticise what Marx says about the determination of the rate of interest but also to raise a general question about it. What the case of financial assets points to is that both the significance and the form of the determination of the rate of interest depend on the form which lending and borrowing takes. It is only in the case where lending and borrowing takes the form of the sale and purchase of financial assets that lending and borrowing of the past (represented by already issued securities in circulation) can affect the terms on which new issues can be floated. But in the case where the creation of credit takes the form of the creation of deposits in financial institutions the terms on which deposits were created in the past have no direct bearing on the terms which new deposits can be created. Unlike the case of financial assets, speculation plays no direct part in the determination of the rate of interest on deposits. Further, the rate of interest which borrowers pay does not have the same status in the two cases. In the case where the borrowing takes the form of the issue of financial assets the rate of interest which the borrower pays is the rate of interest ruling at the date of the issue of the financial asset, and events after that date do not have any effect on the terms of the repayment of the loan. In contrast, the rate of interest which a borrower pays when a loan is granted in the form of the creation of a deposit in a financial institution is the rate at the date of repayment rather than the date of issue of the loan. Apart from these differences, the relation of the two forms of lending to the forms of money is also different. Granting of loans by means of the creation of deposits is associated with credit money, and the rate of interest charged on such loans is, as we pointed out in Chapter 3, a form of seigniorage. In contrast lending and borrowing through the sale and purchase of financial assets has no necessary relation to credit money. What these differences indicate is that the significance and determination of the rate of interest varies with the form which lending and borrowing takes and the form which money assumes. The implication is that there cannot be a general theory of the determination of the rate of interest contrary to what is implicitly assumed in the discussions of the rate of interest.

Now we go on to consider briefly the place and significance of the stock market or the market in financial assets in capitalist national economies. Given the fact that trading on the stock market consists of trading in both new and already issued financial assets, the stock market is, on the one hand, a source of funds for economic agents who are capable of issuing marketable financial assets and, on the other, a mechanism for the transfer of funds between those who buy and sell already issued financial assets. Further, given the fact that equities are both a financial asset in the sense of being entitlements to receive dividends and means—at least potential—for the acquisition of the control of the firms which they represent, the stock market is also a market in the control of firms. The place of the stock market depends on these three factors; they are not equally important and their respective significance varies from one national economy to another.

As a source of funds the stock market is not of the same importance to all economic agents. Households, for example, do not borrow by selling marketable securities, and, although firms do, in general of all the sources of borrowing open to firms the stock market is a minor one in comparison to, for example, financial institutions. And apart from that, the importance of the stock market as a source of funds to firms varies from one national economy to another; it is of greater importance in the US and Britain than in Germany, France, or Japan. The importance of the stock market depends on the nature of organisational links between financial institutions and industrial companies. In the countries where banks have direct organisational links with industrial companies the stock market is unimportant, and the converse is true in the countries where there are no such organisational links. But in all capitalist economies the stock market is an important source of borrowing for public state apparatuses. Whether or not public borrowing dominates the stock market crucially depends on its magnitude relative to what firms borrow through the stock market. In Britain, for instance, trading in government stocks and securities accounts for well over half the total trading on the stock market. In the USA, on the other hand, government securities are not as important as they are in Britain.

An important point about the stock market is that it is not a source of funds alternative to financial institutions. Given that money in capitalist countries takes the form of credit money, all payments associated with transactions in the stock market are in the form of transfer of deposits in financial institutions. What this means is that the stock market in capitalist economies does not mobilise funds which are outside financial institutions; the reason why it does not do so is because there are no such funds left in those economies. Not only that, most of the trading on the stock market is conducted by financial institutions. Thus, for the most part, when firms and public state apparatuses borrow by selling financial assets they in fact borrow from financial institutions. In the cases where new issues are bought by economic agents other than financial institutions borrowing and lending means nothing more than a redistribution of deposits in financial institutions from those who buy new issues to those who sell them.

Given the fact that most financial assets are held by financial institutions, trading in already issued financial assets is, in effect, a method by which funds are transferred from one financial institution to another. If most of the new issues are bought by financial institutions, it may be asked why they do not lend by extending advances, as they do for the most part, rather than by buying financial assets. The difference between advances and financial assets is relevant here, namely that assets which take the form of advances to economic agents, unlike financial assets, are not transferable. The implication is that the capital represented by advances cannot, by and large, be recovered before the maturity of the loan, while the capital represented by marketable assets can be recovered through their sale—hence the economic attraction of marketable financial assets to financial institutions. So far as financial institutions are concerned it is the secondary trading (trading in already issued financial assets) which provides the rationale for primary trading (trading in new issues).

One may also ask why economic agents like firms and public state apparatuses borrow by selling financial assets rather than by directly obtaining advances from financial institutions. So far as firms are concerned, to some extent the issue of equities is an organisational requisite. For a company to be a joint-stock company it is necessary that its shares are quoted and traded on the stock market. Otherwise, as indicated above, the stock market is one of a number of sources of funds available to firms which they may use from time to time. Public state apparatuses borrow by selling securities rather than by obtaining advances because the magnitude of their borrowing is normally larger than what can be provided by an individual financial institution; so borrowing through the stock market is a way of pooling the lending capacities of financial institutions. Further, marketable government securities are one of the main supports of monetary policy, the result being that borrowing by selling such securities is a necessary complement of monetary policy.

The stock market has not always played the same part in capitalist economies. Lenin, in his *Imperialism— the Highest Stage of Capitalism*, argues that the development and the enlargement of banks has meant a decrease in the importance of the stock market, and he identifies the importance of the stock market with the competitive stage of capitalism. Central to Lenin's argument is the assumption that the stock market is an alternative to financial institutions. The assumption may be valid so far as the stock markets before the First World War are concerned but is not so for the present-day stock markets. The latter are adjuncts rather than alternatives to financial institutions. Further, the dominance of government securities on the stock market is a later development. For example, the British government securities were of insignificant importance on the London stock market before the First World War. In conclusion, what one can say is that the functioning and the significance of the stock market in the present-day national economies depends on the following three factors: (1) the existence of joint stock companies; (2) borrowing by public state apparatuses; and (3) the multiplicity of financial institutions.

The analysis of lending and borrowing can never be complete without the analysis of financial institutions. What we want to do now is briefly to analyse the relation between lending and borrowing and the structure of organisation of financial institutions.

Financial institutions cannot exist without lending and borrowing but lending and borrowing can and has existed without financial institutions. Starting with this general remark, one may ask what difference the existence of financial institutions makes to lending and borrowing. The existence of financial institutions is equated here with autonomy of lending and borrowing from other economic activities. In order to answer the question we take the particular case where lending and borrowing is associated with the sale and purchase of commodities. This, in fact, is the case which Marx refers to in *Capital*, vol. 1 when he discusses money in its capacity as the means of deferred payment (the means of payment in the terminology of Marx). The distinguishing feature of this form of lending is that it is subservient to the sale and purchase of commodities. Lending in this case does not take the form of an advance of cash but a delay in the payment for the commodity in question. It, in other words, consists of a temporal discrepancy between the delivery of the commodity and the payment for it. For the present purposes the important point about the trade credit is that it presupposes a double coincidence, namely that the borrower should also be the purchaser of the commodity in question and the lender the seller of that commodity. Here one can draw a useful parallel between trade credit and barter. Barter too, as pointed out earlier, presupposes a double coincidence, i.e. that the seller of a commodity purchases the commodity of the person to whom he sells his own. Double coincidence is a restriction; just as barter restricts the scope of exchange of commodities, so trade credit, in particular, and the pairing of lending and borrowing with other economic activities, e.g. trading, production and consumption of commodities, etc., in general, restrict the scope of lending and borrowing. The lending capacity of a merchant is limited by the requirements of cash for the purposes of the sale and purchase of commodities which is his principal activity. Similarly, the lending capacity of a firm is limited by requirement of cash for the purposes of production. Further, in the case where lending and borrowing is coupled with another economic activity the form of lending is determined by the nature of the economic activity to which lending is subservient. Trade credit is an obvious example of this. The emergence of financial institutions and thus autonomy of lending and borrowing from other economic activities is necessary for the removal of restrictions on the forms of credit, on the one hand, and the removal of the restriction on the volume of credit imposed by the financial capacity of an individual lender, on the other. Both the effect of money on the exchange of commodities and the economic significance of the enlargement of the possibilities of lending and borrowing brought about by the emergence of financial institutions depend on the characteristics of the economy in which lending and borrowing takes place.

An important characteristic of an advanced capitalist economy is that lending and borrowing is not restricted to any particular category of economic agents. This raises the question of the identification of financial institutions from other economic agents, in particular, firms. Firms, like financial institutions, lend and borrow, so just the fact of lending and borrowing cannot distinguish the former from the latter. The main point about financial institutions is that they borrow (we will discuss the nature of this borrowing later) in order to lend, while the same is not true for industrial companies. Thus, the criterion of identification is the form of calculation employed in determining lending and borrowing. It may well be the case that a number of industrial firms actually behave more like financial institutions than industrial companies in their lending and borrowing operations and that the category financial institutions delineated according to the general criterion proposed here actually includes economic institutions which are not officially classified as such.

The exact significance of lending and borrowing crucially depends on the form of money. In the case where money does not take the form of credit money, i.e. when the creation of money is independent of the operation of lending and borrowing as in the case of commodity money, lending means the transfer of something whose quantity does not depend on the operation of lending and borrowing. An example of this is provided by commodity money. Lending and borrowing in the case of a non-credit money is subject to the overall constraint that the volume of lending does not exceed the stock of money in existence. And the lending capacity of a financial institution in that case is limited by the amount of money capital in its possession which may consist of both the money capital the financial institution owns and the amount it succeeds in borrowing from other economic agents. The point is that, in the case of a non-credit money, lending by a financial institution can either take the form of what we may term 'usury' (lending of its own money capital) or intermediation (lending of borrowed money capital). So far as the former is concerned the volume of lending is limited by the financial capacity of the financial institution, and the latter depends on its ability to borrow idle cash.

The significance of lending and borrowing is, in contrast, completely different when money takes the form of credit money. To start with, there is no overall limit on the volume of credit because then the stock of money itself depends on the operation of lending and borrowing. Lending in that case does not take the form of something not created by financial institutions but it simply takes the form of the creation of a deposit. Further, entities like 'own money capital' and 'borrowed money capital' do not have the same significance in the case of credit money as they do in the case of non-credit money. When money takes the form of credit money, the money capital in the possession of a financial institution, in contrast to the other case, is what is created by financial institutions themselves. It consists of nothing more than the financial claims of the financial institution in question on other financial institutions. Thus, taken together financial institutions can increase the money capital in their possession—something which they cannot do when money does not take the form of credit money. Not only that, borrowing by financial institutions does not have the same significance in the two cases. In the case where money is not credit money financial institutions borrow what they themselves do not create. But when money takes the form of credit money, as pointed out earlier, the purchasing power is for the most part held in the form of deposits in financial institutions or claims on them, and when financial institutions borrow they, in fact, borrow nothing other than what they themselves create, namely deposits. Thus, borrowing by a financial institution means nothing more than the acquisition of claims against other financial institutions.

It is common in monetary theory to treat financial institutions as financial intermediaries in the sense that they borrow in order to lend. Once financial institutions are treated as intermediaries it necessarily follows that their lending operations are constrained by their borrowing operations in the sense that they cannot lend more than what they manage to borrow, and the terms on which they lend have to bear some relation to the terms on which they borrow. Under this conception financial institutions, in analogy with telephone exchanges, appear as what one may term financial exchanges: their sole function is to pair potential lenders with potential borrowers. Taken strictly, this conception implies that the forms of credit, i.e. the terms of repayment and the length of time for which credit is given, do not depend on the way in which financial institutions are organised but instead on the preference of potential lenders and borrowers. What we have argued is that the notion of financial intermediation cannot be applied to financial institutions as a whole. One cannot argue that the lending capacity of financial institutions depends on what they succeed in borrowing because they only borrow what they themselves create. Thus, their borrowing cannot be said to constitute a limit on their capacity to lend. Then the implication is that the limit on the power of financial institutions to create credit in advanced capitalist countries cannot be understood by reference to the notion of intermediation.

It is necessary to qualify this. It is not being argued here that the notion of intermediation has no analytical use whatsoever. It is possible to apply the notion of intermediation to individual financial institutions, in particular to those financial institutions whose deposits are not used as the means of payment, in the sense that taken in isolation their lending capacity depends on their ability to attract deposits from other financial institutions. Building societies are a case in point. Institutional trappings aside, building societies are nothing more than a set of accounts in banks, i.e. financial institutions whose deposits circulate as the means of payment. Therefore, a transfer of deposits from banks to building societies mean nothing more than a redistribution of deposits from those who bank with building societies to the accounts of building societies within banks. Building societies when they lend do so by writing a cheque on their accounts in banks. Thus, their capacity to lend is determined by the amount credited to their accounts in banks. We may, in view of the way in which building societies function, refer to them as financial intermediaries on the grounds that their capacity to lend is determined by their capacity to borrow. But the argument here is that the notion of intermediation cannot be used to deduce the limits on the power of financial institutions to create credit in general. In the example we have taken the transfer of deposits to building societies from banks does not by itself mean either a decrease in the deposits of banks or a decrease in the power of banks to create credit. Further, lending by banks, which in the case of credit money takes the form of the creation of deposits, potentially increases the power of building societies to lend in the sense that some of the deposits thus created may be transferred to building societies. If the borrowing of a bank is identified with its deposits—which for accounting purposes are regarded as financial liabilities—then a bank necessarily borrows what it lends. For, as indicated earlier, lending by a bank takes the form of the creation of a deposit which supposedly forms a part of its borrowings. This makes it clear that the notion of intermediation cannot be applied to banks whose deposits circulate as the means of payment.

None the less there are limits on the power of financial institutions to create credit. In the case when money takes the form of credit money there is no externally imposed limit on the power of financial institutions to create credit. Such limits as indeed exist arise out of specialisation of financial institutions in particular forms of lending and borrowing and special procedures concerning the settlement of liabilities among financial institutions. We have already pointed out that banks are normally required to settle their liabilities through the transfer of deposits in the central bank, and this requirement limits the ability of banks to create credit because, *ceteris paribus*, the creation of deposits by a bank normally leads to an increase in its liabilities to other financial institutions without a corresponding increase in the ability of the bank to settle those financial claims. The limit on the power of financial institutions to create credit therefore rests on the simple fact that no financial institution has the monopoly possession of deposits. The absence of the monopoly is maintained partly as a result of legal exclusions and partly as a result of the forms of accounting and calculation which financial institutions employ. In a number of countries the central bank has the monopoly possession of the deposits of public state apparatuses, e.g. in Britain, which means that private banks are automatically excluded from holding public-sector deposits. In the US, on the other hand, though there is no restriction on private banks holding public-sector deposits, the absence of monopoly is maintained by a legal limitation on the number of branches which a bank may open. As for the pertinence of methods of calculation and methods of accounting, financial institutions not only specialise in particular forms of lending but they also employ different methods for assessing the creditworthiness of potential lenders which perpetuate, at least in part, the given range of specialisation. The reason why we have given such importance to the fact that no financial institution has the monopoly of lending and borrowing in the economy is that the source of restriction on the power of financial institutions to create credit is the claims of financial institutions against each other. Needless to add here that such claims can only exist when there is more than one financial institution.

We have neglected the role of central banks so far in this argument. Central banks do impose controls on the creation of credit and the nature of those controls varies from one national economy to another. But the fact is that in most cases it is a bank rather than, say, a department of government which controls the functioning of financial institutions and the power of the central

Credit, Financial Markets, and Financial Institutions   107

bank over other banks and financial institutions rests on its privileged position as a financial institution. The privileged position of the central bank, as we pointed out earlier in Chapter 3, rests on the fact that its deposits have the status of the legal tender and they are used to settle the claims of financial institutions against each other. Thus, the argument is that monetary controls imposed by central banks and monetary authorities are based on the restrictions implied by the multiplicity of financial institutions.

One important corollary of the rejection of the notion that financial institutions function by intermediation is that banks and financial institutions are not at par with each other in their lending and borrowing operations. Often financial institutions are analysed in terms of their balance sheets. In terms of accounting the two sides of the balance sheet, namely the asset side and the liability side, appear at par with each other. To start with one has to question the accounting notion of liability—a notion which is commonly used in the analysis of financial institutions. In terms of accounting the deposits of financial institutions are their liabilities. Liabilities in the sense that they can be withdrawn; but withdrawal of a deposit from a financial institution in an economy where money takes the form of credit money means nothing more than its transfer to another financial institution. Thus, the withdrawal of deposits means nothing more than a creation of a claim by a financial institution against the financial institution in question. This argument remains valid even if the withdrawal of deposits takes the form of their conversion into cash. For cash is created by the central bank, and the conversion of a deposit into cash is equivalent to the creation of the liability of the financial institution in question to the central bank. The implication of the argument is that, taken as a whole, financial institutions have no liabilities and the only effective liabilities of financial institutions are their liabilities to each other.

Therefore, what is required for the functioning of a financial institution is that it should be able to acquire claims against other financial institutions at least sufficient to balance its liabilities to them. So when financial institutions compete against each other to acquire deposits, in effect, they compete to acquire financial claims against each other. Once we analyse the functioning of financial institutions in these terms rather than in terms of the notion of intermediation there is no reason to expect a correspondence between the terms on which financial institutions lend and the terms on which they borrow, i.e. the rate of interest on deposits and conditions for its withdrawal. What follows from this argument is that a financial institution can support its lending activities by offering to accept deposits on a wide variety of terms. The fact that financial institutions specialise in offering a particular variety of deposits does not mean anything more than specialising in a particular way of acquiring claims against other financial institutions.

Now, what we can argue is that the two sides of a financial institution's balance sheet are not symmetrical in the sense that calculations which underlie the two sides of the balance sheet are not the same. The calculations which govern the terms on which financial institutions offer deposits are not the same as the terms on which they extend loans. This means that lending practices of a particular type of financial institution have to be understood in terms of the way in which they assess the creditworthiness of potential borrowers and the way in which they estimate the value of collaterals rather in terms of, so to say, their borrowing operations. Financial institutions specialise both in terms of the way in which they lend and the way in which they borrow. The implication of what we have just argued is that specialisation on the lending side has to be treated as autonomous of specialisation on the borrowing side, and they have to be separately explained. To give an example, the fact that pension funds and insurance companies buy shares in companies while the British clearing banks do not cannot just be explained in terms of the fact that, while the deposits of the latter are withdrawable on demand, those of the former are not.

The analysis of financial institutions here is sketchy. The arguments which are put forward can be summarised in the following terms. The power of financial institutions to create credit depends on the form of money. It is not the centralisation of bank capital which Lenin and Hilferding so much emphasised but the fact that money in advanced capitalist economies takes the form of credit money which is central to an analysis of the credit power of financial institutions. The status of lending and borrowing is affected by the form which money takes. What we have argued is that lending and borrowing—in particular that by financial institutions—acquires a special significance of its own under credit money. As a result, one cannot any longer argue in general that financial institutions in capitalist countries of today function by intermediation.

Part II

Enterprises and Capitalist Calculation

Chapter 7

Calculation as Ideology

The theorisation of enterprise calculation in Marx's *Capital* is both a theorisation of the nature of economic agents and economic 'ideologies' under a capitalist mode of production and of the relationship between economic mechanisms with different theoretical statuses. As we pointed out in the first volume of this work, Marxist theory conceives the economic agent as a 'personification' of a 'place' defined by reference to the mode of production. The general deficiencies of this position have already been pointed out but this conception is relevant here from the particular point of view of a theory of calculation. For Marxist theory 'economic ideologies' are 'representations' of the economic process that are related to the place/personification of the agent. In so far as the agent is a personification (the capitalist as personification of 'capital'), then the unity of the agent is ensured by what the agent personifies. Our task in this section will be to investigate whether the concept of 'economic ideologies' as 'representations of the process' is actually consistent with, what is for Marxist theory, the necessary unity of the agent.

In order to explain the functioning and the transformations of the capitalist mode of production it is necessary for *Capital* to refer to a set of 'laws' and 'tendencies'. These laws and tendencies apply to the social capital, for example, in volume 1 of *Capital* Marx tells us that the analyses presented there apply to 'a fragment of social capital promoted to autonomy'. The import of the reference to social capital is that the laws and tendencies apply in a universal way within a capitalist mode of production, i.e. they apply to each and every 'unit' of capital. Taken in this way laws and tendencies apply to the enterprise in so far as it may be treated itself as a 'fragment' of the social capital. Marx is not wholly consistent in his treatment of social capital but this 'level' of analysis has an important bearing on the position of the enterprise in relation to the laws and tendencies. The primacy of the laws and tendencies means that the enterprise plays the role of 'realising' them. The problem that we will discuss in respect of the relation between laws and tendencies and enterprise calculation is whether the way in which enterprise calculation is conceptualised is consistent with its assigned function of realising the laws and tendencies.

Marx's discussion of 'economic ideologies' in *Capital* is centred around the idea that they are 'false' accounts of the source of the value of commodities. Naturally these 'ideologies' are false because they diverge from the concept of the determination of value in the theory of value, that the value of commodities is determined by the socially necessary labour-time required for their production. We speak of economic *ideologies*. The plural applies to the 'false sources' of the value of commodities and it will be necessary to examine the diversity of these sources and the pertinence of this diversity.

Labour is represented to the capitalist as a cost of production rather than the source of value. This results for Marx from a division in capitalist calculation into costs and mark up. The calculation of costs relates to the demands of reproduction, i.e. every enterprise has to cover its costs to reproduce itself. In this sense it is an exigency of capitalist calculation to calculate costs and to distinguish costs from 'mark up'. Labour-power is purchased by capital and is 'represented' as 'labour', the value of labour-power appearing as the cost of labour. In turn this 'representation' is representation to an agent who is a 'personification' of capital. The 'distortion' lies in the representation of a cost to capital as the 'actual cost' of the commodity. 'The capitalist cost of the commodity is measured by the expenditure of *capital* while the actual cost is measured by the expenditure of *labour*.' (*Capital*, vol. 3, p. 26)

It should be noted that Marx relates this analysis to a specific 'false' source of value:

> Under the item of expenses, which embrace wages as well as the price of raw materials, wear and tear of machinery, etc., the extortion of unpaid labour figures only as a saving in paying for an article which is included in expenses, only as a smaller

payment for a certain quantity of labour, similar to the saving when raw materials are bought more cheaply, or the depreciation of machinery decreases. In this way the extortion of surplus-labour loses its specific character. Its specific relationship to surplus-value is obscured. . . . The relationships of capital are obscured by the fact that all parts of capital appear equally as the source of excess value (profit). (*Capital*, vol. 3, pp. 44–5)

Assuming this 'representation' model, this consequence does not, however, follow. In fact it could be argued that in so far as the agent is conceived of as strictly separating costs of production from 'mark up' there should be a tendency, in accordance with the concepts deployed by Marx, for the 'representation' entirely to divorce the source of surplus from the sphere of costs of production.

While the idea that each component part of capital contributes equally to the generation of the surplus product places the source of value within the 'sphere of production', alternative 'false' sources place the generation of value within the process of circulation. An example of this is that profit arises from the sale of commodities. Again this is argued in terms of a postulated 'position of the agent'. The exigency of 'realising' the extracted surplus value is argued to create the 'representation' of the derivation of the surplus from sale:

In the direct process of production the capitalist already acts simultaneously as producer of commodities and manager of commodity-production. Hence this process of production appears to him by no means simply as a process of producing surplus value. But whatever may be the surplus value extorted by capital in the actual production process and appearing in commodities, the value and surplus value contained in the commodities must first be realised in the circulation-process. And both the restitution of the value advanced in production and particularly, the surplus value contained in the commodities seem not merely to be realised in the circulation but actually to arise from it. (*Capital*, vol. 3, p. 807)

This passage, however, contains an ambiguity which later investigation will show is by no means fortuitous. Although the 'false source' is declared as the sale of commodities the process of production also 'appears', though 'by no means simply', as a 'process of production of surplus value'. That is to say, there is a contradiction between 'representations of the production process' and 'representations of the exchange and circulation of commodities'. It will be necessary to return to this contradiction later in the argument.

False sources are, however, not merely cases of refusals to privilege labour, for another false source privileges not 'labour in general' but the labour of supervision.

> The conception of profit of enterprise as the wages of supervising labour, arising from the antithesis of profit of enterprise to interest, is further strengthened by the fact that a portion of profit may, indeed, be separated, and is separated in reality, as wages, or rather the reverse, that a portion of wages appears under capitalist production as integral part of profit. This portion, as Adam Smith correctly deduced, presents itself in pure form, independently and wholly separated from profit (as the sum of interest and profit of enterprise), on the one hand, and on the other, from that portion of profit which remains, after interest is deducted, as profit of enterprise in the salary of management of those branches of business whose size, etc., permits of a sufficient division of labour to justify a special salary for a manager. (*Capital*, vol. 3, p. 376)

This particular formulation of the 'false source' raises a number of obvious difficulties. Paradoxically Marx argues that it is the separation in capitalist accounting practice of profit of enterprise from wages of superintendence which reinforces the concept of profit *as* wages of superintendence. Precisely the reverse might be expected, for if 'profit of enterprise' is to be represented as 'wages of supervising labour' a conflation of the two categories is effected. Here, in other words, we have a contradiction between 'categories of the practice' and 'representation of the process' thus departing from the 'normal' relation of reflection.

The paradox is deepened, moreover, when this particular analysis is set in its theoretical context. It occurs in Marx's discussion of interest and profit of enterprise and is argued as an effect of the division of the two categories.

Calculation as Ideology 115

Since the specific social attribute of capital under capitalist production—that of being property commanding the labour-power of another—becomes fixed, so that interest appears as a part of surplus value produced by capital in this inter-relation; the other part of surplus value—profit of enterprise—must necessarily appear as coming not from capital as such but from the process of production separated from its specific social attribute, whose distinct mode of existence is already expressed by the term interest on capital. But the process of production, separated from capital, is simply a labour-process. Therefore, the industrial capitalist, as distinct from the owner of capital, does not appear as operating capital, but rather as a functionary irrespective of capital, or, as a simple agent of the labour-process in general, as a labourer, and indeed as a wage-labourer. (*Capital*, vol. 3, p. 374)

Here the division between interest and profit of enterprise is mirrored by a division between a capitalist economic process and a labour process in general, the latter being treated as the ideological consequence of the former division. If, however, this is to be maintained then a number of *non sequiturs* would be committed. How, for example, could a concept of 'profit' be consistent with a 'labour process in general'? Similarly, how could the capitalist, represented as an administrative/supervisory worker, be not only a labourer but a 'wage' labourer?

In this respect if the labour process is to appear as separated from the operation of capital then profit of enterprise should strictly speaking not exist at all. Equally, if the labour of administration 'appears' as identical to other forms of labour, then the pre-condition of the wages of superintendence as source of 'profit of enterprise' no longer obtains, i.e. that the wages of superintendence cannot be categorised as a 'privileged' form of labour.

A further 'source of illusion' is provided by the movement towards the formation of an average rate of profit. The movement towards the equalisation of profit rates involves a dislocation between the rate of surplus value which will vary with the organic composition of capital and the intensity of labour in different sectors of production, and the rate of profit. This dislocation itself leads to an 'appearance' of a complete divorce between the process of extraction of surplus value and the average rate of profit:

Average profit figures practically, in the mind and calculation of the capitalist himself, as a regulating element, not merely insofar as it determines the transfer of capitals from one sphere of investment into another, but also in all sales and contracts which embrace a process of reproduction extending over long periods. But so far as it figures in this manner, it is a pre-existent magnitude, which is in fact independent of the value and surplus value produced in any particular sphere of production. Rather than appearing as a result of a splitting of value, it manifests itself much more as a magnitude independent of the value of the produced commodities, as pre-existing in the process of production of commodities and itself determining the average price of the commodities, i.e., as a creator of value. (*Capital*, vol. 3, p. 849)

Here the postulated mechanism of the *distribution* of surplus value is 'represented' as its source. This mechanism is here applied purely within the sphere of industrial capital, but an analogous mechanism is postulated in the distribution of the social product *in toto*. This involves the distribution of the social product in terms of a threefold channelling of revenues, to capital (profit and interest or, more precisely, *interest* in this form), landed property (ground rent), and labour (wages):

Capital, landed property and labour appear to those agents of production as three different, independent sources, from which as such there arise three different components of the annually produced value—and thereby the product in which it exists; thus, from which there arise not merely the different forms of this value as revenues falling to the share of particular factors in the social process of production, but from which this value itself arises, and thereby the substance of these forms of revenue. (*Capital*, vol. 3, p. 802)

What is most immediately striking about the false sources is their mutual inconsistency. In one sense the concept of labour as a cost of production rather than as a source of value is situated 'at the level of production'. The 'representation' is related to calculations deemed necessary for the reproduction of the enterprise. However, the idea that surplus value is equivalent to the wages necessary for the payment of the labour of supervision places the false source in Marxist terms not within the sphere of production but as the 'product' of administrative labour. The concepts of derivation of value from sale or of the distinction of revenue or profit rates from the process of production assume that the 'false source' derives from a postulation of a role to circulation and exchange which in terms of the law of value should only be performed by the sphere of production.

It is important to stress at this point that we are not aiming to criticise these conceptions of ideology *on the grounds of their mutual inconsistency*. That is to say, we are not erecting consistency into a principle of validity and *ipso facto* inconsistency as a criterion of invalidity. On the contrary, the problem is of a quite different kind. The 'false sources' of value are representations to an agent of the economic process. These 'representations' are assumed to be rendered consistent by reference to the concept of the agent. Economic ideologies are related to a capitalist agent treated by Marx as a 'personification' of the place of capital in the economic process. For example, if we return to the case of the treatment of labour as a cost, this treatment is in no way 'irrational' or a delusion, it is a conception directly related to the labour–capital relationship from the standpoint of the latter. The cost involved in the remuneration of labour-power is treated as the cost of labour and thus surplus value cannot be included because it is *not a cost to capital*. In turn the agent who here 'takes the place of capital' 'reflects' this representation of the process.

This means that, in so far as capital is a unity, (there may be diverse capitals but they necessarily fall under the generic 'capital') and in so far as the place of capital is 'reflected' in the place of the agent as personification, the text of *Capital* itself demands the unity of 'capitalist ideology' as a consequence of the unity of the agent.

It is for this reason that the diversity of the false sources presents a problem for Marx's argument. There are indications of the nature of this problem in the text itself:

> True, the nature of surplus value impresses itself constantly upon the consciousness of the capitalist during the process of production, as his greed for the labour-time of others. . . . But the actual process of production is only a fleeting stage which continually merges with the process of circulation, just as the latter merges with the former, so that in the process of production, the more or less clearly dawning notion of the

source of the gain made in it, i.e., the inkling of the nature of surplus value, stands at best as a factor equally valid as the idea that the realised surplus originates in a movement that is independent of the production process, that it arises in circulation, and that it belongs to capital irrespective of the latter's relation to labour. (*Capital*, vol. 3, p. 44)

Here the pertinence of the unity of the agent to Marx's argument is illuminated by its denial. The capitalist agent is subject both to the ('fleeting') imprint of 'production' but also to the representations of the sphere of circulation. In so far as these representations compete against each other, the dominance of one of them can only be postulated on the grounds of the 'cancelling out' of the other or by the representation of the subordinate in terms of the dominant.

The problem is that the economic process is presented in terms of its distinct mechanisms or moments, production, circulation, etc. With respect to *each* of these moments a correlative 'false' source of value arises as the 'representation' of that moment. It follows that the distinction of mechanisms is reflected in the distinction of 'false sources'. The recourse to the metaphor of the fleeting image is governed by the tautological postulate that the agent 'lives in and through ideology'. At the heart of the problem, therefore, is the Marxist conception of 'economic ideologies'. Marx maintains, as we have seen, that for each of the specific practices in which the capitalist agent is involved, the work of administration/supervision, the marketing and sale of commodities, the calculation of costs, etc., there is a 'representation' of the source of value and surplus value, and that this 'source' is *ipso facto* false.

This formulation therefore treats the 'economic ideologies' as articulated with the economic practices of the agents concerned and thus they exert an 'economic effectivity'. The false sources are thus the medium through which the agent 'thinks' his/her practice. In the case of labour as 'cost of production', for example, 'capital' 'thinks' its relation to 'labour-power'.

This conception raises even more serious problems in respect of the diversity of 'false' sources. It is clear that if we treat the 'false' sources as means by which the agent thinks his/her practice then inconsistency in the 'false sources' implies inconsistency in economic practice. In fact, in so far as each practice refers to a representation of the process as a whole the agent must maintain a

Calculation as Ideology   119

set of wholly contradictory economic strategies.

If the agent derives the source of the surplus product from the *sale* of commodities then any concern with *production* costs should be totally incidental. The same is true vice versa, if the surplus product derives from the supervision of labour then concern with the sale of commodities is not germane. If the rate of profit is conceived as determined independent of the action of the agent then the agent has a *carte blanche* for inactivity.

While this is a *reductio ad absurdum* it does raise serious difficulties. An obvious way out would be to drop the diverse 'false sources', to substitute a single or at least a consistent set of 'false sources'.

One way of attempting this would be to argue that the false sources are unified by a common basis. This common basis is often posed in terms of the 'representation of production relations as exchange-relations'. However, even if a common basis is admitted this in no way solves the problem. The fact that a common basis may be discerned does not effect the 'representation to the agent'. Even if there is a common characteristic to each false source this in no way effaces the diversity of false sources from the standpoint of the agent.

The idea that the 'false sources' derive from representations of exchange is itself manifestly inconsistent with Marx's argument. If we take the idea of labour as a cost of production, for example, and the supposedly consequent 'false source' that each element of capital contributes to the final value of the product *according to its weight in the capital advanced* then it is possible to demonstrate a necessary relation with 'exchange'-relations. This could be done on an analogy with a 'marginalist' form of argument where each factor is employed up to the point at which marginal cost equals marginal revenue.

This argument solves nothing. The reason is simply that no *necessary link* can be established between the conception of labour as a cost of production and the concept that each element of capital contributes to the value of the product in proportion to its initial value. If there is a postulated link it need only be that labour, like all the other elements, contributes to the final value and *ipso facto* to the surplus. This does not require any reference to 'exigencies of competition' enforcing equal proportional contribution to the final value and thus in Marxist terms involves no reference to exchange-relationships. In this sense it is perfectly possible to have what would be characterised in terms of the law of value as a 'false source' without this source in any way involving 'exchange'-relations.

If, therefore, recourse to a common characteristic does not rectify the difficulty the obvious answer would appear to be to dispense with the diversity of false sources *per se*. This would, however, involve a major transformation in Marx's argument. As we have demonstrated, the basic structure of Marx's argument establishes and also requires that the practice of the agent in respect of the process of production and the circulation of commodities is represented in terms of the categories congruent with that 'practice' and its corresponding place in the economic process. If the diversity of the false sources is to be jettisoned, therefore, this involves either a change in the conception of the economic process or a break in the link between the 'false sources' and the economic process, i.e. a rejection of the concept of 'representation of the process to the agents'. However, this in itself would be a radical step, since the theory of the representation of the process provides the mechanism whereby the 'economic ideologies' assert themselves.

It is, of course, also the case that the false sources are treated by Marx as means of *justification* of capitalist economic practice and are often directly accounted for in these terms. However, the attempt to delineate a mechanism via the 'representation of the process' necessarily makes the justifications themselves effects of the representations. Necessarily, if the position of the agents is divorced from the representations it will be impossible to have recourse to such arguments and the economic ideologies would be directly defined as 'rationalisations' in a utilitarian sense.

This conclusion is hardly surprising for, as we pointed out in the first volume, the conception of incarnation/personification of social 'spaces' in no way escapes psychologism. This can be seen very clearly if we briefly consider Marx's discussion of the joint-stock company.

The joint-stock company effects the separation of 'ownership from control': 'the transformation of the actually functioning capitalist into a mere manager, administrator of other people's capital, and the owner of capital into a mere owner, a mere money-capitalist.' (*Capital*, vol. 3, p. 427) This transformation must itself signal a transformation in the representation of the relevant economic categories:

Calculation as Ideology 121

Even if the dividends which they receive include the interest and the profit of enterprise, i.e. the total profit (for the salary of the manager is, or should be, simply the wage of a specific type of skilled labour, whose price is regulated in the labour-market like that of any other labour), this total profit is henceforth received only in the form of interest, i.e. as mere compensation for owning capital that now is entirely divorced from the function in the actual process of reproduction, just as the function in the person of the manager is divorced from the ownership of capital. (*ibid*.)

The final link demonstrates the necessary parallelism between the divorce between a 'pure ownership function' and a 'managerial function' and the fact that now the distinction between profit-interest and wages of superintendence is 'representable' as 'ideologically pertinent'. This in turn involves the category 'interest' functioning in terms of an equivalent personification, the capitalist as 'owner of capital', and wages of management being equally personified in the labourer/manager. The problems associated with this conception are dealt with in Chapter 10 of Volume One of this book, on possession and separation, but what we should note here is the relation between the structure of personification and the correlative definition of 'class interest':

Profit thus appears (no longer only that portion of it, the interest, which derives its justification from the profit of the borrower) as a mere appropriation of the surplus labour of others, arising from the conversion of means of production into capital, i.e., from their alienation *vis-à-vis* the actual producer, from their antithesis as another's property to every individual actually at work in production, from manager down to the last day-labourer. In stock companies the function is divorced from capital ownership, hence also labour is entirely divorced from ownership of means of production and surplus labour. This result of the ultimate development of capitalist production is a necessary transitional phase towards the reconversion of capital into the property of producers, although no longer as the private property of the individual producers, but rather as the property of the associated producers as outright social property. On the other hand, the stock company is a transition towards the conversion of all functions in the reproduction process which still remain linked with capitalist property, into mere functions of associated producers, into social functions. (*ibid.*, pp. 427–8)

Psychologism is here not banished but rather refracted through the categories in which the agent thinks his/her practice. Here there is a parallelism effected through personification itself. Where the functioning capitalist is owner of capital there is an effective conflation at the level of 'representation' between wages of supervision and profit of enterprise. In turn capital is personified in a capitalist agent. In other words representation, personification, and class interests coincide. This is equally true in respect of the separation of ownership from control. The division of profit of enterprise from wages of supervision, corresponds to the class division between rentier-capitalists and managers. Where the personification of capital is separated from the personification of functional supervision, the division of class interests results.

Necessarily the concept of the false sources of value is governed by the philosophical conception of 'economic ideologies' in *Capital*. The 'real' is invoked by Marx as exhibiting the characteristics of a logical process. This leads to the break in Marx with 'epiphenomenal' conceptions of ideology, delusions, dreams, and fantasies, etc. The representation of labour as a cost is thus a 'correct' representation of what is a cost to *capital*, the 'real' itself therefore 'demands' the category 'cost of production'. In turn 'theoretical ideologies' such as the economic theories criticised in the *Theories of Surplus Value* develop these 'necessary categories' in a 'theoretical form'. The reality–ideology correspondence is inescapable. What concerns our argument here, however, is not the circularity of these epistemological and ontological questions *per se* but rather the effect on the Marxist theorisation of calculation.

The correspondence between 'reality' and 'ideology' is therefore only of significance in so far as it results in the diversity of false sources. This diversity, as we have insisted above, relates to the divisions within the economic process, primarily the production process, the circulation of commodities, and the distribution of 'surplus value'. The 'logos' here works in such a way that to each of the phases of the 'metamorphosis of commodities' corresponds a development of its own logic, i.e. a representation of the process as a whole in terms of a premise drawn from a given phase of the production–circulation cycle. In this respect the conception of ideology is 'metonymic', i.e. it involves a representation of 'part as whole'. For this reason it has been necessary to insist on taking the 'false sources' to the letter. In doing so the unity of the agent as the subject of a possible economic calculation must necessarily be broken and the *reductio ad absurdum* is not imposed on this framework but derives from it.

Tendency and calculation

Marx argues that the analysis of the capitalist mode of production must be undertaken through the means of 'laws' and tendencies operating at the level of social capital *and* that enterprises and enterprise calculation are necessary features of a capitalist economy. As we have already seen, these tendencies and 'laws' are conceived of as part of a scientific analysis of the capitalist mode of production and enterprise calculation is conceived as 'ideological'. To this epistemological distinction necessarily corresponds a difference in the terms in which tendencies and 'laws' are cast and those in which enterprise calculation is cast. The former utilise value-terms, the latter price-terms.

Given, however, that enterprise calculation is not treated as epiphenomenal but as necessary it is a prerequisite of the operation of the tendencies and 'laws' that they are translatable in terms of enterprise calculation. Enterprise calculation must realise the tendencies, but to do so 'decisions' taken in terms of prices must correspond to the operation of tendencies and 'laws' cast in value-terms.

Our object here will be to demonstrate that such a 'translation', while necessary for Marx's argument, is in fact impossible in terms of his own position. To demonstrate this we will take three 'tendencies' discussed by Marx in chapter 25 volume 1 of *Capital* which are subsumed under what he calls the 'General Law of Capitalist Accumulation'. In this discussion we will not be concerned with the general character and status of explanation by reference to tendencies, a matter fully discussed in the first volume, but only with the consistency of the tendencies with enterprise calculation.

Marx discusses the organic composition of capital in the following terms:

> The composition of capital is to be understood in a two-fold sense. On the side of value, it is determined by the proportion in

which it is divided into constant capital or value of the means of production, and variable capital or value of labour-power, the sum total of wages. On the side of material as it functions in the process of production, all capital is divided into means of production and living labour-power. This latter composition is determined by the relation between the mass of the means of production employed, on one hand, and the mass of labour necessary for their employment on the other. I call the former the *value-composition*, the latter the *technical composition* of capital. Between the two there is a strict correlation. To express this, I call the value-composition of capital, in so far as it is determined by its technical composition and mirrors the changes of the latter, the *organic* composition of capital. (*Capital*, vol. 1, p. 612)

The organic composition is the division (of the total expended labour-time) between constant capital and variable capital in so far as (this) is defined by the technical composition, i.e. the mutual requirements of means of production and labour-power to operate a given set of production processes. The technical composition is in this definition given, i.e. it assumes a given set of means of production with corresponding employment of labour-power and vice versa. However, the discussion of a 'tendency for the organic composition to rise' cannot take a technical composition as given but must imply a mechanism operating to produce a technical composition which determines that the value of constant capital will rise relative to variable capital.

What is required is a mechanism which leads to the substitution of labour by means of production such that the organic composition 'tends' to rise. However, enterprise calculation will be cast in cost-terms not in value-terms. Consequently, the displacement of labour by means of production would generally be undertaken when the wages of labourers displaced by means of production (cost-saving to the enterprise) outweigh the purchase cost of the means of production. This condition implies that the total of the wages of the labourers employed to produce the means of production must be below the total of the wages of the labourers displaced by the machine since the cost to the enterprise of the machine includes the profit of the enterprise selling the machine. How do these conditions affect the operation of the tendency? (This argument assumes simple reproduction conditions; these are not required in order for the argument to hold but serve to simplify it.)

If substitution takes place in Dept 1 under the conditions of cost calculation specified and if wage levels are uniform throughout Dept 1 then the substitution will result in a *fall* in the organic composition of capital. This is simply because the value of the machine is less than that of the labour displaced by it and thus the value of constant capital falls and *ipso facto* the organic composition of capital.

The organic composition of capital can only rise under two conditions. Either substitution takes place under conditions where the wages of the labourers making the machine are lower than the wages of those displaced. In this case the substitution can reduce costs to the enterprise while increasing the value of constant capital. Or substitution takes place only in Dept 2. (These conditions are derived from the argument of A. Hussain, 'Crises and Tendencies of Capitalism', 1977.)

If these conditions for a rise in the organic composition of capital are to be fulfilled, it will be necessary to show that we can deduce them from the tendencies. However, it is quite easy to see that the terms in which the tendencies are defined preclude such an alternative. The conditions refer to either relative wages within or between departments or to costs of means of production relative to labour-power between departments. The tendencies, however, can, by definition, not derive such conditions because they refer to social capital. There is no theory of the relative costs of constant capital between departments nor of relative wages within and between departments. Consequently, the conditions under which enterprise calculation could 'realise' the tendencies cannot be specified by the tendencies because they cannot deal with relative prices.

The tendency to produce an industrial reserve army is based on an argument that the expansion of production under a capitalist mode of production (expanded reproduction is usually taken by Marx as given) with a given composition of capital leads to labour shortages and increases in wages. This produces a substitution of means of production for labour and a reduction in the demand for labour-power resulting in a pool of unemployed being created. This pool is permanent, being 'in reserve' for expansions in production of a particularly rapid kind (which Marx treats as a 'norm' of capitalism):

Calculation as Ideology

> With accumulation, and the development of the productiveness of labour that accompanies it, the power of sudden expansion of capital grows also. . . . The mass of social wealth, overflowing with the advance of accumulation and transformable into additional capital, thrusts itself frantically into old branches of production, whose market suddenly expands, or into newly formed branches, such as railways . . . the need for which grows out of the development of the old ones. In all such cases, there must be possibility of throwing great masses of men suddenly on the decisive points without injury to the scale of production in other spheres. (*Capital*, vol. 1, p. 632)

It is hard to see, given Marx's argument, why such a permanent pool should exist. Enterprise calculation clearly involves no preference for some cost-savings rather than others and Marx endorses this by assuming that factors of production are applied according to their relative costs. Consequently, the displacement of labour if it has the effect of reducing wages should make labour more attractive as a 'factor' and this should continue to operate up to a point at which costs of labour-power rise sufficiently relative to means of production to justify substitution. Such a process does not engender a 'pool' of unemployed but simply a fluctuating level of unemployment. Furthermore, the 'function' cannot be taken up in enterprise calculation since this presupposes that enterprises 'plan' for such an exigency. Even if enterprises adopted a common time horizon, which is, as we shall show, unsustainable, the argument would not follow, because expansion affects only some enterprises, and in so far as this is predictable will enter into the calculation of those enterprises alone.

It could be argued that this process cannot operate because there is a 'floor' to the fall in wages set by the value of labour-power. Such an objection is unsustainable because what is at issue is not the value of labour-power or real wages but money wages, thus what will be significant will be the money wage at which the 'members' of the industrial reserve army offer their labour-power. Even if this argument were conceded it would make no difference, since if there were a floor it would still imply that any expansion of production ('rapid' or not) would be at constant wage-costs, thus labour-power would *ipso facto* be cheap relative to means of production at some points, implying that substitutions would not take place.

Finally, as is pointed out in the section on laws of tendency in the first volume there can be no 'tendency' towards concentration of production unless a given population of enterprises is assumed. It is clearly a commonplace that both the population of enterprises and what they produce is not given. This is pertinent here because the enterprise need not take its boundary, its continued existence or what it produces as given.

Enterprise calculation cannot realise the tendencies because its effects refer to concrete conditions of capitalist national economies. This is implied in Marx's own analysis, since if enterprises are seen as substituting 'factors' of production according to their relative prices then the direction of substitution will necessarily depend on the pertinent prices at a given point in time. This accounts for manifest inconsistencies in Marx's own treatment of 'tendencies'. Among the factors offsetting the fall in the rate of profit we find 'foreign trade':

> Capitals invested in foreign trade can yield a higher rate of profit, because, in the first place, there is competition with commodities produced in other countries with inferior production facilities, so that the more advanced country sells its goods above their value even though cheaper than the competing countries. (*Capital*, vol. 3, p. 232)

Such a mechanism clearly can in no sense operate at the level of the mode of production; the concept of the capitalist mode of production cannot allow us to deduce the particular economic structures of different national economies which is what is at issue here. The terrain of a theory of enterprise calculation cannot be the terrain of the capitalist mode of production nor, as we shall now attempt to show, can it be the terrain of the capitalist economy in general.

Chapter 8

Problems of a General Theory of Capitalist Calculation

Theories of calculation and domains of application

In Chapter 7 it was argued that the theory of calculation advanced in *Capital* could not provide a satisfactory treatment of the forms of calculation engaged in by capitalist enterprises. This was not argued on the positivist grounds that certain current forms of enterprise calculation do not correspond to the forms specified in the theory but because of a contradiction within the theory between the general conception of calculation and the conception of the domains in which it is to operate. *Capital* regards the separation of enterprises one from another and their interconnection through sales and purchases as a necessary part of capitalist relations of production. Calculation at enterprise level is necessary for this unplanned interconnection to take place and to be effective. At the same time *Capital* regards enterprise calculation as 'ideological', as an experience-effect of the structure with a given general form. This given general form is, nevertheless, assigned the role (as it must be—social relations are effective through commodity circulation and the actions of enterprises) of realising certain tendencies which govern the structure and develop within it. But the given general character of the calculative criteria (effects of the structure) subverts their role as means of realisation of the tendencies. This is because the conditions of 'realisation' of the tendencies suppose the existence of social relations whose form cannot be given as generality and which also contradict the given calculative criteria assigned by the structure. Calculative criteria would have to be non-given in form to respond to these conditions of realisation. But this non-givenness would subvert the form of

Problems of a General Theory of Capitalist Calculation 129

action of the structure which makes the tendencies themselves possible. Furthermore, in our Volume One, Part II we argued that the conditions of 'realisation' of the tendencies, which create the central difficulty for the givenness of the criteria of calculation, are themselves in contradiction with the basic concept of 'law of tendency'.

This argument can now be generalised to consider all theories of capitalist enterprise calculation which assign it a given and necessary form. The problem concerns the contradiction between the criteria of calculation specified in these theories and the conditions of calculation in their domains of application. This problem is common to both the Marxist theory and marginalist/neo-classical theories of the enterprise or economic agent. In both cases the enterprise or agent is a universal calculating subject (by such a subject we mean an entity whose attributes and actions are identical to members of the class of beings in question). For a universal subject of calculation to exist a domain appropriate to that calculation must exist, a domain which is homogeneous and general (which mirrors the identity of the subjects and offers no obstacles to it). This means that in order for all enterprises or agents to use the same given calculative criteria in the same way they must all be of the same organisational form and encounter similar conditions of operation. Universal calculating subjects are, therefore, part of a theory which conceives capitalist economies as existence-as-generality. The domain of application of these theories is capitalist economy-in-general. In this theoretical domain organisational forms and conditions of operation can be given a single and constant form appropriate to the given criteria. An example of such a theoretical domain would be an economy constituted by perfect competition, equal and perfect information, and simultaneous and synoptic exchange of commodities.

The problem with such theories that postulate a universal calculative subject arises when they do not consistently define their domain of application in this way (as generality appropriate to universality), as is the case with *Capital*, or where the attempt is made to extend the theory of calculation to relations beyond the domain on which it is specified. The domains in contradiction are:

> 1 *capitalist economy in general*, where different organisational forms are discounted and conditions of operation are homogenised;

2 *capitalist national economies*, where the forms of organisation of enterprises are affected and differentiated by company law, state policy, taxation, etc., and where the conditions of operation are affected and differentiated by forms of specific financial and industrial structure, etc.

In capitalist national economies the conditions and criteria of calculation cannot be given in general nor can enterprises be assigned a homogeneous form (and, therefore, a single economic rationality with universal effects).

The problems arise when a theory of calculation developed in relation to the first domain is applied to the second. In effect, either the second domain must be negated and reduced to the first, or the theory must state a relationship between the two which gives the discrepancy a theoretical rationale. This rationale can take two basic forms. The first is an epistemological argument that the general domain is an abstraction which is necessary in order to comprehend what is involved in all calculation, for example, the assumption of equal and perfect information. The second is a prescriptive argument that while forms of calculation may exist which do differ from the form given in the theory, that form is the most appropriate, effective, or rational with regard to the activities engaged in (this of course supposes the activities can be considered as the same even if forms of calculation differ). If such a rationale is not deployed then the domain of operation of the theory has been mis-specified and conditions contradictory to or different from the given calculative criteria must be admitted.

We should indicate here that we are not arguing a contradiction between an abstract theoretical domain and reality; *both* domains are theoretical. Capitalist national economy is a concept not a given phenomenon. Theories of calculation which involve a universal subject are concerned with relations at the level of the national economy not because they encounter it as some brute 'reality' but because they attempt to enter into 'practical' debates and discourses about calculative policy. These 'practical' debates and discourses are no more privileged as 'reality' than are these general theories of calculation. They do, however, reveal a central problem for those theories which postulate a universal calculative subject and an economy-as-generality, *the non-givenness of criteria of calculation*.

We will not concentrate on defining the domain *capitalist*

Problems of a General Theory of Capitalist Calculation   131

national economy here; this concept is discussed in the first part and the conclusion to this volume. What matters here is that the forms of organisation and the conditions of operation of enterprises are subject in this domain to determinations the effects of which cannot be deduced from any concept of economy-in-general. Thus, features of this domain are *non-deducible* from the domain of capitalist economy-in-general. Yet they would have to be deducible if these general theories of calculation were to be pertinent to the explication of capitalist calculation at enterprise level.

The bulk of the remainder of Part II will be taken up with a demonstration of the proposition that factors which affect the criteria and forms of enterprise calculation cannot be deduced from any general concept of capitalist economy and with a critique of the notion of a universal subject of calculation. Among the non-deducible factors considered are: the composition of consumption and the structure of markets, technical determinants and the production process, taxation, the organisation of the enterprise, the sources of finance, and relation to the financial structure.

The main problem we will consider in demonstrating our case is that of the measurement of returns to capitalist enterprises and the relation of measurement to capitalist calculation. The measurement of returns to enterprises necessarily involves the categories of 'costs', the determination of the magnitude of the capital involved, and the assessment of the enterprise's assets. All these categories/methods of measure are necessary to arrive at an assessment of the performance of the enterprise in terms of some criterion of 'profit'. Methods of measure regarding these categories are variable and produce different calculative results. All these terms also necessarily refer to determinate (but not given) time-periods. Thus they may take the annual accounting period as a point of reference. This period may, however, be quite secondary to a time-period set by operational calculation, for example, a long-term strategic investment (profit here must be considered relative to the investment cycle). These time-periods, which are crucial to the nature of the calculation, are not given.

General theories of calculation are forced to take definite positions on the operation of measurement. The universal calculating subject is assigned an ideology or rationality and a function which that ideology or rationality is supposed to perform.

The operations of measurement performed by enterprises are then assessed in terms of that ideology/rationality and that function. This assessment generally takes the form of a norm which applies to measurement a rule as to its form or an expectation as to its outcome (given the appropriate form). A commonplace example is the concept of profit-maximising behaviour. Here there is a set of rules for economic practice (for measurement and action) which should, other things being equal, have the effect of maximising 'profit'. Maximisation is a norm. But 'profit' is a category of measurement, it is not homogeneous or unambiguous. The category 'profit' always involves a particular *form* of measurement of returns to the enterprise (definite accounting techniques) and a particular time-period for its application. In effect a theory which postulates a norm of maximisation must suppress or subordinate the pertinence of the specific *form* of the measure (differences of accounting practice) to the determination of the content of the category of 'profit'. It must either adopt a realist position, that there is a definite profit level 'in' the enterprise autonomous from mere accounting conventions, or argue that the postulate applies equally well to the products of different accounting practices (but then there are several possible 'profits' which can be maximised).

Norms of calculation are threatened by the existence of alternative and competing norms. The sole possible responses are to insist on the privilege (i.e. 'correctness') of the general theory postulating the norm defended or invoke a prescription. It may be argued that no determinate 'maximising' position is possible and that instead the results of enterprise calculation may be analysed in terms of criteria of 'satisfactory' solutions to a given 'problem' or sets of 'problems'. The notion of satisfactoriness involves its own problems if it is part of a general doctrine of calculation and conceived of as guiding the behaviour of a universal subject.

In this chapter we will concentrate on the difference in forms of measurement. We will argue that this difference subverts any norm which depends on assigning a single determinate content to the categories of calculation.

The measurement of returns

A general theory of enterprise calculation in capitalist economies can treat the question of the measurement of returns in two basic ways. Either it can seek to define a universal measure of returns

Problems of a General Theory of Capitalist Calculation 133

and a universal norm to be applied in respect of that measure, or it can admit the possibility of a plurality of measures and/or norms. But it must then be able to deduce the plurality from the elements which make up its conception of the capitalist economy in general. This chapter concentrates on the first alternative. The concluding paragraphs then employ the arguments and illustrations which are developed in that discussion to dispose of the second alternative.

The measure of returns is significant here in so far as the use of criteria such as maximising criteria or costs plus mark up are norms applied to measures. If universal criteria of calculation are to be posited it is necessary to have a universal standard of measure of returns to the enterprise. It is, of course, well-known that concepts of returns to the enterprise, such as profit, and of rates of return, such as profit-rates, are subject to a plurality of standards of measure. For example, the recent report of the Inflation Accounting Committee (Cmnd 6225, 1975, referred to hereafter as Sandilands) referred to a number of different concepts governing the measurement of the value of non-monetary assets, of profits, of stock, and of capital maintenance.

In relation to the valuation of non-monetary assets Sandilands cites nine alternative bases of measure. These in turn were broken down into three broad categories which could also function as alternatives to current practice based on historic cost principles where assets are valued at their cost of acquisition and depreciation is calculated by reference to this figure. The three broad criteria used were those based on current purchase price, on net realisable value, and on the value of the asset on the basis of what can be earned by holding the asset. In the first case the asset is valued at what it would cost to purchase at the date when the accounts are prepared; naturally this figure is identical to the asset's historic cost where the asset has been subject to no price changes. In the second case valuation is made on the basis of the resale value of the asset. In this case the general concept is qualified by reference to estimates of the effects of the conditions of sale adopted as the standard. These may refer to whether the sale is assumed to be under the most 'unfavourable' conditions ('forced sale') or it may include allowance for the costs of putting the asset on the market. The third case is based on an estimate of future income flows from holding the asset in discounted terms, 'holding' here indicating either existing use of the asset or alternative uses as the point of reference in estimating income. (Sandilands, pp. 25–6)

Sandilands also outlines five distinct concepts of profit. Each concept shares the same relevant time-period, i.e. in all cases profits are 'for the year'. The first concept defines profits as gains arising during the year which may be distributed while maintaining the amount of the shareholder's interest in the company (defined in Sandilands as share capital plus reserves at the beginning of the year). The second concept is identical to the first with the exception that profit is defined as gains arising during the year which may be distributed while maintaining the 'purchasing power' of the shareholder's interest. Here the initial shareholder's interest is indexed to a set of goods and services charged to be 'representative' of the shareholder's regular pattern of purchases. The third concept of profit outlined designates profit as gains arising during the year which may be distributed while maintaining the productive capacity of the assets held by the company. This latter concept necessarily requires specification since productive capacity can refer to a given volume of output or to the value of output aggegated in money terms. The fourth concept of profit proposes that profit be defined as gains arising during the year which may be distributed while maintaining the purchasing power of the amounts in the balance-sheet representing the assets of the company. While this concept is similar to the previous one it seeks to overcome a difficulty implicit in the third concept. In the latter, it is argued, a distortion may arise since a particular set of assets are indexed on the premise that they will be replaced by the company, and naturally this cannot be assumed to be the case. Here this problem is claimed to be overcome by making the balance-sheet sums the point of reference for indexation (implying a distinct index) rather than specific assets. This procedure would involve a differentiated range of indices for capital equipment and stock but it would also involve logically indexing the sums of cash in the balance-sheet. (Sandilands, p. 37) The final concept of profit outlined in Sandilands is a minor variant of the last concept which simply excludes monetary assets from indexation.

Since profit measures always involve the measure of a surplus over the cost of sales it is necessary to elaborate criteria for the calculation of such costs. This is bound up with a question which has been the subject of considerable discussion during the recent period of rapid price rises, the question of 'stock appreciation'. The element of stock appreciation in profit figures arises on the basis of the historic-cost systems of accounting currently operating

Problems of a General Theory of Capitalist Calculation 135

in capitalist countries since when prices of stock are rising accounts regard as 'profit' the difference between the price of acquisition and the current price. Some commentators do not regard stock appreciation as 'true profit', a view which we will discuss below, and the question of stock appreciation has engendered general discussions of the treatment of stock in accounting practice. For example, two main treatments of stocks are discussed in the Sandilands report, the so-called First In First Out system (FIFO) and the Last In First Out system (LIFO). Both share the characteristic that they do not diverge formally from a historic-cost basis, thus, for example, they involve no direct adjustments for stock appreciation. As the names indicate they differ over the conventions adopted concerning the order in which stock is assumed to be consumed in relation to its time of acquisition.

Under the FIFO method it is assumed that the units of stock consumed during the year are those which have been on hand in the enterprise for the longest period. The reverse is the case under LIFO; as the name indicates, LIFO works on the convention that stock consumed during the year is that stock most recently acquired. Supporters of the argument that stock appreciation should not be treated as 'true' profit give preference to the LIFO method since although it remains within the confines of historic-cost accounting, under conditions of rising stock prices it has the effect of making the charge for stock consumed during the year nearer to the current-cost equivalent than is the case under the FIFO system. This is for the obvious reason that under conditions of rising prices it would generally be the case that the FIFO system produces a lower cost of sales figure, given that it values the former on the basis of stock purchased at earlier dates and which equally might be expected to have been purchased at lower prices. However, it is worth noting that it is not necessarily the case that LIFO eliminates stock appreciation nor that it produces lower profit figures than FIFO does. (For the conditions under which these results would occur see Sandilands, pp. 96–7.)

These examples simply demonstrate the plurality of measures of profit in terms of the cost of sales and the criteria involved in defining a surplus. As we indicated earlier a theorist of calculation in the domain of a capitalist economy has two recourses in respect of such a plurality of measures. Either a 'true' measure of returns has to be specified. Or the plurality of measures must be deduced from the domain of capitalist economies.

We begin the discussion of these options by taking the question of a 'true' measure. The idea that there is a 'true' measure of profit is often reflected in the idea that profit is in some sense an index of the state of the enterprise. In other words profit is in a sense 'in' the enterprise or at least is a sign of a fundamental or essential state thereof. To take an example of the ramifications of this view let us return to the case of stock appreciation. Stock appreciation, as has already been indicated, is related to historic-cost systems of accounting under conditions of rising prices such that the value of stocks at current cost diverges from their cost of acquisition. Many critics of historic-cost accounting under inflationary conditions argue that stock appreciation 'falsifies' profit figures and that a 'true' profit figure should deduct stock appreciation on the basis that a company will necessarily have to purchase new stocks for a new production period at current prices. Consequently gains through stock appreciation are eaten up by the increased purchase price of stocks which the enterprise has to pay.

Much of the impetus behind such arguments lies in the obvious fact that profits are taxed, thus it is put forward that enterprises (mainly in manufacturing industry) are being taxed on 'nominal' or 'fictitious' gains as if they were 'real' gains which are often implicitly identified with operating gains. This view has been criticised by Godley and Wood in their article 'Profits and stock appreciation', and their criticism will serve to introduce the problem of whether we can talk of 'true' and 'false' measures of profit in any absolute sense. Godley and Wood quote Merrett and Sykes's article in the *Financial Times* of 30 September 1974 as an illustration of the view to which we have already referred. The latter argue:

> It has at last . . . become commonly accepted that under inflationary conditions profits must be considered net of both depreciation at replacement cost and of stock appreciation (the difference between the historic and the replacement cost of stocks). Anyone naive enough to suppose that inflation in the cost of assets necessary for the continuation of a business in any sense represents a part of profitability rather than a deduction from it should reflect on the extent to which he himself has really profited by the increase in the replacement cost of his stock of consumer durables. (Quoted by Godley and Wood, 'Profit and stock appreciation', p. 57)

Problems of a General Theory of Capitalist Calculation 137

Godley and Wood show that Merrett and Sykes's argument is completely misleading. They assume a situation where the profit of a hypothetical corporate sector remains unchanged between two periods but is in the first period composed of an operating gain consisting of the difference between company sales and company purchases and in the second period is composed entirely of stock appreciation, the value of purchases and sales being equal. They assume company tax at 33⅓ per cent of accounting profits, stock is treated on an FIFO basis, dividends are treated as two-thirds of profits and all stocks and work in progress are taken as financed by a bank overdraft. They discuss the comparison of the two periods in the following terms:

> The accounting profit of £30 in this period of inflation is as true a measure of profit and as proper a basis for taxation *notwithstanding that it is all stock appreciation* as it was in the previous when there was no inflation. £10 is paid in tax, £20 is spent on dividends (without prices having changed) just as in the previous period; moreover this has been achieved (as before) without changing the net worth of the company, because the rise in liquid assets (the value of stocks) is exactly matched by the increase in liquid liabilities (the value of bank overdrafts). At the end of the period, exactly as at the end of each non-inflationary period the 'company' would cease trading having made a surplus of £30 . . . and precisely eliminate its bank overdraft by selling off all its stocks at cost. (*ibid*, p. 58)

Similarly:

> If (as Merrett and Sykes have advocated, this part of profits being treated as 'unreal'), the company could liquidate at the end of the inflationary period in a net worth condition better than in a non-inflationary period. (*ibid.*)

Godley and Wood argue that the position put forward by Merrett and Sykes primarily suffers from its conflation of problems of the definition of profit with those of liquidity. The essential difference is brought out in their example. The profit figure in their example is independent of the character of its composition and classification, i.e. it is of no interest whether it is composed of operating gains or holding gains. In their example, if the company was liquidated after a non-inflationary or an inflationary period the resources available for disposition would remain unaltered. Liquidity is quite a different problem since it does not refer to a point in time but to a fixed constraint on the disposition of resources in a future time-period. Liquidity arguments here thus presuppose that the company will continue in operation and may presuppose a constant volume of output as a norm. Thus it is only by reference to a norm of continuing operations at a given volume level that a liquidity problem in manufacturing industry can be discussed.

Can we conclude then by saying that it is simply a case that Godley and Wood produce in an absolute sense a 'true' or 'correct' measure and Merrett and Sykes a 'false' one? The answer is 'No' even though this implies no fault in Godley and Wood's argument. They seek to establish that existing norms of taxation of profits need not be changed by reference to the question of stock appreciation and they successfully establish this. This, of course, does not establish the 'correctness' of these norms, which can be shown by considering Merrett and Sykes's argument in more detail.

If we take the passage quoted above it is easy to see that Merrett and Sykes wish to apply a norm whereby business firms are to be supposed to continue in existence as a norm which should govern concepts of *profitability*. For example, in defence of exclusion of stock appreciation they argue,

> Anyone naive enough to suppose that inflation in the cost of assets necessary for the continuation of a business in any sense represents a part of profitability rather than a deduction from it should reflect on the extent to which he himself has really profited by the increase in the replacement cost of his stock of consumer durables. (*ibid.*)

Merrett and Sykes's argument here makes reference not to a state of the company or enterprise but rather to a norm, i.e. that business firms should continue in their existing operations. This is clear in that their continual assumption is that stock appreciation is not treated as a realisable gain but is used (entirely) to finance new purchases of stock with the object of continued production. It is quite clear that such a norm can in no sense be a 'state' of capitalist enterprises. Furthermore, taken to its logical conclusion, it would have ludicrous consequences since it would make the continuation of enterprises an *object of the taxation system*.

The normative character of Merrett and Sykes's argument can be seen even more clearly in a later article, 'The industrial crisis after

Mr Healey's budget'. Complaining that the autumn budget of 1974 failed to introduce replacement-cost criteria into the price code, Merrett and Sykes go on to argue that:

> The logic of allowing stock appreciation for tax purposes while disallowing it for the Price Code purposes can only be based on either political expendiency or a basic failure of comprehension as to the concept of profit itself. In so far as companies are to be financed from external sources by equity capital and debt, the concept of profits on which companies' operations must be based is the concept deemed to be most appropriate to their interests. This must, logically, be replacement cost since it is only replacement cost which represents the profit which (in broad terms) is available for distribution to the suppliers of capital.

Here again the reference point is not to any state of the enterprise but rather to the mode of finance of the enterprise. Merrett and Sykes's argument abounds with obvious *non sequiturs*. Not only do they presuppose a place for external finance but they presuppose the relationship between suppliers of external finance and manufacturing enterprises. It is well known, and we will return to this point below, that relationships between manufacturing enterprises and their sources of finance are subject to considerable variations between nation-states and over time. Obviously, therefore, reference to a particular situation attributing hypothetical practices to suppliers of finance can in no way be used to anchor a 'true' measure of profits.

The same arguments are pertinent to Merrett and Sykes's 'going concern' concept. This might appear to be better based as a premise for measurement but exactly the same problems arise. How, for example, could a decision taken within an industrial enterprise to go into liquidation realising holding gains on stocks be deemed 'incorrect' or a decision to continue in the production of the same commodity or set of commodities be deemed 'correct'? Behind this contrast, in fact, lie distinct types of calculation. A paradox of Merrett and Sykes's argument is that formally it would encourage infringement of their own terms. In so far as stock appreciation is untaxed there would in fact be an impetus to liquidate industrial enterprises in order to realise tax-free gains. This in itself is not of particular significance but underlying it is an important problem to which we shall return. It is clear that the position of industrial enterprises may be measured in respect of their functions as producers of commodities or as a 'collection' of assets which may be treated as financial assets with a given realisable price. It is well known that particular characteristics of national economies, for example the determinants of interest rates, structure the relative positions of these types of enterprise calculation. This point will not be discussed further as it is taken up later in the text, but it is clear that Merrett and Sykes's proposals, in so far as they increase the attraction of viewing industrial enterprises as sources of realisable holding gains with minimal tax liability, have implications somewhat removed from the authors' avowed positions.

We can thus see that the concept of profit in no way sustains a 'realist' conception. The problem with such a conception is that it implicitly refers to a 'state' of the enterprise which is 'reflected' in a 'true' profit figure. Such a reference is, however, unjustifiable. Merrett and Sykes's arguments, for example, do not refer to 'states' but to norms and in the arguments which they deploy the norms are variable in two different ways. In the case of the 'going concern' concept their argument is entirely and incoherently prescriptive. The treatment of enterprises as sets of financial assets in no way implies that they cannot function as industrial enterprises; it simply means that a particular mode of calculation is applied in estimating returns to industrial enterprises. In the case of their reference to the sources of finance, the point of reference for the norm is a hypothetical subject (the 'investor') who is assigned a given functional role ('supplying finance'). The implication here is that the 'true' measure of profit derives from the 'interests' of the investor in so far as infringement of such interests would be 'dysfunctional'.

Obviously such a position merely asserts a set of criteria of calculation as a necessary domain for which the prescriptive criteria apply.

It is worth pointing out at this stage that there is no implication that the procedure of measuring profits and of taxing profits cannot be subject to discussion nor that certain procedures may not be preferred to others. What is at issue here is that a 'correct' procedure cannot be designated by reference to any unitary 'state' of the enterprise. In fact, as we seek to demonstrate in more detail below, the criteria of measurement of returns employed for purposes of fiscal policy can only be a function of political calculations, amongst which are necessarily included economic strategies. This will be apparent from the examples already given, thus the relationship between the 'going-concern' and 'financial-asset' calculation will be structured by economic strategy.

General theories of enterprise calculation in capitalist economies have been characterised not only by the postulation of a 'true' measure of returns but equally by the idea that calculation is governed by a general norm in respect of this measure. The most familiar form which arguments of this type take opposes 'maximising' to 'satisficing' norms. Thus one may conceive enterprise calculation as designed to maximise profits, and prescribe relevant procedures, e.g. that the enterprise should expand output up to the point at which marginal cost and marginal revenue are equated, and correlative conditions, e.g. that the enterprise must be capable of producing measures of the relevant variables deemed intrinsic to such calculations—measures of marginal costs, for example.

These theories are characterised by their direct or indirect hypostatisation of the enterprise as a calculating subject. This is necessarily the case since the norm applies to a measure conceived of as universal. There is a figure for maximum or satisfactory profits under given conditions. There is no objection to this *per se* since for reasons of theoretical demonstration it may be the case that the conditions are specified in such a way as to give a single figure. However, the situation is quite different where the object is to erect a general theory of capitalist calculation. In this case there is no warrant at all for presupposing a universal calculating subject identical with the enterprise.

This can be seen quite simply if we take an example devised by Wiles (*Price, Cost and Output*). He cites a situation in which, to expand output, an enterprise makes a new rights issue. He then goes on to compare the positions of two hypothetical shareholders. It is possible that two hypothetical shareholders will both vote for the rights issue even though the expansion has the effect of lowering the nominal rates of earnings on all shares. The company seeks to offset this loss by offering the issue to existing shareholders at a privileged price such that the yield on the new issues will be competitive with alternative investments. Assuming that the calculation by the hypothetical shareholders is entirely concerned with maximum yield in a given time-period, such a situation would produce different responses given different positions occupied by the shareholders. If one shareholder has, for example, no additional funds for investment then that shareholder faces losses which may or may not be compensated for by the shareholder's ability to sell his take-up rights. A shareholder with surplus funds is clearly in a different position and could, on the basis of such narrow calculations, be expected to support the rights issue. (*Price, Cost and Output*, p. 193) This example simply serves to demonstrate the fact that the enterprise in this sense can in no way be conceived as a universal calculative subject. In this hypothetical case the determination of enterprise policy would depend, given a number of restrictive assumptions, on the relative weight of each 'type' of shareholder and the relative ability of each group to mobilise forces to determine policy.

This problem, in fact, refers to a much more general and significant one. The example above is obviously limited by two major conditions, that the hypothetical shareholders are presumed to be individuals and that their modes of calculation are identical; the *differentia specia* lies in their relations to a rights issue under given conditions as a function of their financial position. However, the provision of finance comes, for example, from diverse types of financial institutions with diverse modes of calculation. As this problem will be discussed more fully later in the text it will not be pursued at any length here but the simple consequence of diversity of calculation can be drawn to illustrate the nature of the problem.

Finance may be provided to an enterprise from a financial institution (e.g. an insurance company) whose own operations require them to have a consistent flow of funds in order to facilitate regular contractual payments which they are obliged to make. Furthermore such institutions have a regular intake of funds which is equally consistent and predictable from regular contractual payments made by its clients. Such an institution requires, therefore, to place large amounts of funds and to ensure a regularity in returns to meet its obligations. This type of institution might be contrasted to a financial conglomerate which operates by seeking funds in the 'wholesale' money market. Such an enterprise will be clearly distinct from the former type of enterprise on the basis that it acquires its funds under highly variable conditions both from the point of view of the period of loans available to it and the rate of interest which it has to pay. It is equally clear that these distinct institutions may have different relations to industrial enterprises. The former type of enterprise is under some pressure to operate a 'going-concern' relation to the enterprise since it is

Problems of a General Theory of Capitalist Calculation 143

generally not faced with major problems in acquiring funds but rather is primarily concerned with placing substantial funds and since its obligations are either fixed or highly predictable it is constrained to achieve a predictable flow-back of funds. This is not the case with the financial conglomerate, which is under pressure to treat the industrial enterprise as a 'parcel' of financial assets. This is because the conglomerate operates under the constraint of obtaining its funds under variable financial market conditions. Therefore, constraints of short-term borrowing might oblige the conglomerate to dispose of all or part of the assets of an industrial enterprise which it controls in order to meet financial obligations. Similarly, the growth of such companies is much more directly tied up with gains on the disposal of company assets since they do not have the same sources of funds in contractual savings that institutions such as the insurance companies do.

Clearly such diverse institutions may apply quite different criteria of calculation in their relations with industrial enterprises, and this will directly affect their relations with industrial enterprises. This in turn will affect their relation to specific practices within the enterprise. For example, these two types of financial institutions operate on different temporalities of calculation. This will directly affect policies such as those affecting the level of stocks held in a given period. In so far as the financial enterprise supplying finance operates on a going-concern basis, it will be more favourable to practices which, for example, base inventory policy on criteria assuring continuity of supply. If, however, such stocks are difficult to resell or involve substantial costs of disposal then such a policy may create serious problems for the conglomerate which, for the reasons already indicated, will put a much higher priority on liquidity. No unequivocal conclusion can be drawn from such a hypothetical comparison but it does serve to show that we may not treat the enterprise as a universal calculating subject.

These considerations affect the relationship of what are traditionally thought of as key operations relating to 'maximising' practice and the plurality of calculative criteria. Traditional 'maximising' or for that matter 'satisficing' criteria have centred on the calculation of costs, 'choice of techniques', pricing, etc. However, once we no longer treat the enterprise as a universal subject it is perfectly possible to see that such criteria may be less significant than the criteria applied to the distribution of 'returns'. For example, it is well known that different criteria of profit are based, as is the case in the Sandilands examples, on different concepts of 'distributable' income. If we take the use of current-purchasing-power methods under inflationary conditions distributable income is related to the index taken to measure 'inflation'. Therefore an index which may be thought to give a lower measure of inflation will give a higher distributable income which will be congruent with calculative criteria in which liquidity plays a central role. It might be objected that a 'going-concern' concept can in some sense be taken as an absolute point of reference for the construction of an index since it is based on preserving the capital and stock on which future income flows depend. But this objection involves a further difficulty since the estimation of future income flows itself depends on the identification of time-periods pertinent to their calculation. No identification of pertinent time-periods can be derived from the notion of a 'going concern' as such.

It is important to stress that the arguments outlined here are applicable not only to 'maximising' theories but also to alternative general conceptions of calculation. A familiar type of criticism addressed to 'maximising' arguments is that they are appropriate only to a particular subject-enterprise, namely where there is an identity of 'ownership' and 'control'. Under conditions in which there is a separation of ownership and control, however, this subject-enterprise is replaced by one in which the calculative criteria are based on the interests of the management, who are assumed to be distinct from 'owners'. As this position will be discussed more fully below we will limit ourselves to signalling the problem of this position in the present context.

One of the arguments often associated with this standpoint (see Wood, *A Theory of Profits*) is that managers of industrial enterprises will seek to limit dividend payments on the basis of maximising internal sources of finance. This practice will be governed by a principle in which dependence on external finance is associated with a danger that the external suppliers of finance are likely to exert pressure on the composition of the management or its policies. Such a conclusion is, however, entirely unwarranted. Presuming such criteria are applied by the management of the enterprises, the conclusion by no means follows. This is simply because there is no 'given' relationship between industrial enterprises and financial institutions. Consequently a situation is perfectly possible where the supply of funds by a financial institution operating on a 'going-concern' criterion may be a condition of preventing the disposal of the company or a substantial proportion of the assets which it deploys in production by a financial conglomerate seeking gains through the disposal of the company's assets.

To take a hypothetical example: assume an industrial enterprise which has renewed its capital equipment on a partial basis such that part of the production process is highly mechanised but other parts retain older equipment. This leads to bottlenecks such that there is no balance between the capacities of the two 'sectors' of the process, and this involves a failure to realise substantial reductions in unit costs. Assume equally that the company's new equipment is easily resaleable with negligible selling costs and equally that it has under-valued property on which the factory stands. The bottlenecks were anticipated, but the installation of the new equipment was on the basis that the company did not have sufficient sources of finance to renew both 'sectors' and that the bottlenecks were expected to be temporary on the basis that under existing trade conditions flows of cash would be sufficient to allow for the renewal of the other 'sector'. Presume that this objective is frustrated by a fall in demand for the company's products as a function of a general recession at the point in time under consideration.

In a case like this the company is obviously vulnerable to take-over from the financial conglomerate, on the basis that it has easily disposable assets some of which are substantially under-valued and that its lower profitability in the relevant period may have depressed its share price. Difficulties in obtaining external finance in a situation of this kind necessarily reinforce the vulnerability of the firm. Clearly, therefore, if external finance were provided on a 'going-concern' basis then the management of the enterprise, assuming the criteria applied by the 'managerialists', would hardly resist seeking such external financing. Nor would they necessarily seek to minimise dividends, for in this situation a dividend policy congruent with financial institutions willing to supply long-term funds would be a condition of emancipating the enterprise from the threat of control by the financial conglomerate. What is clear, therefore, is that the argument founders on its initial premise of a homogeneous space of the relationship between industrial enterprises and financial institutions. Necessarily the conclusion of this argument would apply to the idea that the 'goal' of managers is to maximise the growth of the firm if only because growth is necessarily facilitated by the 'going-concern' concept relative to the treatment of the industrial enterprise as a set of financial assets.

At this point it is worth considering another possible objection. It may be argued that a reductionist treatment of the enterprise is justified on the grounds that 'imperatives of the capitalist market' impose practices on the enterprise which, if not strictly of a profit-maximising type, function as its 'behavioural' equivalent. The implication of such arguments would be that the examination of the theoretical conditions for a universal concept of capitalist calculation are in fact irrelevant. This is simply because such concepts posit calculation as an effect of external exigencies. Such arguments are used in a more or less loose way in a wide variety of arguments. For example, it is a familiar response amongst Marxist writers to proponents of the 'managerial revolution' thesis or variants of it that the 'motivation' of the managers is irrelevant since specific economic practices are imposed on them by the exigencies of the capitalist market.

This argument is often stated in terms of an idea that a 'natural selection' process operates within capitalist markets 'selecting' firms which adopt profit-maximising practices or their 'behavioural' variant. This conception has been exhaustively analysed in an important theoretical paper by Sidney Winter ('Economic "natural selection" and the theory of the firm'). At this point we shall simply indicate some of the problems with the application of such a concept.

In the first place it is easy to see that logically a true reductionist treatment of the problem is untenable. This is simply because the selection process has to 'select' for something. The behaviourist argument, as Winter demonstrates, arises from a series of criticisms of the conception that firms actually adopt profit-maximising criteria. Behaviourist arguments implicitly accept criticisms on broadly 'realist' grounds. The reductionist treatment involves a classic behaviourist distinction between intentions and behaviour such that a whole range of 'intentions' and criteria are potentially compatible with 'profit-maximising' behaviour. Selection in this argument works not on calculative criteria but only on behaviour. This, as Winter points out, is untenable for two related reasons. First, the concept of profit maximising quite necessarily refers to consistent performance over a range of different conditions.

Problems of a General Theory of Capitalist Calculation 147

Friedman, for example, argues that at the level of the calculative criteria we can have practices based on 'habit' or 'chance' which are compatible with profit-maximising behaviour. The obvious difficulty with the behaviourist argument is, therefore, that 'chance' or 'habit' in no way guarantee that 'maximising' behaviour in one set of conditions will necessarily be so in another set of conditions. Second, this problem is compounded by the fact that the mechanism of selection involves adjustments in the economy. If 'selection' is to operate it must involve a situation where 'profit-maximising' firms expand. Consequently random behaviour, which happens to be adjusted to a given environment, is in no way likely to remain 'adaptive' unless a teleology is posited in some sense *in* the environment—a move which would precisely efface the behaviour/selection polarity on which the argument depends. ('Economic "natural selection",' p. 240)

When the 'natural selection' argument, or variants of it, are articulated, its domain of application is stated as that of the capitalist economy in general. Thus, there is an implicit reference to 'competitive pressures' which operate in a consistent way in capitalist economies. As Winter so ably demonstrates, the conditions for the operation of 'natural selection' in respect of profit-maximising organisations are highly restrictive.

The first restriction concerns the status of information in the argument and the problem of establishing a determinate field in which calculation can operate. If, for example, it is assumed that all enterprises face similarly structured problems then profit-maximising decisions will be definable in a determinate way. If this assumption does not apply the enterprise is free to acquire further information concerning the character of the possible problem field and this information would involve costs either directly, or through the effect which seeking information might have on the enterprise (e.g. interruptions of the production process), or through changing the character of the 'problems' facing the enterprise (e.g. consequent change in production methods). It is a standard argument here that this problem builds an indeterminacy into the calculations, since assumptions have to be made concerning the limits which will be imposed on the acquisition of information as, by its very nature, such acquisition is potentially open-ended. It is necessary to be clear on the kinds of problem which this poses. The difficulty lies in the conception of a theory which is supposed to be applicable to the capitalist economy in general. There is no question that assumptions concerning the character of the information deployed in calculation are necessary, but no point of abstraction is derivable from the notion of capitalist economy as such. As Winter points out, 'The concept of profit maximisation must abstract from some information costs, but there is no obviously valid choice of a level of analysis at which abstraction should be made.' (*op. cit.*, p. 268)

Secondly, profit maximisation in 'natural-selection' arguments is 'embodied' in an organisational form, in other words, one speaks of profit-maximising *firms*. If there is to be 'natural selection' for this characteristic then additional characteristics of the firms concerned or in the conditions applying to these firms or in the time-period under consideration must have no bearing on 'survival' and thus on the firms 'selected'. Clearly this involves abstraction both from the financial position of the enterprise at a given point in time and from differential relations to financial institutions. If this abstraction is not made then some firms will survive either because of the time-period employed, or because of their superior financial position at the beginning of the relevant time-period, or because of their superior access to external finance independent of the firms' decision-making structure.

Thirdly, the relative scale of the enterprises must also be treated as having no direct bearing on survival, since if either economies or diseconomies of scale exist the selection will not necessarily be for 'profit maximising'. In the case of economies of scale larger firms will achieve advantages independently of whether they are or are not profit-maximising organisational forms. Assuming that traditional profit-maximising practice is effective in its own terms, it is obviously possible under economies of scale that the scale-effects may more than compensate for the 'divergences' from profit-maximising practices. This may also involve cumulative effects since if the larger unit expands up to the point at which economies of scale cease, and providing the 'divergences' are kept within the relevant limits, then survival will be no indication of a profit-maximising organisational form.

Diseconomies of scale create problems in respect of the selection mechanism. Selection is conceived of as working through a process whereby the profit-maximising firms necessarily generate a higher flow of funds and expand output, thus increasing the supply of commodities at lower prices and consequently eliminating the non-maximisers. Where diseconomies of scale operate, however,

Problems of a General Theory of Capitalist Calculation 149

the expanding firm naturally reaches a point where it encounters penalties for expansion. This clearly implies that the selection process only operates within a given range and consequently that in certain ranges it does not operate at all.

Even with these conditions excluded in a perfect information situation, with firms producing identical goods or perfect substitutes there are still major problems. These arise from the condition stated above that selection is posited as working on *organisational forms* not on *actions*. The import of this is clearly that a firm can *act* in a 'profit-maximising' manner over a particular range of prices and output without doing so over the full range of prices and outputs. For a selection process to operate on organisational forms, therefore, it is necessary for the environment to repeat each possible firm position if organisational forms rather than actions are to be 'tested'. Thus Winter points out that 'The profit maximising argument is false if it is meant to apply to a theoretical world of perfect information, unless every conceivable state of the world occurs not once, but repeatedly, in the selection process.' (*ibid.*, p. 268)

The objection that a definite pattern of calculation is imposed on capitalist economies in general by natural selection thus involves two major problems. First, as selection is for a 'property' of the enterprise's organisational form it is impossible to treat enterprise calculation in a reductionist fashion. It then follows that the problems of a 'true' measure and a 'true' norm cannot be avoided since one would have to specify the character of the property which the environment is deemed to select for and the problems relating to the terrain on which such properties can be specified remain. Second, the natural selection can only function under a series of limiting conditions. But those conditions cannot be derived from the conception of capitalist economy in general. Natural selection cannot then be said to operate in the sphere of capitalist production as such.

Measures and norms applied to them are meaningless without a reference to some definite time-period. Goals of 'growth' or 'profits' are for a given period; correlatively, measures must apply to given periods. The problem involved here is thus identical to the problems associated with the norm and the measure. We pointed out above that if calculation in capitalist economies could be conceived of in terms of a universal practice of calculation this would necessarily involve a 'true' measure of returns, and a 'correct' time-period must be designated. But the notion of a 'correct' time-period is manifestly absurd. A time-period could be judged 'correct' or 'incorrect' only in connection with a particular relationship between the enterprise and its economic environment. Thus to suppose a 'correct' time-period is to suppose an invariant economic environment. Since the economic environment of enterprises cannot be assumed to be invariant there can be no norms of correctness of time-periods of calculation.

The significance of time-periods does not arise from there being such a thing as 'correct' or 'incorrect' but rather from the fact that the adoption of a time-period/norm of calculation has definite effects on the practices of enterprises. To take an example where this is clearly brought out, consider the demise of the British motor-cycle industry and the contrast between the relevant time-periods of calculation of the Japanese motor-cycle producers and their British counterparts.

The question of the time-period taken as relevant for calculation plays a central role in explaining the inferior performance of the British motor-cycle producers and equally helps to account for the cumulative and rapid decline experienced by the British motor-cyele industry. This is clearly brought out in the excellent report prepared for the British government by the Boston Consulting Group, *Strategy Alternatives for the British Motor Cycle Industry*.

In outlining what they call the 'British Marketing Philosophy' the Boston group emphasise that: 'The fundamental feature in this philosophy is its emphasis on model by model profit levels.' (*ibid.*, p. 34) From this overarching premise of policy the group argue four subsidiary policies follow:

> Products should be up-rated or withdrawn whenever the accounting system shows that they are unprofitable.
> Unfortunately the accounting system will be based on existing methods of production and channels of distribution, and not on cost levels that could be achieved under new systems and with different volumes. It will also overlook the effects that each model may have on the costs of producing and marketing models in the range, and on the saleability of other products in the range. (*ibid.*)

The time-period relevant for enterprise calculation here is identical to that taken in the presentation of annual accounts. The

Problems of a General Theory of Capitalist Calculation 151

choice of this period, as the group indicates, necessarily governs a whole range of crucial decisions. Most obviously, as the report indicates, it governs the decisions over the product range supplied by the enterprise. This period of calculation thus leads to a selection of a product range governed by annual profitability considerations and this in turn will govern decisions concerning distribution and production methods. In the former case economies achieved by a higher *overall* volume will be lost due to the fact that applying annual profitability criteria may (and did in this case) cut out models which might be profitable over a long period *and* would tend to reduce unit costs by spreading selling costs over a large volume of units. In the latter case it prevents the company from utilising capital equipment whose use is only economically viable at a higher volume.

In so far as an accounting period which necessarily incorporates reference to these conditions is used as the point of reference then, as the Boston group indicate, the conditions will be reproduced in future decisions. This involves the following pricing policies: 'Prices are set at the levels necessary to achieve profitability. . . . The second order effect that loss of volume may have on costs and hence on profit in the longer term is taken less into account.' (*ibid*.) In the same way in which models are judged on their profitability, marketing and distribution are subject to the same criteria:

> The cost of an effective marketing system is only acceptable in markets where the British are already established, and hence profitable. New markets will only be opened up to the extent that their development will not mean significant front-end expenses investment in establishing s (selling) and d (distribution) systems ahead of sales. (*ibid*.)

The consistent adoption of this relevant time-period for calculation thus involved a cumulative weakening *vis-à-vis* the competitors who oriented their calculation to the achievement of long-term market shares. More inefficient production methods and distributional systems led to more models becoming unprofitable and thus models were withdrawn from production. This involved a larger market for the Japanese competitors who were able to capitalise on further scale economies in both production and distribution. The cumulative gap increasingly forced the British producers, given their pricing policy which necessarily was derived from their calculation period, into requiring higher price premiums over their Japanese competitors. The process of decline continued such that the Japanese were able effectively to compete with the British manufacturers even in the previously most profitable models, thus engendering the current situation where the indigenous industry barely exists.

This example demonstrates the pertinence of the time-period adopted for calculation, but it does not demonstrate that the Japanese producers adopted a 'correct' calculative period in the sense that applies to a norm governing calculation periods in capitalist economies in general. A previous example cited will easily demonstrate this. We stated earlier that industrial enterprises could be the object of radically different types of calculation on the part of financial institutions. It is thus perfectly possible that an enterprise adopting a longer calculation period and, for example, building up stocks to ensure reliability of supply or operating with excess capacity in order to have capacity to meet fluctuations in demand for the enterprise's product, might, under unfavourable conditions of operation, be highly vulnerable to acquisition by a financial conglomerate concerned to realise short-term profits (defined by the difference between selling and acquisition cost) on the enterprise's assets. The effectiveness of calculation designed, for example, to reduce unit costs over a longer calculation period by establishing a stable share of a given market is thus by no means guaranteed. Clearly the question of the time-period relevant to calculation must be referred to the conditions of definite capitalist national economies.

The last example demonstrates that an identification of calculation periods with accounting periods is not 'given' but relates to particular practices of calculation. However, this necessary distinction should not lead us into the position where accounting periods are treated in a reductionist way. Accounting periods are of course, related to important economic and legal constraints. It is a legal obligation under the Companies Act 1948 that every company should prepare annually a balance-sheet and a profit and loss account. There are equally obvious economic reasons for there to be limits on the lengths of accounting periods in either an upward or downward direction in relation to features of capitalist national economies such as distribution of dividends and, in so far as acquisitions of shares are related to profit figures and asset values clearly accounting periods are designed to be congruent with such functions.

This legal imposition has a number of important economic effects which will merely be outlined here as they will be treated in greater detail below. Given that the measures of assets and profits which appear in annual accounts do have a role in determining stock-market valuations, it is easy to see that the appearance of annual accounts may have a significant impact, for example, on the continued existence of enterprises. Take Keynes's well-known argument that, 'There is no sense in building up a new enterprise at a cost greater than that at which a similar existing enterprise can be purchased.' (*General Theory*, p. 151) This might appear to have minimal economic effects; for example, it might appear simply to be an alternative means for an enterprise to expand its output. But from the discussion so far we can see that this cannot be assumed.

There is a difference between expanding an existing enterprise and the acquisition of a new enterprise. To take a point often raised in the literature of economic history, enterprises have determinate managerial and administrative structures: the expansion of an existing enterprises's capacity by the purchase of new capital equipment may not involve any major administrative changes. Acquisition of another enterprise, however, raises the problem of integrating the new enterprise and its managerial and administrative structure into that of the acquiring firm or in some cases vice versa. Naturally it cannot be assumed that such integration is necessarily more inefficent than the expansion of a given enterprise without acquisition but it is clear that acquisition and expansion of an existing enterprise without acquisition are by no means to be assumed to be identical in their effects.

Further, there can be no presumption that the acquiring enterprise will apply similar criteria of calculation to the enterprise acquired. Given the material which has already been presented in the section on calculation and time-periods, it is quite easy to see that differences in time-periods relevant to calculation between enterprises could have highly significant economic repercussions.

In the same passage, Keynes points out another effect of stock-market valuations which particularly facilitate the operations of financial conglomerates of the type to which we have already referred:

> In my *Treatise on Money* . . . I pointed out that when a
> company's shares are quoted very high so that it can raise more

capital by issuing more shares on favourable terms, this has the same effect as if it could borrow at a low rate of interest. (*ibid.*, p. 151, fn. 1)

Stock-market valuations thus play an important role in reinforcing calculation by financial conglomerates aimed at high short-term returns. The achievement of such returns will push up stock-market valuations, having the effect which Keynes indicates. This is particularly important to such enterprises for the reasons which we have indicated, i.e. that they have either no or very limited access to contractual savings or regular deposits like commercial banks and thus operate in the 'wholesale' financial markets under variable conditions. A high stock-market valuation thus has the appeal of providing a flow of funds on terms favourable to the enterprise from the point of view of the time-period applicable to the flow and the effective rate of interest. However, given that a high premium is thus put on a high stock-market valuation, this would lead in fact to a reinforcement of the criteria of calculation already applied by financial enterprises of this kind.

In discussing the problems of a general theory of capitalist enterprise calculation we have concentrated on the question of whether a universal mode of calculation might be established characterising capitalist economies in general. However, at the outset we indicated that it was perfectly possible for a general theory of capitalist enterprise calculation to admit the necessity of a plurality of measures of returns and a plurality of principles governing enterprise calculations. If such a procedure were to be adopted it would be necessary to deduce such pluralities from the conception of capitalist economy as such.

We now wish to establish that such a procedure cannot be undertaken and we will make reference to material already covered with regard to the question of whether a universal mode of calculation might be established.

We pointed out in relation to the question of a univeral mode of calculation that there was a plurality of means of measuring returns to capitalist enterprises. Is it possible to deduce such a plurality from the elements of the domain of the capitalist economy in general? Our examples from the Sandilands report on inflation accounting arose clearly from the question of giving a measure of enterprise returns under conditions of rapid price rises. This was not merely true of the different concepts of profit, treatment of

Problems of a General Theory of Capitalist Calculation 155

stock, and asset valuation presented in the report; it was also true of the modifications to the system of historic cost accounting. Since the Companies Act of 1967 it has been legal to revalue fixed assets on the condition that the amount of the revaluation and the year in which the revaluation was made is shown, or, in the case of a revaluation made in the current year that the name and qualifications of the individual who did the revaluation is shown. (Sandilands, p. 84) An Institute of Chartered Accountants survey conducted in 1973–4 into the question of which fixed assets had been subject to revaluation gave as one of its conclusions that overwhelmingly the most important fixed asset subject to revaluation was property. For example, for the year 1973–4, 151 out of 300 companies in the sample had carried out 'major' revaluations of their property assets and of these 107 had carried out these revaluations in the previous four years, in the same year 10 companies had revalued other fixed assets (5 in the previous four years).

Not surprisingly the revaluation of fixed assets was concentrated on the type of assets whose value had changed dramatically over the relevant period. Changes in the system of historic cost accounting and the set of alternative measures of profit set out in Sandilands were thus developed in respect of a pattern of price changes, of property assets in the former case and in respect of historically high rates of inflation in the latter case. In no sense does this amount to any claim that accounting concepts are 'reflections' of such concerns. On the contrary, there is a long history of disputes in accounting theory over measures of income, capital, etc. However, the transformation of legally sanctioned accounting practices has implications for the presentation of accounts and for the taxation of profits and is clearly related to the specific conditions of historically high rates of price rise. If this is the case then it would be incumbent to show that if reference is to be made to the domain of the capitalist economy in general to account for the plurality of measures and for the entrance of different measures into legally sanctioned accounting practices then such a reference would have to be backed up by the ability to *deduce* levels of inflation, for example, from the conception of capitalism in general. Such a claim is clearly implausible, though some Marxist arguments suggest that 'tendencies' operate to push the capitalist state to raise levels of public expenditure with inflationary effects.

This conclusion may be reinforced if we briefly return to the theoretical dispute over stock appreciation between Godley and Wood on one side and Merrett and Sykes on the other. The question of stock appreciation was taken up in the budgets of November 1974 and April 1975 in which, subject to certain limitations, companies were given the right to reduce the closing valuation of the stocks and work in progress by the amount of the increase in their book value during the year. This dispensation was introduced in the November budget and extended for an additional year in the April budget. However, the dispensation was a deferral of tax, not an exemption. In the Sandilands report the measures were subject to criticism, amongst which was the following:

> The method pays no regard to changes in the volume of stock. Relief is based on the difference between the closing and opening stock valuations irrespective of whether the difference is due to the replacement of stock at higher prices or to the increase in the volume of stock held at the end of the year. Thus a company which allowed its stock levels to run up to an economically inefficient level at the end of the accounting period might be able to claim substantial tax relief for its inefficiency. (Sandilands, p. 201)

Whether the conclusions drawn in Sandilands are in fact warranted is debatable but such a question could only be settled by reference to the economic strategy adopted within a definite national economy. Thus, for example, the import of a major change in legally sanctioned accounting practices would necessarily have important ramifications on economic strategy since it would necessarily favour particular modes of calculation and would equally necessarily involve distributional effects between enterprises. The fact that the government treated the problem as one of liquidity in this instance is thus in part explicable on the grounds that such a treatment leaves more strategic options open than if the problem is treated as one of profitability. Consequently, the task for a general theory of the capitalist enterprise calculation would be to deduce the economic strategies characteristic of definite capitalist national economies.

Epistemology and the terrain of a theory of calculation

In situating our argument concerning the terrain of a theory of

Problems of a General Theory of Capitalist Calculation 157

enterprise calculation we must stress that our position does not involve an *epistemological* critique of Marxism or neo-classical economics. This demarcates our argument from those who seek to link an 'alternative economics' opposed to neo-classical theory, with an 'alternative epistemology'. We may approach the deficiencies of this position by examining a particularly rigorous representative of it, Hollis and Nell's *Rational Economic Man*.

Hollis and Nell counterpose neo-classical economics, which they believe to be founded on an 'empiricist' epistemological basis, to what they call 'Classical-Marxian' economics which is erected on a 'rationalist' philosophical basis. Characteristic of Hollis and Nell's argument is that 'economic science' must have a foundation in an epistemological standpoint. This standpoint, given their rejection of 'empiricism', cannot be 'chosen' for purposes such as its utility in framing hypotheses on the lines of a positivist distinction between 'metaphysics' and 'hypotheses'. To take up such a position would be to adopt the position that the 'validity' or otherwise of a theory could only be established on the basis of 'empirical testing', a view which their book is largely written against. The standpoint is for Hollis and Nell necessarily both 'real' and 'rational'. They reject the 'empiricist' distinction between analytic and synthetic statements such that statements of necessary relationships are simply of a tautological kind. A science for Hollis and Nell rests on what they call 'real definitions' so that the relations of necessity 'in the real' can be analysed by reference to their 'rational necessity'.

Hollis and Nell argue that the fundamental concept of economic science is *production* and that such a concept has both a 'rational' priority and a priority 'in the real'; this explanation of economic phenomena must therefore make reference to this priority. Economic science has a deductive character which can be referred back to this dual priority.

In defence of this view, Hollis and Nell argue that any alternative to such a position will involve pragmatism:

> Why should we claim a necessarily privileged status for 'production' or more exactly, for 'reproduction of the economic system'? The question is as dangerous as it is apparently difficult. For if we cannot provide a satisfactory answer, our whole argument is in jeopardy. . . . We cannot allow the possibility of different fundamental concepts, for different

concepts will give rise to different theories, as different as Robbins and Marx. Pragmatists might simply shrug agreeably and wait to see which worked out best. No such cheerfully casual course is open to us. (*Rational Economic Man*, pp. 242–3)

Hollis and Nell quite rightly object to pragmatism that it is involved in a contradiction which is a well-known characteristic of a relativistic philosophical position. The pragmatist is thus willing to relativise all theories and epistemologies with the exception of pragmatism. In fact their requirement for a standpoint which is 'ontologically prior' has nothing to do with the refutation of pragmatism. Hollis and Nell's own argument against pragmatism is entirely independent of their ontological position. The 'ontological priority' they posit stems from the way in which they use epistemological discourse.

The necessity for a general ontological 'standpoint' derives from the idea that the 'real' constitutes a *totality*. A totality implies an organising principle and in so far as the principle is known both 'real' and 'knowledge' are homogeneous by reference to the organising principle. As we have already indicated, the 'standpoint' adopted by Hollis and Nell is that of 'production' or 'reproduction' and the main competitor to this position discussed in their book is the notion that economic theory should be based on a concept of 'choice'. Their critique of this conception is based on an attempt to demonstrate that 'choice' always implies reference to 'production'.

The formation of relative preferences among goods and services, *if it is to be rational, must* involve solving typical production problems. . . . Preferences for commodities . . . will be based on the way the characteristics of different goods contribute to the objectives of the choosing agent. (*ibid*., p. 243)

Given that the object of the argument is to find a single appropriate epistemological standpoint, there is a counterposition of two homogeneous categories, 'production' and 'choice'. The choosing agent here is clearly engaged in consumption, and as such why 'conditions of production' should be relevant to such an agent is not clear. Obviously agents are not homogeneous. In so far as agents are separated from the means of production it is not clear what pertinence the concern with production might have for their consumption. A rentier does not need to be concerned with production. The argument, however, cannot be sustained by

Problems of a General Theory of Capitalist Calculation   159

reference to agents exerting control over the means of production. They, it can be argued, derive their revenue from their use of the means of production, but here there need be no reference to homogeneous 'conditions of production', only to the determinate means of production over which these agents exert control. Consequently there is nothing in the concept of a 'choosing agent' to imply reference to 'conditions of production' as a homogeneous ontological category and obviously the construction of an appropriate subject suitably designated 'rational' hardly advances the argument.

Hollis and Nell do, however, advance an alternative argument to sustain their position.

> What one wants and what is good for one can, and frequently do, conflict. To function properly and effectively in his appointed roles, a person must maintain both his health and his levels of training and competence: and in either or both of these areas personal preference may be at variance with rational choice. . . . We choose what we do because the context we are in provides us with certain options, certain resources and certain goals. . . . But once we allow that the chooser *must* exist in a specific social context, then the character of the chooser we can assume is limited by the requirements for the maintenance of the context. The conditions of reproduction are prior to because determining those of choice. (*ibid.*, pp. 243– 4)

There are two possible alternative readings of this argument. Either Hollis and Nell are setting out a prescriptive argument that consuming agents *should* take the conditions of production into consideration, in which case reference can hardly be to the 'real' conditions of the subject. Or they are arguing that some kind of natural selection mechanism operates which enforces such 'choices'. In this case the conditions for the operation of the mechanism would be analogous to that which we have already discussed for firms. Selection would have to be 'for' the decision-making structure of the subject not the subject's actions, i.e. we are talking of a 'rational' consumer not someone who 'happens' to be 'rational'. This involves a paradox in Hollis and Nell's argument. They continually put forward a well-known and important line of criticism of neo-classical economics, that the latter posits an infinite field of choice. The neo-classical theory of choice of techniques and of consumer behaviour invokes a potentially infinite set of commodities or production methods which are available to the 'consumer' or 'producer'. They wish to reject such a position but the logic of the natural selection argument is necessarily to involve the positing of such an infinite set of choices as a condition of the argument. As the context cannot in any sense 'give' the consumer's choice it can only be referred to 'reproduction' by reference to exigencies of a natural selection type. If, however, selection is to be for rational consumers and not for actions then, as we have seen above, the environment must reproduce the whole range of possible choices on a regular basis. If selection is to be invoked the 'specific context' must go; the only possible context is the set of all contexts.

These problems do not arise because of Hollis and Nell's theoretical incompetence—even a cursory acquaintance with the book's many lucid and valuable arguments will dispel such an idea—but is an effect of their reliance on epistemology. We have already seen that the search for an epistemological standpoint imposes the necessity of positing homogeneous categories such as 'production' which efface pertinent distinctions, between agents, for example. Homogeneity is further imposed on the economic subject, leading that subject either to be defined tautologically in relation to 'conditions of production' or the positing of unsustainable inferences with respect to the consumption–production relation.

The relevance of the national terrain

We have argued that the terrain on which a theory of enterprise calculation must be established is that of definite capitalist national economies. However, it may be argued that the terrain of national economies has been superseded due to the operations of multi-national companies. These firms, it is claimed, are in no way tied to operations in any given nation-state and their position in the world economy allows them to adopt practices of calculation quite distinct from enterprises operating exclusively within national boundaries.

Two questions, therefore, arise here: are multi-national companies 'autonomous' from nation-states and is there a universal practice of multi-national companies which is radically distinct from enterprises working exclusively within national boundaries? The multi-national company is a slightly misleading

Problems of a General Theory of Capitalist Calculation 161

term in so far as such enterprises are always combinations of parent companies and subsidiaries; in this respect what is pertinent is that parent companies are almost always based in advanced capitalist national economies. There is no 'multi-national' base such that multi-national enterprises are indifferent to the nation-state in which the parent is located. This is reinforced by pertinent differences between international companies on the basis of the characteristics of the national market in which the parent company operates. Thus the considerably larger scale of the internal American market would seem to give American international firms a decisive advantage over European competitors in labour-productivity terms by allowing for the advantages of longer production runs to be reaped. (Pratten, *Labour Productivity Differentials within International Companies*, p. 61)

Multi-national companies are equally differentiated in respect of the character of parent–subsidiary relationships. Swedish international companies, for example, usually use their subsidiaries as marketing operations, production being concentrated in Sweden. British subsidiaries do not, however, seem to give any privileged status to the parent company in respect of their purchases. (Pratten, *A Comparison of the Performance of Swedish and UK Companies*, pp. 65–6 and Parry, 'The international firm and national economic policy: a survey of some issues'). Such differences arise from differences in the character of the national base of the parent. In this case there is some evidence that the relative efficiency of plants in the 'home' country of the parent was important and that while Swedish plants were regarded as more efficient by the managers of their international firms, the reverse was true in the British case.

It is possible to argue that multi-national companies do not have a universal mode of calculation. How far, however, are there features specific to multi-national companies, and what is their significance? A common argument is that the multi-national firm is in a unique position by being able to switch production facilities from country to country to take advantage of wage differentials or differences in labour relations, for example. This difference is a difference referring to the scale of operation of the switching of production facilities. There is no difference in principle between multi-national firms and firms whose operations are limited to particular nation-states. Switching is not costless for it will involve costs of running down or liquidating a subsidiary, costs of setting up or expanding subsidiaries. Calculations of this type are therefore not radically different whether they are made within a given nation-state or between nation-states. Furthermore, these costs will be affected by the particular national economies in which switches take place. Switching clearly involves the possibility of reprisals, costs arising from the effects of redundancy legislation, etc.

Multi-national firms are equally claimed to be differentiated by the ability to dictate pricing policies to their subsidiaries with the object of tax avoidance, where the company takes advantage of differences in tax rates and makes corresponding adjustments in income flows. Again, however, this does not differ in principle from the practices of firms operating in national markets who may similarly adjust income flows.

Multi-national firms are claimed to exert significant effects on national economies by being in a privileged position to speculate in currency and it is often argued that such firms have a substantial effect on movements of exchange rates. Such practices involve speculating in currency, but the whole character of speculation would tend to contradict such an argument. Central-bank interventions are designed to control the effects of speculation by leaving the speculator open to risk of losses by purchases or sales of currency in the 'opposite direction' to the speculator. This assumes that the volume of purchases and sales of the central bank and speculators is relatively small. Substantial falls which cannot be offset by central-bank activity generally arise from substantial holders involving themselves in continued selling and making losses on such selling. In this situation the central bank cannot impose the loss penalty as a sanction since the sellers are already willing to tolerate substantial losses and have already done so from the previous sales. This situation, for example, occurred in the recent substantial fall in sterling with sales mainly coming from OPEC governments. (Harris, 'Cross your fingers—and get them burned'). Holders on this scale are almost invariably public authorities and other central banks.

While this brief survey can in no sense claim to tackle the problems raised by multi-national firms, our object has simply been to show that their existence need not involve the positing of an alternative terrain for theoretical investigation to that of definite capitalist national economies.

Chapter 9

Enterprise Calculation and Production Methods

In the example of the British and Japanese motor-cycle industries cited above, it was possible to discern not only a marked difference in the relevant time-periods adopted for calculation but also a marked difference in the character of the production methods adopted. In the Japanese case both high-output volumes and high volume per model made it economically feasible to use capital equipment representing a substantial initial cost. The high volume naturally meant that the high initial cost was spread over a large number of units, thus indicating the link observed in many spheres of production between the employment of capital equipment representing a high initial cost and the volume of output of the enterprise. In discussing this example we pointed out that it could by no means be assumed that enterprises adopting practices of calculation similar to those of the Japanese enterprises in this case were necessarily guaranteed similar results. The constraint that we indicated related to the mode of calculation applied to the enterprise by financial institutions but it is worth considering here another aspect of the problem.

It might be possible to argue in relation to that example that in so far as calculation *was* premised on what we have called a 'going-concern' basis, industrial enterprises would 'converge' upon production methods such as those represented by the case of the Japanese motor-cycle industry. This would indicate that enterprise calculation in the case of industrial enterprises would be characterised by high volumes and low unit costs and would involve capital equipment designed progressively to mechanise production operations and the transfer of products within the production process, provided 'going-concern' criteria were adopted.

We argue that such a view is fallacious and that advanced capitalist economies are characterised by forms of industrial enterprise calculation which engender a diversity of production methods. This, however, should not lead to a view that production methods of the broad 'type' characterised by the Japanese motor-cycle industry do not have *under certain conditions* numerous important advantages.

In the motor-cycle industry case the fact that the value of capital equipment deployed by the Japanese firms was much greater than with the British firms did not prevent the former achieving substantially lower unit costs. This is for a number of reasons. Mechanisation has the advantage that it can greatly increase the integration of a production process. Mechanisation of a process is usually characterised by machines performing a variable range of specialist tasks. These tasks can thus be given quite a precise allocation of the total production time. Furthermore, production time will be reduced in so far as machines can be designed to produce to particular specifications in the operations they perform. This means that variability in operations should be minimised.

This gives two major advantages from the point of view of integration. First, since the tasks can be allocated a precise time-period in the production process, it is possible to arrange the series of operations in such a way that they can be co-ordinated with each other so that the minimum time-period is spent on each. Second, if the operations can be performed precisely the production time lost because particular parts are defective is cut out. Such integration is linked with mechanisation since the transfer of tasks from labour to machines is a condition of the advantages of integration being achieved. In the case of the specification of the operations the use of labour involves two problems related to variability: variation according to the manual dexterity and relevant knowledge of the labourer and variation as a simple effect of physiological causes (tiredness, boredom, etc.).

Of course, there is no simple counterposition of 'labour' to 'machinery' at issue here. The most common forms of mechanisation do involve only a limited degree of mechanisation, and differential combinations of labour and machinery necessarily produce different degrees of variability in operations.

The integration of the production process, however, does not simply involve the direct production operations but equally involves the transfer of the product from one production stage to another. Mechanised transfer is clearly necessary for integration in so far as a specific flow of materials at specific time-periods to different operations can be programmed, thus enabling each piece of equipment to operate as far as possible in a continuous way throughout the production period. Again, in so far as the transfer of the product is by the use of labour the predictability necessary for integration is endangered.

An integrated production process is thus aided by the mechanisation both of direct operations on the product and of the transfer of the product. The dependence on labour necessarily builds greater variability into both performance of operations and transfer. This variability is in turn related to variations in economic class struggles affecting working practices internal to the enterprise and the supply of labour.

In the former case economic class struggles will affect both interruptions of the production process through strikes and stoppages and equally will regulate the pace of work within the production process itself. Strikes may not only lengthen a given production period but may have even greater effects on the integration of the production process. Strikes, for example, may have uneven effects on the production process such that only particular processes are affected. This, in turn, can clearly lead to shortages and/or bottlenecks. The effect of mechanisation on the enterprise's labour requirements are highly variable. The primary advantage for the enterprise, however, is in reducing the manual skills and specialist knowledge required by the labourers. This would primarily function through the fact that if the integration and consistency of the process of production is to be a major, sought-after effect of mechanisation then correlatively the tasks performed by labourers should be simplified. This would have the effect of insulating the enterprise from shortages of labour in grades of labour with such skills or knowledge and thus prevent the consequently lengthening of the production period for a given volume of output.

The advantages of integration may also be accompanied by economies both in the use of raw materials and in the use of capital equipment. The mechanisation of direct production operations may economise on raw materials for the reasons already suggested in respect of the integration of the production process. If variability of the production operations is minimised by mechanisation then the number of defective operations should be reduced with consequent savings on raw materials. Similarly, mechanisation may allow for operations which reduce waste of raw materials. The same effects operate in relation to transfer of products where mechanisation may allow for reductions in wear and breakages. The same goes for capital equipment—variability in operations may produce greater wear on capital equipment, damage to raw materials or semi-finished goods in transit may have similar effects.

For these reasons mechanisation of the production process can be linked with lower unit costs. One axis of this process is that a higher volume can be produced in a shorter production period. This is partly due to the obvious speeding up of both the direct operations of the process and the transfer of materials. It is equally due to the possibility of integration such that each part of the process is working at a continuous speed, and shortages and bottlenecks which would lengthen the production period do not occur. On the other axis is the economy in the use of equipment and raw materials to which we have already referred, since a given investment in equipment and raw materials is 'represented' in a correspondingly higher volume of products.

Advantages are not merely restricted to unit costs, however, for they are frequently accompanied by advances in quality. This is for reasons already indicated; the predictability of both operations and the transfer of materials means that engineering tolerances can be more precise and that 'high quality' can be maintained with low unit costs. To return to the motor-cycle-industry example, the Japanese industry was both more highly mechanised and exhibited quality advantages. British bikes were consistently more unreliable than Japanese, engendering a higher level of warranty claims, had consistent design problems involving oil leaks, for example, and often did not incorporate technical improvements which were taken-for-granted features of the Japanese bikes, such as electric starters. (Boston Group, *Strategy Alternatives*, pp. 27–8)

Particularly central to the calculation of capitalist enterprises is the question of reliability of supply of finished products and the related question of the relation of the enterprise to its suppliers. These questions are often not given the prominence they deserve because the consistent supply of products is often taken for granted in advanced capitalist national economies. Any consideration of calculation in capitalist enterprises necessarily must involve the enterprise's relation to the sale and distribution of its products. One of the advantages of mechanised production is the capacity to produce high volumes of standardised products at predictable prices and qualities. This has clear advantages in terms of sale and distribution; the distributor is able to meet demands of consumers quickly, is able to keep inventories at a low level and is involved in no problems in obtaining the product. The same considerations apply to replacements; here too the reliability of supply of components will be a characteristic of highly mechanised production. The importance of these considerations is emphasised in products such as motor-vehicles where control over the distribution system is crucial. In so far, for example, as dealers operate exclusively with the products of a given enterprise a failure of that enterprise to maintain consistent supply may lead it to forfeit control over the dealership, with the consequent effects on market shares.

Similar considerations enter into the determinants of the relationship between the enterprise and its suppliers. The enterprise will necessarily require regular supplies of raw materials and semi-finished goods utilised in the production process. The high-volume mechanised producer has two central advantages for the supplier, the volume demanded and the regularity and consistency of that demand. Thus not only does the supplier have a reliable market he may also be able to schedule production in an efficient manner because of the predictability of the demand of the purchasing enterprise. This in turn may have cost advantages for the purchasing enterprise, giving the latter a privileged status *vis-à-vis* the former.

It might be thought that costs associated with the circulation of commodities are objects of capitalist enterprise calculation while economies in the use of raw materials or in the use of capital equipment involve calculations of a 'technical' character. Such a distinction is untenable. Economy in the use of raw materials or reduction in the wear on capital equipment might be measured in terms of the volume of finished products for a given use of raw materials and/or capital equipment but such calculations are not directly made by capitalist enterprises. The calculations of capitalist enterprises are made in terms of a given set of prices. To take the example of economisation in the use of raw materials, if it involves the employment of new capital equipment then the decision to employ such equipment will be conditioned by the relative cost of the equipment in relation to the cost reductions effected by producing a given volume of output with a smaller volume of raw materials. As the economisation on the use of raw materials is not a direct objective of the capitalist enterprise whether it does or does not take place will necessarily relate at any given point in time to the particular set of capital equipment employed by the enterprise. For example, the new equipment may be non-complementary with the existing equipment, involving as a condition of its use that the existing equipment be disposed of, possibly involving a loss due to the equipment being disposed of on a 'forced-sale' basis.

Is it the case, perhaps, that while the enterprise does not make calculations directly in technical terms it does so 'indirectly' by virtue of the fact that prices 'reflect' technical exigencies? This position is equally unsustainable. If we take the example above it is possible to envisage a situation in which the capital equipment required to effect the economisation on the use of raw materials is not directly purchased by the enterprise but acquired as part of the purchase of another enterprise. The 'price' of such capital goods will thus be affected by the capitalised value of the acquired enterprise if a cash purchase is at issue or the relative capitalised values if a share exchange or share and cash offer is involved. In such cases the 'prices' vary with these relative capitalised values of the acquiring and acquired firm, values which are by no means technical in character. For instance, and we will examine this in more detail below, larger, stock-market-quoted industrial enterprises are generally capitalised at a more favourable ratio to their earnings than smaller, quoted companies and this advantage is substantially more marked between quoted and unquoted companies. The relative prices facing different enterprises by no means involve a universal set of determinants. There is no underlying determinant of prices, prices are set by different determinants and can perform variegated functions. Thus the price of capital equipment is composed of heterogeneous determinants as the above example indicates. Similarly, the character of capital equipment utilised in a given industry will not necessarily be subject to 'technical' exigencies such that the enterprise using the most advanced equipments are those which survive. In this respect Hannah cites the case of the cotton industry:

> In cotton spinning, for example, the financially weak firms were often those which had suffered from speculative company promotions and not necessarily those with uneconomic

equipment; in this industry, therefore, the competitive process working though bankruptcy might have had adverse effects on overall production efficiency, had it not been tempered by the planned scrapping of uneconomic equipment. (*The Rise of the Corporate Economy*, p. 158)

We cannot therefore counterpose 'technical' calculation to capitalist enterprise calculation as if production-process decisions enter the former sphere and 'costs of circulation' enter the latter. Since both are subject to capitalist enterprise calculation they involve cost-calculation in terms of a set of prices whose determinants are heterogeneous.

The clear advantages possessed by high-volume, highly mechanised production processes are nevertheless quite compatible with a situation in which considerable diversity of production methods is discernible within capitalist national economies, and it will now be necessary to demonstrate the reasons for this diversity.

When we stressed the importance of the integration which could accompany mechanisation of the production process we implicitly referred to a *system* of mechanisation. That is, our point of reference was to mechanisation of processes where each operation was mechanised in relation to a plan, where particular processes were inserted into a flow of materials, where shortages and bottlenecks were eliminated, and where each process worked at 'optimal' speed. The operation of such a system generally, however, presumes that the system is incorporated in the setting up of an entirely new production process, possibly simultaneous with the opening of a new factory. In a situation of this kind the mechanisation of production can be planned as an interrelated system, though it is worth noting that it by no means follows that new factories are necessarily examples of integrated technical systems (for evidence which runs counter to such a notion see Gregory and James, 'Do new factories embody best practice technology?').

Such situations clearly depend on a high rate of growth in the economy or in a particular sector of it. Installation of new equipment generally takes place within a given range of existing equipment where only part of the existing equipment is renewed. This may lead to problems of unevenness in the production process which may arise from the fact that in any production period output of different sections of the production process can be radically different. Such a situation could easily exacerbate the problem of shortages and bottlenecks whose overcoming appeared to be the main virtue of mechanisation.

Thus the impact on unit costs of partial increases in the level of mechanisation might well be unfavourable. Unevenness in the production process may involve large stocks having to be carried, since the part of the production process operating at a higher optimal output may produce volumes beyond the processing capacity of the remaining equipment. The unevenness may equally result in a reverse situation where the newly mechanised section has to operate at substantially below its capacity in order to avoid considerable accumulation of stocks. In either case the introduction of the new equipment will not lead to any substantial fall in unit costs since the volume of units produced in any given time-period is set by the least efficient equipment. This may mean either that the enterprise has to commit a larger part of its capital to holding stocks thus increasing its fixed costs and *ipso facto* its unit costs, plus any additional costs required to expand its storage capacity, or that the cost of the new equipment cannot be spread over a substantially larger volume because of the constraints imposed by the other equipment.

Such unevenness clearly has cumulative effects in so far as it means that the enterprise, by being unable to reduce unit costs, may equally be unable to generate sufficient funds to renew the other equipment to produce a congruent system. In some cases this problem may be compounded by design problems. It is often the case that new *pieces* of equipment create problems relating to inadequate design. Bright cites the case of the introduction of atomic energy plants during the Second World War where the range of instruments was increased without a correlative reduction in the size of the relevant dials. This resulted in the instrument panel used being over 500 ft long. Similar problems occurred in relation to the monitoring of dials. In so far as needles indicating norm values and deviations from norm values each point in different directions, monitoring could only take place by studying each individual dial. These problems were tackled in various stages: first, marks on the dials were made directly to indicate norm values; then, the dials were rotated so that norm values occupied the same place on each dial; finally, recorders were used to indicate deviations from norm values in the print out (see *Automation and Management*, p. 18). Thus, even with individual pieces of

Enterprise Calculation and Production Methods   171

equipment all operating problems cannot be anticipated, and this compounds the problems of reducing unit costs.

Unevenness is, of course, not limited to operations within the firm but relates to the demands on both suppliers and distributors of changes in capital equipment. The latter case will be dealt with below. In the former case a substantial increase in output involves attaining a reliable supply. Thus, the effectiveness of high-volume production will be necessarily affected by the structure of the supplying industries.

These types of problems will impinge on the enterprise in many ways, two of which are pertinent here. Either they will enter into initial calculations concerning policy in replacing equipment such that equipment changes are made on the basis of attaining congruence with the existing set of equipment in operation. Or constraints operate by reducing the flow of funds to the enterprise, inhibiting or preventing further renewal of equipment.

Highly mechanised, high-volume production necessarily requires continuity of production to be effective. This puts a particularly high priority on maintenance of equipment. These problems are in fact more considerable in a highly integrated plant since, given its substantially higher volume, the impact of bottlenecks and shortages are exacerbated. This is equally true of the production of defective units since, given the speed of operation of the equipment and its high output, defective products may involve the scrapping of a substantial volume of output.

In so far as the latter facet refers to individual pieces of equipment it is equally applicable to the case of unevenness where the more efficient pieces of equipment are run at their optimal volume. The major problem with an integrated system is preventing cumulative breakdowns. Changes in work practice can be effected to deal with these problems; thus to avoid the cumulative effect of breakdowns maintenance work can be carried on during periods when the machinery is not operating. However, again, unevenness in relation to design can create several problems in respect of maintenance. The high emphasis on continuity means that repairs must be carried out as rapidly as possible; clearly machine design which favours accessibility to the relevant parts will facilitate such practices, but here again unevenness in design may not produce the requisite specifications.

Uneven degrees of mechanisation are necessarily related to the character of the products of given sectors. For a number of reasons different products lend themselves to mechanisation in differing degrees. An excellent example of the effects of the character of the product in this respect is the contrast in the scope for mechanisation in the production of electric light bulbs and of footwear which is given in Bright's classic account in *Automation and Management*. This example is particularly pertinent because both products are 'mass' products, so that we are not dealing with a specialist product but one in which large volumes are sold.

Notwithstanding the fact that both products are sold in high volumes, there is a marked degree of difference in mechanisation in both cases. A crucial difference lies in the degree to which each product lends itself to standardisation. Whereas electric light bulbs could be reduced to a basic design with a small variation in sizes, footwear is directly constrained by variations in sizes such that even the most popular men's sizes account for only 10 per cent of total sales and in the case of women's shoes the corresponding figure is only 3 per cent. The problem, however, is less difficult to deal with from the point of view of standardisation than from the nature of the materials involved. Not only are leather hides of variable quality, but also quality varies from one part of the hide to the other and, for example, the strength and flexibility of leather is greater with the grain than at right angles to it. Manufacturing also creates manifold problems:

> Many shoe forming operations require complex motions. There is scarcely a straight line or a reference plane in a shoe. A number of compound curves and many simple curves must be formed. The planes of the various parts of different sizes and styles of shoes do not lie at regular angles, or even at consistent angles to each other. Reproducing the required production motions by machinery with the ability to vary the motions for different sizes is an extremely difficult design problem. Many of the operations require motions with six degrees of freedom: that is, the materials must be manipulated along a straight line in each of the three dimensions and also rotated around each of the three axes. These motions may be required singly; more often they are necessary in various combinations. (*Automation and Management*, p. 32)

Both the character of the material and the character of the product require the most complex types of equipment. To mechanise the selection of hides and of parts from hides requires

Enterprise Calculation and Production Methods 173

the use of machinery with sensing mechanisms able to make precise discriminations. To produce the shoe requires a machine capable of multiple operations of a diverse kind. These exigencies exert a dual constraint on mechanisation from the point of view of enterprise calculation. Most mechanisation is of a much simpler type than that which would be required in this instance and is directly linked with the specialisation of tasks. Machinery is called upon to perform a fixed set of operations, drilling of holes in materials to particular specifications, cutting of materials to specific shapes and dimensions, etc. More complex tasks necessarily require the building in of more elaborate decision-making mechanisms and this complexity is further increased if the tasks to not occur in a constant order. Given that equipment of this kind is exceptional, then aside from its complexity, which may increase its cost, the cost-reduction effects linked with the high volumes do not arise.

The high cost of equipment might, however, still be spread over a large number of units as this is a 'high-volume' sector. This is problematised by the scattered distribution of sales in relation to different sizes which has already been indicated. This builds in a further difficulty since it means that the equipment must incorporate a capacity to deal with a wide variety of sizes or that the equipment is specialised to deal with individual sizes. In either case cost constraints are encountered. In the first case the additional complexity of the machine may push up its cost. In the second case, the machine must deal with a smaller volume of products in any given time-period.

This problem is compounded, Bright argues, by the conventions of measurement adopted in relation to shoe sizes. Differentiation of sizes is based on an arithmetical progression such that shoe lengths are differentiated on the basis of increments in the length of the shoe. This has the effect of divorcing shoe sizes from any constant relationship between length and girth. This problem is resolvable if size differentiations were made on a 'geometric' basis, i.e. if size differences were percentage increases, since here the constant relationship between length and girth would be maintained. However, as we indicated earlier, capitalist enterprise calculation is not concerned with direct 'technical' calculations but with cost calculations in respect of a given set of prices.

The impact of this concern with costs can be clearly seen in this case. The existing means of differentiating shoe sizes is necessarily accompanied by a correlative investment in equipment. Shoe manufacturers invested in a large number of 'arithmetic lasts' precisely differentiated by the size to be produced. Given the lack of a 'representative' size and the unmechanised character of production there is a need for the large number of lasts to be held by manufacturers. Consequently such lasts represent a substantial proportion of the enterprise's capital equipment in this sector.

A radical change of methods necessarily involves the obsolescence of lasts and may have quite drastic effects on the enterprise's financial position. The lasts are no longer objects of calculation in respect of the continued production of shoes by the enterprise using existing methods, they are now assets which simply have a resale value. Such a resale value will necessarily be variable according to the capacity of the industry, whether there is a market in second-hand equipment, etc., but clearly the enterprise is faced with the problem that it is operating on a more or less 'forced-sale' basis. This is simply because the use of arithmetic lasts would in no way be complementary with the mechanisation of production and consequently it would not be possible to phase out the sale of the lasts. Any calculation of the conditions of introducing new equipment would thus have to include possible losses from the writing down of the value of capital equipment.

At a different level of calculation the market structure of the industry could equally function against the mechanisation of production. The lack of use of expensive capital equipment would function both to increase the number of enterprises in the industry and equally would facilitate entry into the industry. Such a situation has the effect of engendering overcapacity in the sector as a whole and equally creates a situation where distributors adopt practices geared to a diversity of sources of supply. The position of distributors compounds the problems of introducing mechanisation in another way. To take the case of the British footwear industry: while supply is fragmented in many small units distribution outlets are heavily concentrated in the hands of a few large enterprises. Such unevenness allows for situations where the distributors can impose inventory costs on the manufacturers by placing orders in small lots, and can impose irregular patterns of demand by switching to imported products, for example (for the British case see Smith, 'Footwear under scrutiny').

This is compounded by the differentiation of the product by reference to 'fashion' such that production outputs for any given style may be reduced because of the short period during which any

Enterprise Calculation and Production Methods   175

particular style is marketed. A set of forces is thus consistently working to prevent mechanisation of this sector. These forces can be said to exert a 'ratcheting' effect on calculation. A given material and product establish the necessity for investment in a set of equipment. In so far as this equipment is non-complementary with the new production methods adopted then a 'writing-down' loss can occur. High-volume production encounters the obstacle of a market structure of small units and the uneven relation between manufacturers and distributors which allows the latter to transfer costs to the former. Of course, we are not positing any teleology here, it is simply the case that modifications to this particular structure are difficult to effect for the manifold reasons which we have already suggested. Clearly, a major change here would depend upon a change in materials, notably the move to a liquid compound as the material would allow for methods analogous to the production of plastics to be adopted. The use of moulds would effect a great simplification of the operations required to produce the product.

The material constraint thus operates even though between sectors overall volumes of output to units may be roughly similar or at least comparable. Such constraints are not simply effects of variability in standardisation of the final product. In the case of the mechanisation of electric light bulbs, for example, an obstacle was created to further mechanisation by the lack of a wire which would resist sagging at high temperatures. This meant that concentration of wires into coils allowing ease of mechanical assembly was periodically blocked.

A problem connected with considerations of standardisation is that mechanised production processes appear to function more effectively when producing either a single product or a limited range of products. This is for reasons already indicated. Mechanisation is generally limited to a specific set of functions, costs of equipment rising where a wide range of operations and functions are incorporated into the process. Equally, where the production process is integrated it is designed to achieve either the production of a specific product or of a specific balance between products.

Bright cites an example of the latter in an enterprise producing a main product, mattresses, and a subordinate product, cushions. The production process was designed to produce the two products in the proportion of 85:15. At a particular point in time an increase in the demand for cushions relative to mattresses led the enterprise to alter the ratio to 70:30. The consequence was a severe bottleneck in the production of cushions. This arose from the fact that the employment of direct labour was geared to the previously operative ratio but given that cushions are smaller and have more perimeter area they require more finishing and, given the production methods operated by the company, this required greater application of direct labour. Mechanised systems are equally vulnerable to changes in design. Again Bright reports a case where the size of the front bumpers was altered while that of rear bumpers remained unchanged. This disrupted practices in a plating plant, since the transfer equipment was designed to transfer the same number of front and rear bumpers in the plating racks. While the equipment was capable of holding nine rear bumpers it could only hold seven front bumpers of the new larger design. Such changes necessarily engender the kind of shortage/bottleneck problems to which we have already referred. (*Automation and Management*, pp. 212–13)

Given that highly mechanised production processes are designed to produce large volumes, this constitutes problems for the production of small runs. This is generally because systems of a mechanised type often require considerable set-up time or lengthy periods before the system functions properly. Such time represents a fixed cost which is only economically spread over a large volume of units produced. It is often difficult to meet this situation by varying output in an upward direction for specific runs. An integrated process may in fact only be integrated within a given range of output and certain pieces of equipment may be capable of more variation in output than others. Equally, running equipment at beyond optimal speeds leads to a risk of breakdowns or defective products whose cost impact is, as we have indicated above, magnified under conditions of high-volume output. The small run can, of course, be subcontracted to smaller units but this possibility again refers to the level of calculation concerned with the industrial structure of the sector.

The 'subcontracting' option clearly depends upon the existence of other smaller units willing to take up such orders. A condition of the adoption of a mechanised production system may thus be that within the sector smaller enterprises exist so that the larger enterprise can meet small orders without facing cost penalties. While the considerable variation in the scale of enterprises is a commonplace of studies of industrial structure, it is equally clear that it can enter as a pertinent determinant of the relevant set of prices within which an enterprise operates a decision to change its methods of production.

Subcontracting is clearly not the only way around the problem. It is perfectly possible to duplicate production lines or to run lines adjusted to different optimal volumes if the range of capital equipment available allows such an option. Such a policy, however, is clearly not restricted to the boundaries of a given enterprise. Following the lines suggested by Keynes's remark cited earlier, additional lines can be acquired by acquisition of other enterprises. Such a situation is demonstrated by the disjuncture between concentration of industrial output measured by the share of plants and the share of enterprises. A recent study by S. J. Prais (*The Evolution of Giant Firms in Britain*) indicates, for example, that while the share in net output of the hundred largest manufacturing establishments remained unchanged between 1930 and 1968 at 10·8 per cent and was subject only to a variation of approximately two percentage points over the period as a whole, the share of the hundred largest manufacturing firms rose from 23 to 41 per cent in the same period. (pp. 45–6)

Limits on the mechanisation of the production process through inflexibilities of the kind to which we have already referred do not, however, pose any absolute limit on mechanisation. They do, however, exert important effects on the level of calculation. A major obstacle clearly arises in assuring the regular turnover of the product. Lengthening of turnover times creates problems due to involuntary stock building which may take the form of increased fixed costs of storage space and associated labour costs if problems of turnover persist. Equally, of course, enterprises are not simply concerned with reducing the production time for a given volume of output but equally the turnover time for that volume. This clearly means that the character of the enterprise's relationship to the sale and distribution of its product is subject to variable effects in relation to the character of the production methods used.

The enterprise operating highly mechanised production methods has a strong impetus to standardise products and to get customers to accept a smaller range of products. Clearly, a number of tools are open to the enterprise to effect such practices, notably price discounts and other types of preferential treatment for customers purchasing large volumes of each range consistently. Equally, as the Japanese motor-cycle industry case discussed above indicates, high-volume production necessarily is accompanied by attempts to maintain a target market share. Such calculations need not involve a given market size but may be at a level where calculations concerning the growth of the market are involved. Maintenance of market share is equally crucial as it allows the enterprise to integrate its production and distribution systems. This is important even when the problems of inflexibility can be mitigated within the production process. Inflexibility is less of a problem where products may be produced for inventory and this is in turn facilitated by standardisation and interchangeability such that components can be drawn from stock for incorporation in a range of products. Necessarily, however, this only works within certain ranges and in turn may involve complex market calculations. For example, the production of components for motor-cars in the American market is accompanied by calculations of the relative prices of new and second-hand cars by the American car producers, such calculations being required to identify the market for their components.

In examining the advantages which might be claimed for highly mechanised plants we cited the emancipation from constraints of variability in the performance of tasks by labour and of constraints set by the supply of labour. Supply of labour, however, will necessarily be conditioned by the practices and strength of trade unions and unions will equally establish codes of 'acceptable' working practices. Mechanisation is usually accompanied by a substitution of capital equipment for labour such that, while labour requirements for a given volume of production may not fall over a long period, initial effects may be to displace labour. Given that substitution is implied in the initial calculations, it is clearly important from the position of the capitalist enterprise that it is able to displace labour, i.e. effect redundancies. Similarly, the enterprise will require that manning practices are geared to the calculated displacement effects.

Continuity of production is equally a high priority and here certain systems of labour organisation are requirements of attaining such a norm. As we indicated earlier, the high-volume norm is usually associated with substantial fixed costs.

Notwithstanding the advantages which, under specific conditions, mechanised production exhibits, we have demonstrated that such methods are subject to particular and distinct constraints on their effectiveness. At different levels of operations these constraints enter into the calculations of capitalist enterprises and condition the adoption of specific production methods. From what we have so far argued it is clear that we cannot talk of 'tendencies' operating in the selection of production methods in the capitalist economy. The conditions for the operation of such tendencies would depend broadly on three important conditions, that the character of the composition of consumption be deducible from general features of the system, equally that production techniques be deducible, and that the relationship between industrial sectors be deducible.

The necessity of the condition that the composition of consumption be deducible can be easily seen from the above discussion. When we contrasted the conditions of mechanisation in the footwear industry and in the production of electric light bulbs we saw the impact both of the character of the product and the materials utilised. These conditions do not have comparable effects on mechanisation. The constraints set by the character of the product worked on the limits of standardisation, and the constraint set by the material worked on the complexity of operations required of machinery in the production process.

Given these constraints on mechanisation, a 'tendency' can only be defined by reference to the composition of consumption. This is clearly because, given that determinants of the level of mechanisation lie in part in the character of the product and material utilised, then a 'direction' to methods can only be derived by reference to products produced and materials utilised. We can see the effects of this condition by looking at the conditions of the minimum optimal scale of output in different industrial sectors. As indicated above, the advantages of mechanised production processes assert themselves, in particular, through the reduction of unit costs. These effects vary from sector to sector. Scherer gives, for example, an estimate of the cost penalties of operating at below a minimum optimal scale defined on the basis of engineering criteria. The measure used took the percentage cost penalty of operating at a scale one-third of the defined minimum. Considerable variation was encounted between sectors, thus while non-rubber shoes exhibited a cost penalty of only 1·5 per cent on this basis, in Portland cement production the corresponding figure was 26 per cent. ('The determinants of industrial plant sizes in six nations')

Presuming that the composition of consumption is deducible, however, measures of the differential effects of scale would not directly indicate the character of the methods used, because such a measure only gives the cost effects given technical criteria over a particular range of outputs. Obviously the range of outputs characterising a particular sector is quite a different question which cannot be inferred from a measure of the minimum-optimal-scale plants compatible with the volume of the domestic market. For example, Scherer's figures indicate there is no correspondence between cost penalties of operating at one-third of the minimum plant scale and the number of minimum-optimal-scale plants compatible with the scale of the domestic market. ('The determinants of industrial plant sizes', pp. 137, 141)

As we pointed out above, market structure is directly related to enterprise calculation. Thus, the character of the market structure will itself be related to and affect the level of mechanisation within a given sector by, for example, providing opportunities for subcontracting work which may be a condition of existence of the large enterprise adopting a higher level of mechanisation—such a relationship reinforcing and acting as a condition of existence of a given industrial structure.

If, therefore, the cost advantages of mechanised production are, under specific conditions, linked to volume, the effects of scale are variable. But what are the major obstacles to deducing the composition of consumption? It is clear that such a deduction in this case cannot merely utilise a set of rules to be applied to a given consumer choice. Since the composition of consumption is at issue, arguments which presuppose a given composition cannot, by definition, serve the purpose.

Two broad possibilities present themselves, which are variants of each other. In one case we can refer consumption to 'needs' meaning by the latter some type of 'physical' subsistence level. This position can be disposed of on two simple grounds. First, it is well known that 'minimum' standards of nutrition are by no means universally applicable. Second, even if the subsistence level is definable in a non-circular way there must be a specifiable mechanism which links the structure of consumption to social classes.

This is the case in Marx's arguments concerning the effect of the industrial reserve army. Here there is a distinction posited between consumption of 'necessities' by the working class and of 'luxuries and necessities' by the capitalist class. The terms are defined tautologically since a component entering capitalist consumption but excluded from working-class consumption qualifies as a luxury. It is worth noting that Marx's argument not only involves non-deducible conditions, population levels, absence of trade unions, mobility of labour, etc., but equally treats the calculation used in wage bargaining in a reductionist manner. Wage levels are treated by Marx as representing a set of commodities by which the value of labour-power is defined. However, wage bargains are made in money terms not in terms of a set of commodities and there is no necessary correspondence between a given wage level and the value of labour-power. The effect of Marx's treatment is to invoke a necessary correspondence between wages and the value of labour-power.

A circular treatment of a similar kind invokes 'cultural' standards in criteria of 'subsistence'. No independent criteria are stated here, however, for the determinants of such a 'cultural' standard, and thus *ad hoc* and circular arguments, are invoked. Thus, the fact that the English worker's consumption of beer and the French worker's consumption of wine reflects their 'cultural needs' is a function of the fact that one drinks beer and the other wine. Such a construction, again, can in no way *deduce* a composition of consumption since it necessarily presupposes such a composition.

A key problem here lies in the concept of use-value, which implies such circularity. Marx tells us in volume I of *Capital* that 'A commodity is, in the first place, an object outside us, a thing that by its properties satisfies human wants of some sort or another.' (*Capital*, vol. 1, p. 35) The differentiation of commodities mirrors the diversity of 'wants', thus inferring function from existence. Thus, Marx's argument involves a double circularity, 'necessities' are defined by reference to the function of reproducing labour-power, the diversity of commodities by reference to the diversity of 'wants'.

Even if problems concerning the deduction of the composition of the social product were to be soluble, the definition of a 'tendency' with respect to production methods would still have to deduce a 'tendency' with respect to techniques. This is simply because techniques have different effects on the general character of production methods.

We showed above that the adoption of particular methods of

production could be related to the distribution of enterprises in a given sector of production. This did not function in a unilateral manner. A larger number of small units might be an obstacle to the introduction of more highly mechanised methods, by preventing an enterprise concentrating sufficient production in a given plant and thus allowing capital equipment of a higher value to be employed. Equally the existence of small firms could allow a large enterprise with a 'high-volume' plant to subcontract small orders thus enabling it to satisfy distributors without cost penalties.

It is well known that technical innovations have very different effects on the structure of industrial sectors. Machines today can be equipped with small electric motors. Such an innovation favoured smaller units by reducing the minimum capital level required to utilise such motors. Before the introduction of small electric motors which could be attached to specific machines, the electric motor drove a central transmission belt and individual machines were driven by leather belts coming from the central transmission belt. This necessarily meant that not only was there the initial cost of the central transmission belt required to undertake production using electrical power but a minimum number of machines would have to be used to spread the cost. New materials can have similar effects. Thus, moulding in plastics has the advantage for the smaller unit that it does away with a set of auxiliary departments such as those concerned with machining, polishing, and finishing which are required in producing metals by casting. (Prais, *The Evolution of Giant Firms*, pp. 52–3)

Such innovations exert their effect on the structure of an industrial sector by their impact on the minimal level of capital required to enter the sector. Innovations can, however, exert effects by reference to their availability to enterprises. In this respect Hannah contrasts the position in the nineteenth-century cotton industry, where 'Specialist machinery builders would supply factory equipment incorporating the latest designs of, say, power looms and the steam boilers and engines to drive them and this encouraged the entry of new firms on equal terms with the existing ones', with the tobacco industry where at the turn of the century the Wills company obtained exclusive control over the only efficient cigarette-making machine available at the time. (*The Rise of the Corporate Economy*, pp. 15–16)

It is important to stress here that there is no necessity to treat technical innovations as entirely unpredictable or contingent,

Enterprise Calculation and Production Methods 183

reflecting a romantic conception of 'scientific discovery'. The pattern of research-and-development expenditure is in some respects consistent, and expenditure is highly concentrated on a sectoral basis. In 1968, for example, four sectors of British manufacturing industry accounted for over 80 per cent of research-and-development expenditure: aerospace (40·8 per cent), pharmaceuticals and toilet preparations (16·6 per cent), electronics and telecommunications (14·6 per cent) and industrial engines (10·7 per cent). ('Resources devoted to research and development by manufacturing industry'). Equally, both the direction of research and the taking up of innovations do relate to relative price levels and movements.

In the USA recent attempts to impose legislation on energy use, for example, require each manufacturer's cars to have a production-weighted average of 20 mpg by 1980 and 27·5 mpg by 1985. Clearly, one strategy for the enterprises concerned would be to make smaller cars and to make cars lighter by using new materials, a clear direction for research. However, it is well known that smaller cars have a smaller profit per unit, thus there is an impetus to meet the specifications without varying the size of the car. This structures an alternative direction of research towards improving the efficiency of the engine. An instance of this is the introduction of the electronic-spark-timing control which permits the engine to be tuned to a leaner air/fuel mixture, improving economy and performance, a measure already introduced by the Chrysler corporation on its medium and large saloons. (Done, 'Electronics advance')

Price constraints and a given structure of consumption necessarily exert barriers to the introduction of innovations. Battery driven electric cars, for example, are limited by a relatively low maximum speed (40–50 mph) and range (40–60 miles per charge) and a carrying capacity limited to two people. Current norms in the use of motor vehicles involve them serving the dual function of means of transport to work, involving corresponding spatial layout of urban areas, and as a means of leisure transport. The limited range and speed of the battery car would clearly limit its use in the second capacity and impinge on its competitiveness with cars using conventional internal combustion engines. (Central Policy Review Staff, *The Future of the British Car Industry*, p. 17) Cost problems equally affect the introduction of such engines on public transport systems, the current diesel engines used on London transport, double-decker buses, weighing 7·4 tonnes, are capable of carrying 4·4 tonnes of passengers, a corresponding electric bus, weighing 8 tonnes, is capable of carrying 1·65 tonnes of passengers. (Fishlock, 'The glamour goes out of technology')

Innovations are more rapidly sought and applied where existing production and operational facilities can be utilised. This is the case with the stratified charge engine in motor vehicles, which has the potential advantage that it may be able to use lower grade fuels and which can be manufactured on existing engine production facilities. (*The Future of the British Car Industry*, pp. 19–20) Similarly, the British Rail Advanced Passenger Train has the advantage that it involves no writing off of the railways' investment in track and signalling systems.

However, the reference to given structures of consumption and investment in no way sustains the objective of deducing the character of technical innovations. This is compounded by the major role played by government in either directly funding research expenditure in the case of defence, for example, or more indirectly in the case of medical research. The latter case, for example, has led to research oriented to new products, either new drugs or new modes of surgical treatment. The position which has kept this sector as one of the main 'R and D' sectors is, however, dependent on a number of important political conditions. Such practices have arisen from the dominant role of medicine as a 'curative' practice and has involved the downgrading of interest, in particular, in research into environmental causation of diseases. In respect of the latter a wide variety of evidence suggests that environmental determinants are significant in determining a wide variety of diseases, including major 'killers' on which a substantial proportion of medical research is devoted. (For summaries of evidence see Draper, *et al.*, *Health, Money and the NHS* and Powles, 'On the limitations of modern medicine'.) The important difference here lies in the fact that research on new drugs or surgical treatments is designed to produce new products in a particular terrain where a substantial proportion of research expenditure is currently deployed. Research on environmental causation, while not excluding the development of new medical products, necessarily exerts an effect on the introduction of new products in other areas and equally on the transformation of social practices independent of any introduction of new products. Such a situation demonstrates both the impact of a political practice

Enterprise Calculation and Production Methods   185

allowing *de facto* allocation of resources to rest with the medical profession and the tendentiousness of referring products to 'needs' or 'wants'.

The deduction of the composition of consumption and of technical innovations would, however, not of themselves 'give' a set of production methods. This is because, as we have indicated above, the structure of specific sectors would have to be known. The distribution of enterprises by size within a sector, as we indicated above, affects the nature of the production methods utilised. This means that effects are exerted on the interrelation between sectors. Obviously, for example, a reduction in the cost of capital equipment will lower the capital required to enter a sector and may, by reducing the cost advantage of an integrated mechanised system, prevent either the introduction of the latter or its spread within the sector. Equally, as we have indicated above, enterprises do not encounter at any point in time an infinity of either technical or, *a fortiori*, economic 'choices' in respect of the techniques available to them. Necessarily, therefore, the character of the available choices will be set by a determinate set of inter-sectoral relationships.

The theoretical demonstration of properties of reproduction schemas can of course assume the givenness of the composition of the social product, or assign it arbitrarily. The problem for a theory of calculation as an effect of the structure is that the composition of the social product affects calculations and in some sense that composition must be considered an effect of the economy itself.

The relationship which obtains, therefore, between enterprise calculation and production methods adopted can only be analysed by reference to the terrain of capitalist national economies. Any attempt to argue that there are 'tendencies' in relation to the latter must founder on the impossibility of deducing the necessary conditions. Calculation itself cannot yield any tendency since the object of cost calculation in capitalist enterprises is not to reduce the cost of any particular elements of the production process (means of production, labour, etc.) but to reduce costs *in toto*, it being a matter of indifference as to the source of such cost reductions. If, therefore, and this is debatable (see, for example, Hussain, 'Crises and tendencies of capitalism'), technical innovations are primarily 'labour-saving' or 'capital-saving' this cannot be accounted for by any *a priori* preference on the part of those responsible for enterprise calculation.

Some Marxists and some proponents of a kind of 'alternative economics', such as Hollis and Nell, argue that the 'standpoint of reproduction' should be adopted as a point of reference from which theory can be constructed in a deductive manner. The standpoint of reproduction implies that a given set of economic relations and their conditions of existence at a given point in time are granted a direction such that conditions of existence and conditions of perpetuation are identified. Such a position means that even if the plurality of determinants and effects of prices are admitted a given relation between modes of calculation will be 'frozen' by the identification of conditions of existence and conditions of perpetuation. We would wish completely to reject such a position on the grounds that no set of practices of calculation nor any relationships between practices of calculation imply any teleoloy whether of perpetuation or dissolution. The implications of this rejection will be taken up in the conclusion of this section and in the conclusion to the work as a whole.

The problem of the connection between forms of political calculation in capitalist social formations and the calculation of capitalist enterprises is one of great complexity and only some indications can be given here. The adoption of specific production methods may involve the displacement of labour, but this in itself does not imply any particular displacement of labourers. This is clearly affected by the length of working hours. However, there is no indifference in capitalist calculation to the impact of displacements of labour on displacements of labourers in so far as legal constraints operate in respect of them. These constraints may be absolute in any given time-period such that conditions of notice are required to dismiss labourers or such that cost constraints may operate in the form that compensation is required to the labourer in the event of dismissal. The distinction between labour and labourer is one involving the constitution of a legal subjectivity.

The calculation of the capitalist enterprise involves either the taking of such constituted subjectivity as given or operating in the rules of variability accompanying its constitution or application. The *constitution* of such subjectivity, however, is not an object of enterprise calculation here but of political calculation, since the constitution of subjectivity of a legal character does not lie at the level of the enterprise. Such subjectivity, it should be stressed, is not universal, i.e. we have no reason to hold that there is a subject 'appropriate to capitalist societies'. The latter idea arises from the

Enterprise Calculation and Production Methods 187

realist treatment of the subject which defines the unity of the latter by reference to its 'eccentricity' in relation to 'the real', a view which has been thoroughly criticised elsewhere. (Hirst, 'Althusser and the theory of ideology') Such definitions of subjectivity may well depend on variegated rules of constitution according to the sphere concerned. The definition of a right of compensation, for example, where it is accompanied by discretion over the level of compensation on the part of the judiciary, involves them in defining a point of reference by means of the conception of a 'subject of consumption'.

The condition of such subjectivity has clear and important effects upon the economic strategy functioning as a component of political calculation. Thus, since the labourer has a set of 'rights' and 'obligations' set by various rules, the constitution of these rights and obligations exerts constraints on the character of economic strategy. Obligations do exist to employ individuals on the part of government agencies (in respect of the handicapped, for example); the extension of such obligations would clearly have important effects on economic strategy. To take an example of current relevance, reductions in planned government expenditure have fallen on capital programmes rather than on current expenditure and have been designed to avoid displacing labour. Such policies can operate partly because of the nature of economic practice within the state sector excluding the nationalised industries, i.e. because of the so-called 'labour-intensive' character of social services, health and education, etc. How far, however, such 'labour-intensiveness' is not purely a 'technical' characteristic is debatable. It can easily be seen that in so far as economic policy imposes heavier constraints on expenditure on capital equipment than on labour this itself exerts a 'labour-intensive' effect.

We have seen, therefore, that the study of production methods utilised in capitalist national economies must be related to the analysis of enterprise calculation. It is quite impossible to establish the priority of particular types of production methods under conditions of capitalist national economies. Increased mechanisation of production methods does clearly yield certain definite advantages to enterprises adopting them under specific conditions. But the scope for mechanisation is highly variable according to conditions of materials utilised, structure of the industrial sector, relation to distributors, etc. Such constraints on mechanisation are consistent with the variability in cost-penalties associated with different spreads of volumes produced in different industrial sectors.

This argument applies *ipso facto* to the postulation of necessary tendencies in respect of production methods. Such tendencies have to be established on the domain of the capitalist economy in general, but, as we have demonstrated, the character of production methods utilised depends on reference to determinants which are not general features of the capitalist economy but are specific and variable features of definite capitalist national economies.

In Volume One we demonstrated the necessity of treating political practice in a non-reductionist manner. The constitution of legal subjectivity in political calculation exerts important effects on the character of production methods utilised. The level of statutory working hours clearly affects the relationship between the displacement of labour and the displacement of labourers. Given that unemployment is an object of political calculation, we can see that a given level of statutorily defined working hours imposes constraints on economic strategy. Such constraints may be seen to operate in the British case in the creation of 'labour-intensive' practices within the 'non-industrial' sector of state employment.

Enterprise calculation is in no way reducible to technical determinants, and the reference to the terrain of capitalist national economies is thus enjoined by the necessary operation of enterprise calculation in the conditions of particular capitalist economies.

Chapter 10

A Critique of the Enterprise as a Universal Calculating Subject

In Chapter 8 we criticised the idea that the capitalist enterprise could be treated in terms of a universal calculative subject. In this section we aim to extend this argument. We will seek to demonstrate that while different conceptions of the 'enterprise-subject' have been put forward they share a common set of concepts. Some elements of the debate between different concepts of the enterprise-subject do raise important questions for a theory of enterprise calculation but these are not resolvable on the terrain of the capitalist economy in general. The terrain of theories of the enterprise-subject is that of the capitalist economy in general, the enterprise-subject is thus an invariant characteristic of the capitalist economy. We argue that theories of the enterprise-subject either are prescriptive or posit economic conditions which cannot be derived from the conception of the capitalist economy in general.

The most familiar notions of the enterprise-subject derive from an argument initiated by Burnham's *Managerial Revolution*. In its simplest form the argument suggests that one enterprise-subject is replaced by another. The enterprise-subject replaced is one owned and controlled by either a single individual or a family, the enterprise-subject replacing it is one related to a separation of ownership and control such that the owner becomes a pure rentier and decisions concerning the disposition of the means of production lie with professional managers who are employees of the enterprise. Linked to this differentiation is a distinction of economic subjectivities. The owner and the manager do not simply have a distinct legal relation to the means of production but their distinct legal status is 'reflected' in their economic practice.

The 'owner', for example, is often conceived of as pursuing

'profit-maximisation' policies on the grounds that he has a direct interest in revenues accruing to the firm. The 'manager', however, is seen as having quite distinct goals; these may be related to sources of pecuniary advantage such that the manager's remuneration might be based more closely on the volume of sales than on 'profits'. Alternatively, expansion of the volume of sales may be a means of greater security than 'profit maximisation', thus the 'manager' may seek such a goal as a means of securing his job, or managers may be claimed to be motivated by 'non-economic' considerations, etc.

A wide variety of 'options' can be taken within this framework. It can be argued that the distinction is irrelevant since enterprise practice is determined by 'exigencies of the capitalist market', a view which has been discussed above. Alternatively the premises may be accepted but the effective relevance of the distinction may be challenged, hence the response that no 'separation' has occurred since managers are substantial owners of equity. Equally, the specified goals of the subject can be argued to be such that they are *de facto* equivalent in various ways, e.g. in effect 'profit maximising' and 'growth of sales' are equivalent. Obviously this does not exhaust the possibilities, but what is clear is that the debate is carried on in a framework where the enterprise is conceived as a subject and then as adopting distinct goals and means in economic calculation. To discuss this position in more detail in relation to the question of enterprise calculation it will be necessary to take up arguments which seek to demonstrate that systematically different enterprise-subjects operate in the domain of the capitalist economy, i.e. that different enterprise-subjects apply different criteria to enterprise calculation. A systematic and thorough attempt to do this is provided by Adrian Wood in *A Theory of Profits*. Wood attempts to produce a theory of the place of profits in enterprise calculation and to derive implications of such calculations for capitalist national economies and for government policy. We will be primarily concerned with the first aspect of his work.

He outlines a number of elements which he regards as central to the neo-classical theory of the firm which is the object of his attack. It is important to realise that, while these elements may not directly be articulated as a theory of the enterprise-subject, they are consistent with such a theory. In other words, Wood's theoretical position and the position which he characterises as neo-classical are alternative theories of the enterprise-subject.

The neo-classical theory involves, in Wood's view, the assumption that, 'Expectations of the future while uncertain, must be "objective" in the sense of being common to all agents in the capital market. In other words, everyone must have the same view of the magnitude and uncertainty of the future returns from any particular investment project.' (*A Theory of Profits*, p. 6) This condition is important simply because it establishes a universal subject of calculation which is particularly important in this framework in respect of the relative position of 'borrowers' and 'lenders'. If there is a 'factual' separation between ownership and control, 'borrowers' will be the professional management of the firm, but in so far as expectations of returns to particular investment projects are shared the implication is that no distinction in terms of criteria of calculation can be based on particular positions in the capital market.

A second important condition concerns the pertinence of the source of investment funds. Given the previous condition, it can be deduced that the assessment of an investment project is entirely independent of the sources of funds for that project. This means that the source of finance is a matter of indifference since lenders and borrowers share a common assessment of any given investment project. It would therefore be contradictory to invoke any relationship between the assessment of an investment project and the sources of funds for that project since such a position would posit a pertinent difference in the position of 'lenders' and 'borrowers' such that the assessments were governed, at least in part, by their structural positions.

Linked to this assumption is the argument that for any investment there is an appropriate rate of interest determined by 'risk' and expected returns, and that lenders will finance any investment project at the appropriate rate of interest. This assumption follows from the previous one in so far as the sources of funds are a matter of indifference to the investor so that, if commonality of assessments of investment projects is assumed, then any project will carry its appropriate interest rate and will obtain funds accordingly.

The commonality of calculation assumed in the first condition involves a similar commonality with respect to the question of revenues to shareholders. Investment projects should thus be undertaken up to the point at which the expected rate of return, subject to an adjustment for uncertainty, is equal to those available to shareholders in alternative investments. This result automatically follows since the borrowing agents will not exert any special preferences for investments in the enterprise in which they may be employees. But there is an additional condition of operation of the 'constraint' type. It is assumed that if practices such as the above are not carried out then the shareholders can 'declare their own dividends' by selling their shares and thus can impose a constraint on a 'management' using different criteria. Although it will not concern us in detail, it is worth noting that the invocation of this latter condition is contradictory to the other assumptions which involve the importance of the commonality of calculation. The condition, of course, only operates in so far as the former assumption is null, and its importance is therefore an index of the weakness of the theory.

The enterprise-subject here is thus one in which the 'separation of ownership and control' is posited as non-pertinent except in so far as it is involved in the constraint on dividend policy. These two arguments have thus a somewhat different status, for the latter construct can be referred to its specific conditions of existence for validation which the concept of the enterprise-subject defines as divergences by reference to the universality of the subject.

Wood's criticism of the tenability of these assumptions rests on an alternative enterprise-subject. Consequently, his argument is required not merely to impugn the theoretical value of the neo-classical theory, but to do it in such a way that the viability of reference to an alternative enterprise-subject is established.

In relation to the first assumption, Wood argues that the commonality of calculation in respect of investment projects,

> Fails to recognise that in reality expectations are inevitably 'subjective' in the sense that they are specific to the individual and liable to vary among individuals. For different people commonly entertain very different opinions about the magnitude and uncertainty of the future returns from any investment project, a fact which not only damages the neoclassical position but also, and more generally, makes it difficult to see how there could be any neat and tidy model of the capital market as a whole. (*A Theory of Profits*, p. 6)

At this level Wood merely sceptically invokes a potentially infinite plurality of criteria linked to a solipsistic 'subjectivity'.

However, as we indicated above, his concern is to support an alternative enterprise-subject. To do this it is particularly necessary to indicate systematic differences between calculating subjects, in particular between 'owners' and 'controllers'. A systematic difference in respect of 'risks' may be related to the differentiation of legal statuses involved. Thus Wood points out that the risks associated with liquidation of a company are quite distinct for managers and owners. For the latter losses are only incurred in so far as the disposal price of the enterprise's assets are insufficient to realise the shareholder's capital. For the former, however, the loss necessarily arises from the fact that the manager's position is tied up with the enterprise as a going concern not with its value as a set of assets with a disposal price. These distinct concepts of risk may equally involve distinct targets. The manager's interest, for example, would lie in preventing the liquidation of the enterprise and such a target might well diverge from the strategy 'preferred' by the 'shareholders'. A prime candidate for the manager's target would be sales volume, on the grounds that the larger unit could have a lower probability of either liquidation or of being acquired in a merger. Although both cases are not equivalent 'risks' the take-over of a company may be thought to threaten the management's disposition over the means of production.

In so far, however, as considerations of statistical probability are invoked here as criteria of calculation, the argument would need to be qualified by reference to the range in which 'large size' provides an insurance against take-over. A recent study by Singh indicates that between 1967 and 1970 the probability of take-over was lower for the smallest quintile in the four industries (food, drink, clothing and footwear, and non-electrical engineering) in his survey. From the third quintile upwards, however, probability of acquisition declines with increased size. ('Take-overs, economic natural selection and the theory of the firm', p. 505) Singh's explanation for this pattern lies in the fact that either the smallest firms are family firms or there is no market for their shares. In so far as the latter firms could be said not to have effected a 'separation of ownership and control', then it could be argued that within the relevant range of enterprises Singh's conclusions are instances of the process described by the 'managerialists'. However, the situation is much more equivocal. The attempt to derive forms of calculation from the divorce of ownership and control using arguments of a statistical probability type runs into the problem of defining a 'representative period'. This is particularly important with respect to mergers, since it is well known that they have moved in waves and that the character and incidence of mergers has varied markedly from 'wave' to 'wave'.

The dropping of the assumption of universal criteria of assessment necessarily involves dropping the assumption that the source of finance is unimportant. Given the postulated differentiation of criteria of calculation, the source of funds does become an important issue in the assessment of investment projects. For Wood this involves the idea that managers *do* exert a strong preference for internal sources of finance and wish to minimise dependence on external finance. This is essentially for reasons associated with the retention of control over investment projects. A high level of external finance involves a commitment to contractual payments of interest at a given point in time. If dividend levels are stable the result of high levels of external finance will be to exaggerate short-term fluctuations in profit levels. Consequently, if the enterprise is to realise its long-run investment programme it will have to hold a higher level of financial assets. This is undesirable for the enterprise on the grounds that it infringes its main 'targets' of growth of sales and generation of internal sources of finance, by virtue of having to maintain a higher level of liquidity than would be the case if a lower level of external finance were the norm. (*A Theory of Profits*, p. 29) A more serious problem in this respect arises from increased dependence on the capital market such that the enterprise

> Is more vulnerable to the sort of collapse which is caused by a chain reaction of refusals to lend based on the self-justifying expectation of a company's imminent demise. For companies which are heavily dependent on borrowed money commonly fall victims to sudden changes in the confidence of lenders about their future credit-worthiness. (*ibid.*, pp. 29–30)

Investment projects would equally not be assessed independently of the source of finance of the enterprise as indicated in the third assumption. Broadly speaking, willingness to provide external finance is posited as standing in inverse relation to the gearing ratio of the enterprise. The latter relationship is an effect of the contractual obligations involved in fixed-interest securities.

In the case of the final assumption, a divergence between 'managers' and 'shareholders' can arise as an effect of the postulated premium on internal finance. Managements must be expected to seek to minimise dividends since the higher they become either the lower is the level of new investment open to the enterprise or the greater the dependence on external finance—both conditions which, for reasons already indicated, the management could be expected to avoid.

Given that Wood's argument accepts both a separation of ownership and control and that such a separation produces distinct calculating subjects, it is necessary for his argument to refute the constraining effect referred to above. A relatively minor problem in this respect is that sales of shares necessarily involve transaction costs which would in general be more significant the smaller the sale was. These costs might be offset if the sale were conducted by a large stockbroking firm since a larger overall clientele would give the former a higher probability of a matching bargain. (see Wooley, 'The economics of the UK stock exchange') Offsetting this, however, would be the effect on the share price of a 'mass defection' from the shares of a particular enterprise.

A more fundamental problem with 'declaration of dividends' by shareholders arises from the character of the stock market. The 'declaration-of-dividends' concept involves the idea that a divergence from a 'correct' investment strategy will be reflected in a company's share price because of the sale of shares. Such a conception necessarily abstracts from the speculative practice which characterises the stock market and from the fact that the flow of income from funds re-invested in a given enterprise is more predictable than flows arising from purchase and sale of shares. Given such a situation declaration of dividends is a risky procedure and its incidence is likely to be consequently reduced.

The provision of external finance need not derive exclusively from the issuing of fixed-interest securities but can arise from new share issues. The latter, of course, do not involve the drawbacks which Wood posits as associated with fixed-interest securities, i.e. they involve no contractual obligations to make payments in any given accounting period. Wood argues, however, that they are a minor source of finance and that this can be explained by reference to their unpopularity with long-term shareholders.

This derives from the fact that a new issue is generally associated with a fall in share prices. Wood adduces three basic reasons for such a fall in price. First, the new issue necessarily involves the rearrangement of portfolios, since to meet the costs of purchasing the new issue it will be necessary to sell shares. Rearrangement involves costs, and some compensation for those costs might be expected. Second, if the new issue is to be taken up by existing shareholders then this will involve an increase in the concentration of their holdings. But, in so far as diversification implies a reduction in risks such an increase in concentration should also involve a compensation. Finally, if considerations of this kind do operate then a new issue may be deemed unlikely to be taken up entirely by existing shareholders. Consequently a price reduction may be required in order to attract buyers who would not have bought the share at its previous price. This effect is, of course, not invariant. It is possible that a new issue can be made with no price fall or even with a price rise if the enterprise is able to convince potential shareholders that, given the additional capital, it can undertake investment programmes which will yield particularly high returns. The limit to this, in Wood's view, is that it is difficult for companies to convince the shareholders concerning such opportunities since the latter are not well informed about the future potential profitability of the enterprise.

In considering Wood's arguments, it is worth reiterating that an implicit enterprise-subject is counterposed to that posited in neo-classical theory. Furthermore, such a subject is supposed to function in what we have called the domain of the capitalist economy in general. For example, the differentiation of criteria of calculation between 'lenders' and 'borrowers' implies that the latter are subjects whose positions are invariant to the capitalist economy. Wood is not entirely consistent on this point, for his treatment of new issues does allow for a differential relation between management and long-term shareholders depending on the share price at which a new issue may be floated. However, generally the 'positions' accorded to the subjects are of an invariant character. If this position is to be sustained it is necessary to accord determinate modes of calculation to these positions as necessary correlates of them.

In addition to the differentiation of risks referred to earlier, which related to the differential effects on 'lenders' and 'borrowers' of the liquidation of a company, Wood argues that a further differentiation arises from the capacity of the 'lender' to spread risks in ways which are not open to the 'borrower'. This might be sustained by arguing that the shareholder has the whole range of marketable assets within his 'purview', while the enterprise is engaged in a determinate range of lines of production. This comparison is, however, somewhat specious. Clearly, it is quite open to an industrial enterprise to acquire a wide range of both industrial and non-industrial enterprises. Furthermore the fact that we have an 'enterprise' and a 'shareholder' here does not at all imply any differentiation in the capacity to avoid risk. Risk calculation is here premised on the notion that a diversity of investments reduces risk; the condition involves the argument that as far as possible the spread of investment should be in areas independent of each other or preferably negatively correlated with each other in terms of levels of returns in any given period (deck chairs and plastic macs, etc.). (see Prais, *The Evolution of Giant Firms*, pp. 92–8) Under such conditions it is clearly irrelevant whether we have a company or a shareholder, since if the company follows this view of risk it will seek to acquire enterprises as far as possible unrelated to its own line of operation. Of course, it is perfectly possible that the *de facto* capacity to adopt such risk-avoidance policies of different 'shareholders' or economic enterprises may be quite distinct, but this is not capable of being inferred from the general 'lender' or 'borrower' status and necessarily refers to the conditions of capitalist national economies.

Diversification, of course, will involve costs and it is perfectly possible to argue that certain conditions put particular industrial enterprises at a considerable advantage. A capitalist enterprise with a stock-market quotation can acquire another enterprise through an exchange of shares or a share-plus-cash offer. The price of the acquired company will thus be reduced if the price/earnings ratio of the acquiring company is higher than that of the acquired company. In such a situation the cost of acquisition and diversification is reduced for the acquiring company. Such an advantage is not open to a shareholder making acquisitions in cash and consequently bearing a higher cost for 'risk avoidance'.

This possibility should lead us to reflect on the difference postulated between 'lenders' and 'borrowers' in respect of the criteria applied in the assessment of investment programmes. The case that such divergences are systematic might rest on the character of the information available to lenders. Here it might be argued that if an industrial enterprise aims to expand in its existing area of manufacturing operations then the assessment of such a project involves precise knowledge of the enterprise's position in a given sector. This might involve knowledge of the efficiency of the enterprise's production operations, plans for new capital investment, likely scale economies, the likely expansion of the market internally and externally for a given product. It could be argued that such information is likely to be possessed by the management of the enterprise but not by potential investors and that there is thus a possible divergence in their assessments of a given investment project even if their 'target goals' are identical.

However, there is no way in which projects of this kind can be claimed to be privileged. If we take the example of the acquisition through exchange of shares it is possible to see that this use of the enterprise's funds sets up an entirely different relationship between enterprise and investor. The information required to assess such a project is both simpler and more determinate. It is well known that the earnings of quoted companies are capitalised at a much more favourable ratio to earnings than unquoted companies. The fact that such an acquisition may represent a capital gain for the acquiring enterprise involves no knowledge of the particular sector involved, and consequently the project may have an identical assessment by both 'lenders' and 'borrowers'. The point with this is that, as in a number of examples above, the postulation of 'positions' of lenders and borrowers in the domain of the capitalist economy in general involves an indeterminacy, since the positions, while not empty, are variable in terms of the criteria of calculation associated with them.

The invocation of the case of mergers between enterprises raises an important question in relation to Wood's argument. Wood excludes mergers by exchange of securities on the following grounds:

> As far as the present theory is concerned, this sort of operation is completely irrelevant. For it represents no more than an
> arbitrary alteration of the demarcation lines between companies. Moreover, new issues of this kind raise no additional finance for the companies involved (in the sense that they permit no increase in the sums of the capital outlays of A and B). (*A Theory of Profit*, p. 21)

From what we have already discussed, we can see that Wood's assertion is false. The acquisition by a firm with a higher price/earnings ratio of a firm with a lower price/earnings ratio *ipso facto* increases the finance available to the acquiring enterprise by the increased capitalisation of the earnings of the acquired enterprise. More important, these effects cannot be treated as 'arbitrary' distributional effects since they are of considerable significance in respect of production methods utilised.

It could be argued, for example, that the acquiring enterprise could achieve a similar effect simply by increasing its own profitability. However, to do this without acquisition would necessarily involve either the enterprise effecting gains on financial assets or improving production methods and the distribution of the products manufactured. Acquisition has the immediate advantage that, given the relative price/earnings ratios, the acquiring enterprise obtains the capital equipment of the acquired firm at a discount, and while the acquiring firm may be able to obtain favourable conditions for the purchase of capital equipment (though this is unlikely due to the fact that regularity of orders is not a feature here) the effect of the former advantage is likely to outweigh the latter.

As we pointed out in the discussion of production methods, renewal of capital equipment in the direction of more-mechanised production processes has highly variable effects depending on the sectors in which enterprises operate, and the scope for successful investment of this type is therefore limited. Of course, the acquisition process does not produce unlimited gains for the enterprise, but within a relevant range there will be a virtuous circle effect. This derives from the observed effects of the scale of the enterprise on the price/earnings ratio. This is most marked in the difference between quoted and unquoted firms. Prais estimates, for example, that unquoted firms would typically be capitalised at eight times their net profits while the corresponding figure for quoted firms would be approximately sixteen times. Naturally, the differences between quoted companies is much less marked, but fall in earnings yield with size is still discernible. (*The Evolution of Giant Firms*, pp. 110–11)

Given such a situation, acquisition can clearly lead to a virtuous financial circle whereby a lower earnings yield accompanies larger scale such that acquisition allows for cumulative gains where the acquiring enterprise not only obtains the gains associated with the acquisition but may move to a lower earnings yield allowing for larger gains to be obtained in future acquisitions. Since there are other financial advantages associated with scale such a strategy has a number of attractions.

A key element of Wood's argument is designed to demonstrate

the reason why capitalist enterprises preferred internal sources of finance. This argument is linked to the 'ownership-and-control' arguments on the grounds of perceived risk to the enterprise, in particular of dependence on the capital market where fixed-interest securities are a major source of finance. Of course, it is important to point out that, while fixed-interest securities do represent a contractual obligation of the enterprise, this does not necessarily mean that such obligations have to be met at a given point in time. It is perfectly possible for the interest payments to be 'rolled up'.

More important, however, it is difficult to consider the impact of fixed-interest finance on enterprises in terms of a given level of profits or of a *given* financial position. To do so would be to abstract from the advantages of fixed-interest securities to enterprises. These advantages are particularly pertinent since they are compounded in the case of larger enterprises. As we indicated earlier, the larger enterprise is usually the classic terrain for the ownership/control thesis since it is here that the 'corporate form' is claimed to dominate, vesting control of the means of production in the hands of professional managers.

A major advantage of issuing fixed-interest securities such as debentures is that interest on them is chargeable against profits. Obviously, this makes them more attractive than alternative sources of finance, particularly internal sources. These advantages are compounded by the fact that fixed-interest securities represent a cheap form of finance. Over the whole period from 1951 to 1970, for example, the real rate of return on industrial debentures was barely positive and was negative for each year from 1970 to 1974. (Prais, *The Evolution of Giant Firms*, p. 104)

These advantages can be articulated in an important way with the question of mergers raised above. The legal situation, in fact, encourages mergers, since modifying the capital structure of an enterprise directly to avoid tax is illegal. This does not apply to the issue of debentures to acquire another enterprise, consequently capital restructuring can be effected by mergers and, as we have already seen, they do have independent advantages for some enterprises. (*ibid.*, p. 105)

As we have already indicated, there is evidence that the financial advantages are more marked for larger enterprises which have been characterised as the classic terrain for managerialist arguments. Part of the reason for this advantage necessarily flows from the character of the 'investors'. It is now a commonplace that investment in capitalist enterprises has increasingly switched from individual to 'institutional' investors. In particular, insurance companies and pension funds receive continual flows of funds from contractual savings and have concentrated funds on a substantial scale. Receiving substantial flows of funds, they are concerned to place funds in large blocks. This necessarily benefits the large units whose requirements are more substantial. Similarly, the institutions require a regular flow-back of funds to meet contractual obligations, and the larger units are characterised by less variability in their revenues from period to period. Equally, of course, the larger enterprise may have other advantages associated with the security of the investment.

Such practices on the part of the institutions may well reinforce the financial virtuous circle to which we have already referred, since acquisition is further facilitated by cheap finance. Such advantages apply to share issues where the fixed costs involved in the issue are spread over a larger issue, resulting in a smaller cost per share issued. These manifold advantages have in the British case contributed to the growing importance in the last twenty years of fixed-interest securities as a source of finance for capitalist enterprises.

We have thus established that reference to an enterprise-subject will not allow us to produce a theory of capitalist calculation on the domain of the capitalist economy in general. There is no unequivocal set of practices for enterprises, managers, 'lenders' or 'borrowers', etc. We cannot establish priorities for internal over external sources of finance or vice versa, since the domain of the capitalist economy in general will not allow us to answer these questions.

Chapter 11

Enterprise Calculation and Sources of Finance

In this chapter we will be concerned with the effects on enterprise calculation of the sources of funds to enterprises and the adoption of 'financial calculation' by industrial enterprises. We will presuppose the theoretical arguments deployed in respect of money and financial institutions in Part I; specific reference will be made to that section where relevant.

This chapter concentrates on capitalist industrial enterprises and their sources of funds; financial institutions enter primarily as suppliers of funds. Capitalist industrial enterprises have three major sources of funds. First, internal finance is derived from profits made by the enterprise. These profits are only directly relevant to the financing of the enterprise if they are disposable, i.e. after tax. This means that the form taken by government allowances has a bearing on the finance of enterprises. Where the allowance takes the form of an offset against tax, the benefit necessarily accrues proportionately more to enterprises making higher profits in terms of the accounting conventions adopted. This necessarily does not apply to grants made directly for specific purposes, to encourage enterprises to move to areas of high unemployment through direct cash grants, etc.

The second major source arises from funds lent at interest for given time-periods. These can take a wide variety of forms. A marketable security bearing a fixed interest rate redeemable at the end of a given time-period may be issued by an enterprise. A loan may be obtained for a fixed term at fixed or fluctuating interest rates. An overdraft facility may be obtained from a bank where both the amount borrowed and the interest rate fluctuates. These sources of finance involve a contractual obligation to repay the sum borrowed but, as we have pointed out above, the lending institution may use discretion as to whether to enforce the contractual obligation.

The third major source is a new issue of shares by the enterprise. Obviously, unlike the provision of funds at interest, the issue of shares involves no contractual obligation on the enterprise to make payments; dividend payments are, at least formally, discretionary. Equally, new issues may involve a creation of voting rights in respect of the control of the enterprise.

We need to enquire whether the alternative sources of finance exert any pertinent effects in respect of enterprise calculation and in turn to enquire into the pertinence of the differentiation of sources. To do this we will examine two major issues in enterprise calculation, the time-period relevant for calculation and the 'level' of calculation. The former refers to the period adopted as the frame of reference for a 'target'. In the example cited above, of the Japanese and British motor-cycle industries, the difference was between a time-period geared to a 'market-share' concept and one geared to an accounting profit/accounting period concept. The former refers to the scope of calculation and may be divided as above into the intra-market level and the inter-market level. Intra-market level involves the analysis of the commodity/set of commodities at sector level, i.e. in respect of 'similar' products, or at inter-sectoral level where the commodity is situated in respect of its place in the expenditure of a given market. Inter-market level involves the same questions but with the addition that variations in national and/or regional markets are incorporated and a strategy is designed in relation to entry into markets, succession of entry, etc.

Necessarily there is a relationship between relevant time-periods and level of calculation. Time-periods, for example, are not homogeneous in so far as a time-period relevant to market-share calculations is not simply 'longer' than one linked to accounting periods. In the case of market-share calculations the accounting profitability in a given time-period is necessarily subordinated to the overall unit costs and corresponding volumes linked to the market-share target over the relevant period. Taking the accounting period as the relevant time-period necessarily involves linking production of particular commodities to an assigned estimate of individual profitability of those commodities, i.e. calculations which enter into the 'longer' time-period are simply not made. The level of calculation adopted implies a relevant time-period because some 'levels' of calculation are not pertinent in respect of some time-periods. An analysis of the enterprise's product or set of products in respect of prospective growth of sales in relation to the overall distribution of expenditure in a given market involves a time-period beyond that of any given accounting period. This equally applies in respect of inter-market-level calculations; a strategy of reducing unit costs can, for example, be based on an analysis in terms of a relevant succession of entry into different markets. When unit costs are significantly linked to volume of output, therefore, entry into a 'less competitive' market could allow volume to be expanded more easily, thus laying the foundations in reduced unit costs for entry into 'more competitive' markets. Clearly again, the reference to succession involves a reference to more than one accounting period.

In analysing the relationship between source of funds and relevant time-periods and level of calculation it should be stressed that we are seeking a possible condition of the latter not a determinant. In other words, time-periods and levels of calculation do not arise from sources of funds; neither are the latter their only conditions. The level of calculation and the relevant time-period are necessarily related to programmes of investment and the pricing, marketing, and distribution practices of the enterprise. Such programmes necessarily imply requirements of funds and a temporality of returns both in terms of criteria applied to the programme and in terms of cash flow. The temporality of returns will be affected by the enterprise's pricing policy and in turn this will structure the assessment of the project, the 'adequacy' of returns, and the cash flow anticipated in respect of the project.

Involved, therefore, will be questions both of the level of funds required and the time-period governing the flow of the funds. What are the pertinent differences between the possible sources in relation to these requirements? It is worth pointing out that profit for a given accounting period and internal company reserves are not to be distinguished on the grounds that they involve no costs to the enterprise while the other two sources do. This is because of the overlaying of money by credit relations referred to in the section on money and financial institutions, thus profit and internal reserves necessarily represent loanable funds with consequent potential returns.

Finance of investment projects by internal sources derives primarily from the enterprise's retained profits. In the case of industrial enterprises these will consist of operating gains, through the sale of commodities produced by the enterprise, holding gains arising from increases in the value of assets (property, stock appreciation, etc.), plus returns on financial assets held. Internal sources of finance are distinct in respect of the variability of returns. In the case of the other two sources the flow of funds is predictable. This is because in the case of fixed-interest securities or term loans the relevant flow of funds is set in the terms of the loan and is thus a constant even if the rate of interest is variable. In the case of share issues, the likelihood of floating the issue at the given share price is relatively predictable under given market conditions and can be subject to insurance in respect of underwriting, etc. Given that internal sources of funds derive from the operations of the enterprise itself, variability in flow of finance is directly linked to variability in returns to the enterprise. The extent of this variability will, of course, differ from enterprise to enterprise. How far it can be offset will vary with the position of the enterprise. As we pointed out above, there is no reason in principle why an enterprise should not be able to diversify its holdings in an identical way to a shareholder, but the *de facto* situation of each enterprise will involve a specific limit on diversification and a specific variability of returns. This means that the statistical link between diversification and reduction of variability of returns, while applicable in principle, may not have application in enterprise calculation. Of course, variability is not limited to operating gains but may be exaggerated or reduced by holding gains or returns on financial assets.

There is equally a specific drawback to reliance on internal sources of funds. This arises because of the existence of credit money. The availability of credit means that the expansion of the output of a given enterprise does not depend on internal finance. This means that where scale economies operate enterprises availing themselves of credit may gain at the expense of those utilising internal funds, since the former have the possibility of more rapid expansion of output. This applies under conditions where credit is available but is particularly important where credit money operates.

In the case of commodity money, as argued in the section on money and financial institutions, there is no creation of credit but simply a transfer of funds representing returns to enterprises (and individuals) which are not re-invested. Marx explains the source of these funds in the disjuncture between the accumulation of funds within the enterprise and the requirements of expanded reproduction. In the absence of credit-creation, therefore, the limit on funds is set by the conditions of this disjuncture. This necessarily means that the volume of credit available is restricted to the total of such funds. No such constraint operates in the case of credit money, where the constaints over the volume and time-period of loans that apply in the case of commodity-money no longer apply.

The provision of finance through loans at interest can take a number of forms. The issue of securities bearing fixed rates of interest necessarily has the advantage that the cost of a fixed volume of funds is given. However, such securities are marketable, and it would be incorrect to argue that their market price and the corresponding interest rate is irrelevant to enterprise calculations. This is because the rate of interest on newly issued securities will be adjusted to the prevailing market interest rates, thus the price of marketable, fixed-interest securities conditions the cost of finance of new issues. The fixed-interest security has the additional advantage from the point of view of enterprise calculation that its redemption is at a given date. A term loan from a bank fulfils a similar function in this respect, but with the major difference that interest rates will be variable. The variability is important here for it may force the enterprise into seeking additional finance to meet contractual obligations in the form of interest payments.

New issues are in a different category on the grounds that their success in raising funds depends upon the state of the stock market and will vary from company to company. New issues are easier to use as a source of funds when share prices are high. This facility will vary between enterprises because particularly 'desirable' shares can normally be floated on favourable terms. As a source of finance new issues do not involve contractual obligations either to repay capital or to pay interest or to pay a fixed cost for finance.

How are these differences pertinent to the level and time of calculation? Internal finance is subject clearly to problems of variability, but equally reliance on internal finance has another serious effect on the time and level of calculation. In respect of the latter pricing policies are necessarily adjusted to the strategy. For example, if a given market share is a target, prices may be adjusted to allow 'penetration' of the market and consequently flows of funds will be reduced. Where internal sources of funds are relied on, therefore, there is a dual function played by the internal sources of finance. As sources of finance they are necessarily required to meet the capital-expenditure and working-capital requirements of the enterprise; this in turn involves the adoption of a pricing policy to facilitate a 'target' flow of funds in a given time-period. Reliance on internal sources involves the possibility of the function of obtaining funds running into contradiction with the pricing function outlined in the market strategy. An exemplification of this arose in the case of the motor-cycle industry, where the lines produced and their prices were linked to the flow of funds derived from internal finance. The Boston Group raised the criticism in this case that the identification of the calculating period with the accounting period led to the continuation of practices which engendered the relative weakness of the British industry. In this case a strong argument could be advanced to support this claim, but it would be difficult to generalise it. This is because a given source of finance does not of itself *involve* a period and level of calculation.

The impact of loaned funds clearly depends on their volume and temporality. Their advantage is that they allow for the partial separation of the pricing policy from the source-of-funds function; these two are linked where internal funds are the primary source. Equally the provision of loaned funds for a term equivalent to the calculation period overcomes the variability of flow which may be associated with internal finance. This latter condition is important since if the period of the loan and the calculation period are not identical then additional sources of finance will be required. If they are sought in further loans then the conditions of these loans may be subject to variability as to the term of the loan and the rate of interest charged to the borrower. The marketability of fixed-interest securities means that there is no guarantee that new issues will be financed on the same terms as previous issues. Here it is worth noting that inflation is particularly important in respect of this effect. Inflation is often argued to make fixed-interest securities more attractive because it reduces real interest rates often to negative levels (see our own argument above) but in terms of long-term calculation it does involve a serious problem. Price rises necessarily mean that loans may be required to finance stock appreciation, in particular, which, as we indicated above, is a liquidity problem. This involves obtaining loans which would not be required if prices were more stable, and from the point of view of the enterprise engenders problems with the variability of sources of funds. Necessarily, therefore, the significance of funds lent at interest for calculation can only be assessed if the terms of the loan are taken into consideration, thus a global figure of debt in the composition of enterprise finance is meaningless when it is not accompanied by information as to the term of the loan concerned.

As we have already pointed out, funds loaned out at interest have, under British conditions, the major advantage that interest is chargeable against tax. The significance of this is in the context of the comparability of internal and external sources of funds. As was pointed out above, the overlaying of credit relations means that internal sources of funds and external sources are equally pertinent choices, and so the fact that the tax concession is applicable to funds loaned at interest puts them at a discount compared with internal sources of finance.

New issues are subject to variability since the finance which can be raised from the issue of a given volume of shares depends on the prevailing prices for the shares concerned. These will vary between enterprises but also with the overall level of prices on the stock market. The variability here is associated with the alternative sources of acquisition of financial assets, and therefore the character of the market for financial assets will condition the variability associated with new issues. New issues possess the advantage that if they can be floated at a favourable share price they represent a cheap source of finance.

It is, therefore, not possible to single out a source of finance which is ideally adapted to a particular temporality or level of calculation. While variability is reduced by seeking funds loaned at interest this variability is by no means eradicated. The term of the loan may or may not be identical with the relevant calculation period, but even if it is the *de facto* term can be reduced by the exigencies of inflation. This statement holds whatever specific use the enterprise makes of its borrowed funds (capital project, working capital, etc.), since what is relevant to the calculation period is the total flow of funds in that period.

As we have demonstrated, the variability of access to sources of funds means that distinct sources can operate at given points in time. Equally, the differentiation of sources plays a role in the acquisition of enterprises. An enterprise with a favourable valuation ratio could acquire other enterprises 'at a discount' if the acquired enterprises' earnings were capitalised less favourably.

Such an advantage is not open to an enterprise acquiring another by issue of debentures or in a cash acquisition. As was pointed out previously, however, an acquisition through a debenture issue can, under British conditions, be used as a means of altering the enterprise's capital structure in order to avoid tax. In this respect the differentiation of sources relates both to particular conditions and to the particular functions which specific sources may fulfil.

We will now consider the character of the sources of finance available to British industrial enterprises. An important feature of British industrial enterprises is the relatively high dependence on internal sources of finance. The self-financing ratio (undistributed income, including income from depreciation and income from abroad, plus capital transfers as a percentage of capital spending including stock appreciation) of UK industrial and commercial companies varied from a low of 72 per cent to a high of 112 per cent over the 1970 to 1975 period. The figure for British enterprises was higher than those of the industrial and commercial sectors of the USA, Japan, Germany or France during the same period, with the exception of 1974 when the American figure was identical to the British figure. These figures vary from year to year, and the international differences are increased or reduced in a similarly variable manner. In general the American and German figures were closer to the British, the French were slightly below the American and German figures, and the Japanese substantially below. (Johnson, *Anatomy of UK Finance 1970–75*, table 2·34, p. 75)

This might seem rather paradoxical in view of the much-heralded argument that British industry is undergoing a profits crisis. We will not attempt to examine the labyrinth of alternative measures of 'profit' here but one point is worth noting. The self-financing ratio includes income from abroad, and this source has been progressively more important in recent years; income from abroad made up 24 per cent of the income of UK industrial and commerical companies in 1972 and 32 per cent in 1974; UK gross trading profits made up 70 per cent of the corresponding income figure in 1972 and 60 per cent in 1974. (*ibid.*, table 2·8, p. 66)

Another measure of a different kind relating to the source of funds is the so-called 'gearing ratio'. This measures the ratio of total debt (contractual commitments) to the shareholders' funds. As we saw in Wood's analysis, the gearing ratio is often treated as significant as an indicator of risk. Thus, a number of commentators argue that as debt involves contractual commitments to repay capital and to pay interest at given dates a higher gearing ratio increases the vulnerability of the enterprise. Because what is regarded as important here is the contractual commitment, the term of the debt is not examined. This emphasis is misplaced because it presupposes some 'norm' relationship between financial institutions and industrial enterprises. As we have already pointed out, the formal contractual obligations may or may not be taken up, and rolling up of interest payments may, for a number of reasons, be a preferred strategy for financial institutions at particular points in time.

As far as the ratio of total debt to shareholders' funds ('primary gearing') is concerned the idea of a 'norm' level is contradicted by the large variation in gearing ratios. For example, while the primary gearing of the UK, US and German industry was fairly similar between 1970 and 1974, the Japanese level of primary gearing was on average six times the level of those countries over the same period. (*Anatomy of UK Finance 1970–75*, table 2·39, p. 77) It is questionable how far the primary gearing ratio is significant. It is demarcated theoretically because of the legal difference between debt and equity, but necessarily debt includes loans of differing terms and securities of differing maturities. A loose measure of the terms of loans is given in the distinction between 'long'- and 'short'-term debt.

If we examine the variation in 'secondary gearing' ('short-term' debt as a percentage of 'long-term' debt) then a somewhat different picture emerges. Although Japan still has the highest secondary gearing ratio, it was never more than one-third higher than the British figure for the 1970-4 period, while the American figure for secondary gearing was only half the British figure. Consequently, American and Japanese enterprises were utilising a higher ratio of 'long-term' debt to 'short-term' debt than the British, a distinction effaced by the overall gearing ratio.

Part of the reason for this configuration lies in the character of the lending institutions. The provision of bank credit in Britain has primarily been on a 'short-term' basis and this in turn has involved specialisation in their calculation, with the result that the clearing banks are not equipped to assess the economic position of industrial and commercial companies over long periods. The other main financial institutions are significant for finance through new issues of fixed-interest securities, and we shall deal with the latter below.

The insurance companies and pension funds are characterised by drawing their receipts through contractual saving and making similar contractual payments. Their calculation is designed to switch funds according to the various rates of return on financial assets.

They are involved in the purchase of equities, sometimes on a large scale, but this has little bearing on the financing of industrial companies. This is essentially because the equity market is primarily a secondary market dealing in 'old' issues. The impact of the secondary market on new issues is indirect; that is, to the extent that trading in issued securities sets the general level of share prices it affects the fate of new issues.

In discussing the impact of sources of finance on calculation we indicated that the volume and predictability of a source of funds were the most significant criteria. In volume terms new issues have not been important in recent years as a source of funds for industrial companies. Thus even in a 'peak' year for issues (1972) new issues made up 12 per cent of Gross Domestic Fixed Capital Formation. (*Anatomy of UK Finance 1970–75*, table 2·26, p. 73)

Where consistency is the concern the main issue is whether the stock market can be relied upon as a source of finance from new issues. Militating against this is the practice of insurance companies and pension funds to switch funds between different financial assets. The insurance companies' net acquisitions of public-sector debt fluctuated from 12 per cent of their net acquisitions in 1970 to 68 per cent for 1975, while net acquisitions of company securities fluctuated from 57 per cent (1972) to 4 per cent (1975). (*ibid.*, table 4·14, p. 150) It must be noted that the fluctuations are exaggerated by a particularly rapid increase between 1974 and 1975 in the holding of public-sector debt to a figure 30 per cent above that for any other year in the 1970–5 period, and that acquisition of securities did rise to 22 per cent in 1975 from the low of 1974.

There is a similar picture for the pension funds; public-sector debt fluctuated from a low of 2 per cent of net acquisitions in 1972 to a high of 36 per cent (1975), while company securities fluctuated from a high of 66 per cent (1970) to a low of 12 per cent (1974). (*ibid.*, table 4·18, p. 152) The 1970–75 period is characterised by an increasing share of new issues being taken up by rights issues, i.e. issues by established, quoted companies. Johnson discusses this pattern in the following terms: 'The primary market is thus becoming less a way for growing unquoted companies to enter the big league, and more a means for quoted companies to increase their equity base.' (*ibid.*, p. 139; see also table 4·44, p. 161)

New issues are thus a source which can be relied on not as a *regular* means of raising finance but as a means which can be adopted as relatively cheap finance during periods of high equity prices. The primary exception to this rule would appear to be established firms whose issues are likely to be generally treated favourably.

We have treated the question of the source of funds to industrial enterprises in respect of the finance of their manufacturing activities; we will now go on to examine the role of *financial capitalist calculation* in the operational calculation of industrial enterprises.

This problem is often effaced because distinctions such as those between industrial and finance capital are seen as distinctions between types of enterprises. Thus 'finance capital' is identified with banking, and other financial institutions, and 'industrial capital' with industrial enterprises, etc. The calculation of such enterprises is seen as corresponding: financial enterprises adopt 'financial' calculation and industrial enterprises 'industrial' calculation, etc.

Underlying these distinctions is a general 'productionist' view of capitalism shared by authors of diverse positions. The norm of capitalism is thus treated as the pursuit of operating gains through the production of commodities. We have encountered this kind of position in various guises already. It is implicit in the arguments of Merrett and Sykes as it is in those of 'orthodox' Marxists.

There are two central flaws with the argument. There is no reason why capitalist enterprises should *a priori* privilege one source of returns rather than another. Furthermore, the effect of the overlaying of credit relations is that means of production 'double' as 'productive' and 'financial' assets.

Means of production can thus be assigned a value in respect of calculation based on the enterprise as a concern producing commodities. In this respect, for example, the depreciation of capital equipment is conceived of in terms of a given working life in which the asset functions as a means of production. In relation to this mode of calculation a resale value for the asset is only relevant where an estimate applies to the end of its 'working life'. However, it is equally possible to treat means of production as assets with a resale value on which a return can be obtained.

These latter types of calculation are often related to the calculation of financial conglomerates involved in 'asset stripping'. In the 'productionist' treatment, whether Marxist or non-Marxist, such operations are often thought of as not strictly capitalist but adventurist.

But there is no reason why an industrial enterprise should not make such calculations, or why it should not treat means of production as financial assets. Financial capitalist calculation by industrial enterprises is by no means restricted to treating the means of production as assets with a resale value. Financial capitalist calculation may be pursued without any object of selling means of production entering into it.

This type of practice has already been exemplified in the practice of acquisitive industrial conglomerates. Such conglomerates utilise both financial and industrial capitalist calculation. In the latter case acquisition may be linked to integration of production processes or to rationalisation of capacity, i.e. calculation linked to reducing unit costs. Financial capitalist calculation, however, applies to the use of the financial valuation of the acquiring enterprise as a means of acquisition of assets.

We discussed this process above in respect of the effects of enterprise scale on the price/earnings ratio. A similar effect can occur as an object of financial capitalist calculation. In other words, the acquiring enterprise actively seeks an enterprise with a lower price/earnings ratio with a view to acquisition. The acquisition improves the earnings per share of the acquiring company and can lead to a 'virtuous' circle process of expansion. Lynch describes the process in the following terms:

> The combination of this process over time creates a pattern of growth in earnings per share which may cause the market to place a higher price-earnings ratio on the common stock of the acquiring corporation. This price-earnings ratio is, in turn, the vehicle which enables the process to continue. It would appear that this feedback effect from earnings per share growth through acquisition to price-earnings ratio, if indeed it exists increases the market value of the acquired firm without any change in its 'economic value' as an operating unit. (*The Financial Performance of Conglomerates*, p. 6)

Lynch gives the following simple example of the operation of such a process:

A, with $1 million in earnings after tax, 1 million shares outstanding, and therefore $1 in earnings per share, has a price-earnings ration of 20. B has exactly the same current earnings, shares and earnings per share but has a price-earnings ratio of only 10. A has a total market value of $20 million; B has a total market value of $10 million. A acquires B in a stock for stock transaction based on the market values of the securities of the two companies. After the acquisition A has 50% more shares outstanding and total earnings have doubled. Earnings per share have therefore increased to ($2,000,000/1,500,000 shares) = $1.33. (*ibid.*)

These practices are often taken to be 'speculative' operations, i.e. involving short-term, unstable, and non-recurrent gains, but there is no warrant for this. Entering into calculations of this type may be an attempt to ascertain that the acquired enterprise will be capable of realising a *consistent* flow of earnings as an industrial enterprise. Such calculations, however, work on the basis that the controllers of the conglomerate enterprise do not directly enter into industrial calculation concerned with the production of specific commodities. What is involved in this process is the carrying on of an industrial conglomerate enterprise governed by financial capitalist calculation.

This type of calculation is geared to the calculations of potential shareholders. This is the case because the earnings-per-share indicator will be pertinent to the shareholder, since it is immediately calculable in a way that the analysis of the production of specific commodities is not. This is particularly important considering the calculative practice of financial institutions, a practice primarily of a financial capitalist nature, where the returns on financial assets are relevant but their source is not.

A process of expansion of this type is thus based on the selection of appropriate enterprises for acquisition, not on what is normally thought of as 'industrial' calculation. Naturally, the extent of such practices will vary with particular conditions of the capital market. They are facilitated by a market where there is an extensive secondary market in securities. It is generally considered that such practices are facilitated by periods of high share prices since the prices of the stock of such conglomerates are thought to be more volatile than those of 'non-acquisitive' enterprises.

Chapter 12

The Sraffa Model as a Theory of Reproduction Prices

Piero Sraffa's *Production of Commodities by Means of Commodities* has generated a considerable secondary literature, some of which has occupied a prominent place in recent debates among economists over the Marxist theory of value. What has been designated, by Marxist opponents, as the 'neo-Ricardian' critique of Marx's theory has concentrated on the technical validity of value, defined in terms of labour-time, as the measure of the prices and proportions in which commodities exchange. It has been argued that value, in this sense, is formally redundant for a theory of reproduction prices, that under certain conditions there may be commodities with positive prices and negative values and that it is possible for an economy to exhibit both a negative surplus value and a positive rate of profit (see, for example, Hodgson, 'Marxian epistemology'; Meek, 'Introduction'; Steedman, 'Value, price and profit' and 'Positive profits'; Wolfstetter, 'Surplus value'). Marxist critics of Sraffa and derivative work have tended to reply that while the Sraffa system may be formally adequate, in the sense of being a logically consistent theoretical system, it is nevertheless formalist, incomplete, and essentially a-historical in that it fails to conceptualise social relations of production, their historical character, and their effects. They have argued that Marx's theory of value cannot be reduced to an algebraic theory of exchange and exchange-value, that the 'neo-Ricardian' approach effectively reduces capitalist relations of production to a matter of the division of the net product, and, most importantly, that the concept of value is crucial in explaining the way that exchange-relations are governed by production-relations. Many of these critics do point to weaknesses in the neo-Ricardian position, but the main effect of the Marxist response to Sraffa has been a defensive and essentially dogmatic reassertion of the problem of value as posed in *Capital* and of Marx's solution to it.

The object of this chapter is neither to defend Marx against Sraffa and the 'neo-Ricardian' critique nor to question the technical validity of Sraffa's and 'neo-Ricardian' analyses. Marx's theory of value has been subjected to fundamental criticism in the first part of Volume One of this work and it needs no further discussion here. Rather than question the technical character of their arguments, this chapter will consider the conceptualisation of the economy in terms of which Sraffa and the 'neo-Ricardians' pose their problems of the algebraic properties of an economy in the state of general economic equilibrium. What is at stake in these problems is a theory of reproduction prices, of the quantitative relations between prices, the level of wages, rate of profit, and other economic magnitudes which must hold in conditions of general equilibrium. It is a theory of reproduction prices in the sense that the exchange of all commodities at those prices would allow all production processes to reproduce themselves or, more generally, to grow at the same rate. Sraffa posits an economy of interdependent processes each defined by definite labour-time and commodity input-and-output coefficients. These coefficients, together with the level of wages (or rate of profit), are supposed to determine the set of reproduction prices for the system. Processes in this sense are not enterprises. The effect of positing an economy of processes as object of analysis is therefore to preclude consideration of the pertinences of the organisation of production at the level of enterprises (the calculations, accounting procedures and decisions of capitalists, struggles between capitalists and workers, etc.) and of the conditions of the circulation of products between economic agents. Although this chapter concentrates on the work of Sraffa and derivative positions it should be noted that a more sophisticated mathematical foundation for a theory of reproduction prices has been developed elsewhere, notably in the work of von Neumann ('A model of economic equilibrium'). Nevertheless, von Neumann's work will not be considered here. This is for two reasons. First, because the way in which Sraffa, unlike von Neumann, explicitly poses the problem of the determination of prices as a function of the division between wages and profit has aroused the interest of Marxist economists and provided the foundation for the so-called neo-Ricardian critique of

The Sraffa Model as a Theory of Reproduction Prices   217

Marx's theory of value. Second, our analysis is concerned more with the mode of conceptualisation of the economy involved in the project for a theory of reproduction prices than with the technical, mathematical apparatus in which that project is realised. The technical superiority of the von Neumann model, therefore, is not significant for the argument developed below.

If the Sraffa economy may be considered as a model for capitalism it is only for the following reasons: (1) the distribution of the surplus product takes the form of the exchange commodities; and (2) wages and profit are the principal income categories. The main argument of this chapter is that the analysis of price formation and distribution in Sraffa and similar work has no pertinence to the analysis of price formation under capitalism. We consider first the effects of the way the problems of price determination and of distribution are posed by Sraffa and then proceed to examine some rather odd features of the Sraffa model in more detail, the irrelevance of the composition of the surplus product to the division between wages and profit, the simultaneous determination of the prices of commodities and the money-value of the capital advanced for their production, the treatment of joint production as an attempt to handle depreciation, and, finally, the fact that the standard commodity as a unit of measurement is of no importance in analysing the formation of prices. These discussions allow us to establish in conclusion that the analysis of price formation in Sraffa cannot be pertinent to price formation under capitalism. The argument here is that the mode of conceptualising the economy involved in a theory of reproduction prices is incompatible with the conditions of existence of capitalist production, conceived as a field of production organised around capitalist forms of possession of the means and conditions of production and the correlative separation of the labourers from those means and conditions. This is not a 'realist' critique since it is not concerned to argue that existing capitalist economies fail to exhibit the properties posited by Sraffa; nor does it attempt an alternative general theory of price determination. On the contrary, it measures the theoretical presuppositions of the Sraffa model against the conditions of existence of capitalist production established in other sections of this work, in the analyses of money and of capitalist calculation in this volume and the discussion of possession and separation in Volume One. It is these conditions which determine how the problem of the formation of prices under capitalism should be posed, as a function of capitalist calculation and its exigencies, on the one hand, and of the conditions in which exchanges take place, on the other. Since universal conditions of exchange and a universal form of capitalist calculation cannot be derived from the conception of capitalist production as such, it follows that the project for a general theory of price determination, applicable to all conditions of price formation, must be misconceived.

Distribution and price determination

In this section we consider the consequences of the way in which the determination of prices is posed as a problem by Sraffa and derivative work. The problem is constituted on the basis of an economy specified in terms of a set of processes of production and a division of the surplus product between workers and capitalists (the latter being represented by processes). In a Sraffa economy there are no units of production or enterprises. There are only processes of production each defined by definite labour-time and commodity input-and-output coefficients. These processes, and therefore the composition of the product, are assumed to be given, subject only to the restriction that the means of production consumed in the course of production are themselves reproduced. The total product net of what is consumed in the process of production constitutes a surplus that is distributed between two categories of economic agent, workers and capitalists, in the form of wages and profit. The social product is assumed to be distributed through commodity exchange. The division of the product between wages and profit is therefore determined by prices. The problem of the determination of prices, therefore, amounts to specifying a pattern of distribution which prices are supposed to accomplish and then finding a set of prices which effect that distribution. Thus, equilibrium prices in a Sraffa economy perform the following functions:

    1 they distribute products so that each process may be repeated;
    2 they define a real wage rate, that is, they allow workers to appropriate a part of the surplus;
    3 they distribute the surplus left after the deduction of wages among processes (capitalists) in proportion to the capital

The Sraffa Model as a Theory of Reproduction Prices

advanced (wages are paid *post festum*, so they do not form part of the capital advanced).

Sraffa shows that the determination of prices cannot be independent of the pattern of distribution of the surplus and further that, given an appropriate unit of measurement (the standard commodity), there is a linear relation between wages and the rate of profit.

In its emphasis on the problem of distribution between wages and profit, Sraffa's analysis returns to one of the central concerns of classical political economy. Political economy is concerned with the problems of the wealth of nations, with questions of economic policy and the management of national economies. It is in connection with the distribution between the classes who form the nation that the nature and source of profit (and rent) arises as a problem. Sraffa, in effect, answers that the condition of existence of profit is to be found in the presence of a surplus, and that its magnitude is determined by the division of the surplus between wages and profit. For Sraffa the distribution of the social product is a function of prices which are themselves determined by the conditions of production, on the one hand, and the division between wages and profit, on the other. The problem of distribution is, therefore, first and foremost a problem of distribution between classes. It is presumably the fact that he allows the problem of distribution to be posed in this way that accounts for the interest shown in Sraffa's work by so many Marxist economists.

But the emphasis on the problem of distribution also accounts for another striking feature of Sraffa's work which it shares with political economy, namely, its lack of concern with the organisation of production. That statement may seem perverse in view of the role attributed by Sraffa and the classics to the conditions of production and to the expenditure of labour in particular. But what does this emphasis on the conditions of production amount to? Merely that prices are supposed to be determined by abstractly defined coefficients representing production processes and the pattern of distribution between classes. In the classics there is little discussion of the organisation of production as such and certainly nothing to compare with Marx's extensive analyses of capitalist production processes. Although his discussions are to a considerable extent hegemonised by the theory of value, Marx shows in the first volume of *Capital* how the 'technical' conditions of production, the forms of organisation of the labour process, their development, and possible transformations, are dependent on capitalist possession of the means of production and the manner in which labourers are separated from those means. It is this concern with the conditions and effects of the capitalist organisation of production that is so largely missing from classical political economy. Ricardo, for example, considers the effects of machinery, but his discussion is entirely concerned with its distributive effects on the interests of the different classes of society and its possible contribution to increasing the net social product. The conditions of production are important for their effects in the sphere of distribution and they have no significance for the classics outside of those effects. The role assigned to the conditions of production by the classics receives its clearest expression in Sraffa's text and in derivative 'neo-Ricardian' analyses. There the methods of production are reduced to the sets of commodity input-and-output and labour-time coefficients which define the distinct production processes. These coefficients, together with the division between wages and profit, uniquely determine all prices in the system. The conditions of production then consist in nothing more than a set of linear algebraic equations. However much these equations may be said to involve quantities of 'iron', 'wheat', 'pigs', or whatever, no features of the conditions in which these things are produced or enter production are pertinent to the analysis other than in their algebraic representation. In particular, then, the conditions in which capitalist production is organised in enterprises has no pertinence to the analysis of Sraffa economies. The converse of this point, to which we return below, is that the analysis of price determination and distribution in Sraffa economies is of no direct help in analysing the formation of prices in capitalist economies.

The Sraffan and 'neo-Ricardian' problem of distribution involves a general theory in which, as we have seen, the determination of the pattern of distribution is equivalent to the determination of a set of prices through which that distribution is to be effected. In this respect Sraffa shares with the classics and with marginalism the problem of a general theory of distribution as effected by the determination of commodity prices. Sraffa's analysis of the significance and effects of the conditions of production and the division between wages and profit has provided

The Sraffa Model as a Theory of Reproduction Prices 221

the foundation for what is often regarded as a devastating critique of neo-classical economics (see Dobb, 'The Sraffa system', for a concise summary). The details of this critique do not concern us here. What must be noted is that the Sraffan critique of neo-classical theory is internal to the terrain of a general problem of distribution. A general problem of distribution by means of price determination supposes a general answer in the form of a principle which governs or is realised in all particular cases of price determination and all economic transactions. To pose a general problem of distribution or of price determination is therefore to suppose that the economy is itself governed by a single general principle. This problem returns us to the conception of the economy as a totality, and its attempted solutions take the form of an identification of the organising principle which is supposed to govern the functioning of that totality. We have criticised the conception of the economy as a totality in Volume One of this work and we have shown that both Marx's theory of value and the marginalist alternatives involve equivalent, though distinct, essentialisms. Sraffa's organising principle is different from that of neo-classical economics and it differs in certain particulars from those of Marx and Ricardo. Nevertheless, it is the postulate of the economy-as-totality required by the posing of a general problem of distribution that allows an answer to take the form of an analysis of particular 'states' of that economy. In an equilibrium state prices and therefore the pattern of distribution are simultaneously determined—by the law of value, by the conditions of production and the division between wages and profit, by the marginal productivity of the factors of production, or whatever. Otherwise the pattern of distribution and prices will depart from those given by the organising principle. What must be noted here is that the notions of disequilibrium or non-equilibrium as states of an economy themselves depend on the conceptualisation of the economy as a totality. It is precisely the conception of the economy-as—totality governed by an organising principle that allows the conception of non-equilibrium as states of the economy representing departures from the equilibrium state and effected by disturbances in (or to) the functioning of the organising principle of the economy. If the economy is not a totality then the notion of equilibrium or non-equilibrium as states of the economy can have no meaning. It is, therefore, not a pertinent criticism of Sraffa and related positions that they posit an equilibrium state of the economy, and it is not a pertinent defence to say that the analysis of equilibrium allows for the analysis, as determinate departures from it, of other states of the economy. What is important is the conceptualisation of the economy-as-totality, which ensures that the notion of general equilibrium occupies such an important place in economic theorising. It is this conception which allows the definition of an equilibrium state as a pertinent object of analysis and the correlative conceptions of non-equilibrium states precisely as departures from it. We have shown in other chapters that the notion of economy-as-totality cannot be sustained and that it is strictly incompatible with any conception of the effectivity of capitalist calculation at the level of the enterprise.

We now consider some of the features of the Sraffa and related models in rather more detail.

The division of the surplus between wages and profit

The first feature to notice is that the composition of the social product is in no way pertinent to its division between wages and profit. The surplus product may consist both of basics, which enter directly or indirectly into the production of all commodities, and non-basics. At the beginning of chapter 2 of *The Production of Commodities* Sraffa gives the example of an economy in which the surplus product consists of wheat and iron. Thus part of the surplus received by workers may contain quantities of iron. What do the workers do with it? Later in the same chapter Sraffa notes that treating the whole of the wage as variable has the drawback 'that it involves relegating the necessities of consumption to the limbo of non-basic products'. (*ibid.*, p. 10) But whether means of consumption are regarded as basics or not the fact remains that the surplus distributed between wages and profit will contain basics that are not means of consumption. What are the workers supposed to do with them? (In fact, since the economy is assumed to be in a self-replacing state it is not clear what the recipients of profit are supposed to do with them either.) The problem here is that consumption functions as a purely notional category in the Sraffa model. It is certainly effective in the sense that workers' consumption takes up part of the gross product and also in the sense that there may be luxury goods (non-basics) which do not enter into the production of other commodities. But it has no role to play in the determination of the structure of demand. Whatever

The Sraffa Model as a Theory of Reproduction Prices 223

its composition the surplus product, after replacement of what is consumed in production, is divided between wages and profit. In effect, the subordination of consumption to the structure of production is simply established by fiat in the Sraffa system.

The simultaneous determination of all prices

Second, Sraffa assumes that prices are equilibrium prices and these prices are arrived at algebraically. The process of formation of prices is a mathematical process not an economic one. The analysis tells us what the equilibrium prices are but it does not tell us how economic agents arrive at these prices. The significance of this point will become clear when we consider that the algebraic method of determination of prices implies that the money value of the capital advanced in each process is not given. It is determined simultaneously with the prices of the commodities that the capital advanced helps to produce. The money value of capital advanced in the production of steel is determined side by side with the price of steel itself—and similarly for all commodities and processes in the system. Capital is advanced before production commences, but its magnitude in money terms is not known until the product is brought to the market. This analysis poses no problems so long as the economy is assumed to be in a state of equilibrium, since in that case the prices of products relative to those of their means of production do not change. Thus the analysis is not affected if it is assumed that the value of the capital advanced and the prices of the commodities that capital has helped to produce are determined simultaneously. But that argument is not valid if an equilibrium state of the economy is not assumed. The value of the capital advanced is given at the start of production and this value is in no way affected by the price obtained for the commodities which the capital advanced helps to produce. In general it is necessary to distinguish between two magnitudes: (1) the prices of the means of production at the beginning of the period of production; and (2) those at the end of the period of production. The cost of production is determined by the former and not by the latter. But it is the latter which is important in determining the costs of reproduction. Only in a state of equilibrium can the significance of the difference between these two magnitudes and their effects be ignored. In equilibrium the procedures whereby economic agents arrive at the determination of prices are of no pertinence since all commodity prices necessarily realise the effects of the organising principle governing the functioning of the economy.

The Sraffa model is of a stationary economy and what is analysed is a once and for all act of production. However, many derivative 'neo-Ricardian' models attempt to analyse similar economies in a state of equilibrium growth. In these cases prices perform two different functions: they equate the rate of return on capital advanced in all branches of production and they make it possible for all branches to grow at the same rate. In this latter capacity the prices of production are prices of reproduction. 'Before' and 'after' do have a limited pertinence in a growth economy but the presumption of equilibrium still ensures that the cost of production of a commodity is identical to the cost of its reproduction. The distinction between prices at the beginning and at the end of the production period thus has no pertinence for the analysis of such economies.

Joint production

Joint production refers to processes in which there are several distinct products, for example, mutton and wool, beef and leather, sausage and ice-cream. But the real interest of joint products does not lie in these examples but rather in 'its being the genus of which Fixed Capital is the leading species'. (*ibid.*, p. 63) Suppose, for the sake of exposition, that the economy is analysed in terms of an accounting period of one year. How are we to treat of those means of production with a life of more than one year or of those processes which take more than one year to complete? Sraffa treats durable instruments of production as part of the annual intake of a process and treats what is left of them at the end of the year as a portion of the annual joint product of the process in question. Thus a machine with a lifetime of ten years would be treated as a new machine for its first year, a new one-year-old machine for its second year, and so on. Similarly, for a process taking more than one year to complete the partially finished products after each year of operation may be treated as products in the same way. In this way all processes can be broken down into a series of analytically distinct processes each taking one year to complete, and all durable means of production broken down into a series of analytically distinct means of production. Any means of production, partially finished product, or whatever, appearing at the end of a production

The Sraffa Model as a Theory of Reproduction Prices   225

period has a reproduction price, and the totality of reproduction prices ensures the reproduction of the system of production processes in the economy.

The treatment of partially used fixed capital as joint products appears to dispose of the distinction between fixed and working capital, since it allows all components of the capital advanced to be analysed in terms of a life of one production period only. Alternatively, the theory of joint production may be regarded as a means of analysing depreciation. (*ibid.*, ch. 10) The treatment of a machine as a series of distinct products, one for each year of its employment, allows reproduction prices to be calculated for each year of operation. The differences between the new price and these reproduction prices then gives the depreciation to be allowed on the machine. Finally, it is possible to show that in joint-production systems there may be commodities with positive prices and negative labour-times, and that there may be systems in which the surplus embodies a negative labour-time—so that there will be positive profit and negative surplus value. (Steedman, 'Positive profits'; Morishima, *Marx's Economics*, ch. 14)

The details of these arguments need not detain us here. What must be noted is that the erasure of the distinction between fixed and working capital and the technical quibbles over Marx's handling of the relations between profit, prices, and values all depend on the absence of enterprises or units of production. It is this absence that determines both the impertinence of the distinction between fixed and working capital and the possibility of reducing all processes to a single common period of production. The distinction between fixed and working capital is an accounting distinction in capitalist enterprises and it cannot be erased by treating the former as joint products. The problem of the valuation of partially used machines arises only because the accounting period does not coincide with the period over which the machine lasts. The problem of valuation, in other words, is an accounting problem for enterprises, and if it is treated in this way then there are no negative values. The reason this accounting distinction is not pertinent in Sraffa's analysis is that there are no enterprises or units of production but only processes. If there are no enterprises then there can be no place for accounting distinctions. Or again, the fact that the economy may be reduced to processes having the same period of production does not depend primarily on the conception of joint production but rather on the absence of units of production. Processes can be treated as partitionable with a view to equating periods of production and to that extent are arbitrary constructs. But capitalist enterprises cannot be treated as partitionable in this way because the boundaries of enterprises are not arbitrary constructs. They are drawn on the basis of profit and loss calculations and not with a view to equating periods of production.

The standard commodity

> The necessity of having to express the price of one commodity in terms of another which is arbitrarily chosen as standard complicates the study of price-movements which accompany a change in distribution. It is impossible to tell of any particular price-fluctuation whether it arises from the peculiarities of the commodity which is being measured or from those of the measuring standard. (*The Production of Commodities*, p. 18)

The 'peculiarities' to which Sraffa refers will be considered below. The significance of this passage lies in its suggestion that analysis of the properties of the system presents the problem of an invariant standard of prices, that is, of a standard that, for a given set of production processes, is invariant to changes in the distribution of the surplus. Sraffa shows that such a standard commodity can always be defined. The importance of establishing a standard commodity is specified as follows:

> It is true that, as wages fell, such a commodity would be no less susceptible than any other to rise or fall in price relative to other individual commodities; but we should know for certain that any such fluctuation would originate exclusively in the peculiarities of production of the commodity that was being compared with it, and not in its own. If we could discover such a commodity we should therefore be in possession of a standard capable of isolating the price movements of any other product so that they could be observed as in a vacuum. (*ibid.*)

The problem with this argument is that it cannot establish the need for an invariant standard of prices. Notice first that the fact that relative prices change when the wage rate is changed does not in itself require an invariant standard of prices. The pattern of relative prices does not depend on the unit of measurement adopted, and relative prices are determined without reference to the

The Sraffa Model as a Theory of Reproduction Prices 227

standard commodity. The standard commodity as unit of measurement is therefore of no importance in analysing the formation of prices in a Sraffa economy. Thus, if the analysis is concerned with the determination of prices and effects of changes in the wage rate on relative prices, then the search for a standard commodity is pointless. Second, the idea of isolating the price-movements of individual products 'so that they could be observed as in a vacuum' is an extremely curious one. In a Sraffa economy all prices are determined simultaneously by the coefficients representing the conditions of production and the division of the surplus between wages and profit. The algebraic determination of prices ensures an inescapable interdependence between the prices of distinct commodities. In this sense the idea of isolating the price-movements of one commodity from those of all other commodities so that they could be observed 'as in a vacuum' has no meaning and it certainly provides no reason for requiring an invariant standard of prices.

In fact, the idea of isolating the price-movements of one commodity from those of all other commodities can be seriously entertained only if the simultaneous algebraic determination of prices is thought not to represent the real determinants but rather to obscure them—that is, if the real determinants are thought to lie elsewhere. In order to identify these determinants it is necessary to return to the 'peculiarities' of the production of commodities referred to above since it is precisely in terms of those 'peculiarities' that the need for a standard commodity is argued.

The peculiarities in question here arise from the manner in which processes and prices may be represented in the economy of single-product processes analysed in Part I of Sraffa's book. In such an economy each process may be completely specified by the coefficients representing the labour-time and commodity-inputs necessary to the production of one unit of output. The capital advanced per unit of output is then given by the sum of commodity-input coefficients multiplied by their prices, while the labour cost is given by the wage level and labour-time. The unit price of the commodity produced is therefore jointly determined by a set of quantities that are fixed, the commodity and labour-time coefficients, and also by quantities that are variable, i.e. wages, the rate of profit, and the prices of commodities that constitute the capital advanced. The direct contribution of labour costs to the unit price therefore varies directly with wages themselves. But the contribution of the capital advanced and the profit return on it does not vary directly with the rate of profit since its magnitude depends also on the prices of the means of production employed. Investigation of the determinants of those prices will reveal that they depend on the labour costs and returns on capital advanced in their production. This suggests that the 'peculiarities' of a commodity pertinent to an investigation of the effects of changes in distribution may be represented in the form of a series of labour-time contributions: first, the labour-time directly employed in its production; second, the labour-time directly employed in production of its means of production; third, the labour-time directly employed in the means of production of those means of production; and so on. The price of a commodity can then be represented as the sum of a convergent series of the form:

$$p = w(a_0 + a_1(1 + r) + a_2(1 + r)^2 = \ldots)$$

where the a_i represent labour contributions at different 'layers' of production, w represents wages and r is the rate of profit. Sraffa refers to this as a dated labour series, since the first coefficient gives the labour-time directly employed in the production of one unit of the commodity concerned, the second gives the labour-time directly employed in production of the means of production of that commodity, and so on.

Now, the 'peculiarities' of the production of commodities to which Sraffa refers are not the coefficients representing labour contributions at different layers of production but rather the inequalities between them. If the coefficients were all the same for a particular commodity, then its price relative to the price of its means of production would be invariant to changes in the level of wages. This condition defines the standard commodity in the Sraffa system: it is a commodity for which the ratio of its price to the price of its means of production is invariant to changes in the wage rate. It is easy to see that any commodity which requires no means of production other than itself must be a standard commodity. Sraffa shows that a composite commodity of this kind can always be found by algebraic manipulation of the equations representing the conditions of production of basics in the economy. The standard commodity has no 'peculiarities' and it therefore provides Sraffa with the means of representing prices of other commodities as determined solely by labour contributions, the wage rate, and the rate of profit. If wages are measured in terms of

The Sraffa Model as a Theory of Reproduction Prices

the standard commodity, then there is a linear relation between wages and the rate of profit. It follows that all prices can be represented as determined solely by labour contributions and the wage rate.

We can now return to the significance of the definition of the standard commodity in the Sraffa system. We have seen that it has no importance for the analysis of relative prices. The standard commodity is certainly necessary for allowing the connection between wages and profit to be represented as a linear relationship. But what is so special about a linear relationship? It has no significance for the analysis of the functioning of the economy. Since it is established by definition that the surplus is divided between wages and profit, there is nothing to be gained by showing that in terms of one particular unit of measurement an increase in money wages implies a corresponding decrease in the rate of profit or vice versa.

The key to the definition of the standard commodity does not lie in its analytic utility with regard to the determination of wages, prices, and rate of profit. But it does allow prices, wages, and profit to be expressed in terms of labour-time. Why is this important? Given the definition of the economy as, in effect, a set of linear equations in which prices, wages and rate of profit are simultaneously determined, there will be a variety of different ways in which some of these variables can be represented in terms of other variables. Since the representation in terms of labour-time has no analytical significance, it can only be regarded as important for some other reason, namely, as showing that prices, wages, and profit can indeed be expressed in terms of labour-time. It is only the qualitative, if not the ontological, primacy of labour in his conception of the economy that accounts for the importance of the standard commodity in the Sraffa system. For this reason it would be an error to regard Sraffa's book as a radical critique of the Marxist theory of value.

The Sraffa model and capitalist production

The results of the preceding discussion may be summarised as follows. We have seen first that Sraffan analysis presents a general theory of distribution as effected by the determination of commodity prices. The project for a general theory involves the conception of the economy as a totality. The notion of totality entails an organising principle of that totality which, in this case, governs or is realised in all particular cases of price determination. The effects of the specific conditions of price formation in each individual case must therefore be subsumed into the effects of a single general principle of determination. In this respect Sraffa's analysis occupies a terrain that is common to classical political economy and to marginalist and neo-classical theories of distribution. Second, the composition of the surplus is not pertinent to the division between wages and profit. In effect this means that consumption is determined by the conditions of production. The role of the conditions of production in the determination of prices is therefore established by fiat, since the structure of demand is reduced to an effect of production itself. Third, price determination is a mathematical, not an economic, process. The simultaneous algebraic determination of all prices means that temporal differences have no significance in their determination. In particular, the distinction between the prices of means of production at the beginning of the production process and their prices at the end has no pertinence. Fourth, the reduction of all production to the same period of production and the erasure of the accounting distinction between fixed and working capital are consequences of the fact that there are no enterprises or units of production but only processes. Finally, we have seen that the standard commodity as a unit of measurement is of no importance in analysing the formation of prices and that what importance it does possess is because it allows wages, prices, and profit to be represented as the products of labour-time.

The role of the standard commodity needs no further discussion, but the remaining points are sufficient to show that the analysis of price formation in Sraffa has no pertinence for the analysis of price formation under capitalism. The object of analysis in this case concerns the field of application of capitalist relations of production in which production takes the form of the production of commodities and is organised into a multiplicity of enterprises separated from each other and each constituted by a definite form of possession-in-separation of the means and conditions of production. The unity of the enterprise is the unity of a capital, and the elements of production, including labour-power, enter the production process in the form of commodities purchased by the capitalist. Effective possession involves a capacity to control the functioning of the means of production in the process of

The Sraffa Model as a Theory of Reproduction Prices   231

production, that is, it requires the performance of certain technical functions by or on the part of the possessing agent, the direction and supervision of the labour process, and, since we are dealing with commodities, the calculation of monetary costs and returns. If those functions are not performed by the capitalist or on his behalf then he ceases to have effective possession of the means of production.

Now, the project for a general theory of distribution through the determination of prices involves the conception of the economy as a totality in which, as we have seen, all instances of price formation must be governed by the organising principle of that totality. Thus, to posit a general theory of distribution as pertinent to the analysis of capitalist price determination is to suppose, on the one hand, that enterprises are separated from each other and that therefore calculation must be effective at the level of the enterprise and subject to exigencies constituted at that level; but it is to suppose, on the other hand, that the effectivity of calculation and the exigencies to which it is subjected are reducible to the realisation of a pre-given general principle. We have seen in the chapter on capitalist calculation that Marx's conception of capitalism as subject to the action of definite tendencies involves a contradiction of this kind. But the problem here is in no way peculiar to Marxism. It arises for any analysis which posits a conception of the economy as a totality as pertinent to the analysis of price determination under capitalism by posing the problem of a general theory of prices.

Second, it is clear that a Sraffan economy is essentially non-monetary, in the sense that there are no monetary or financial exigencies pertinent to the determination of prices and the pattern of distribution. The theory of money is discussed in other chapters and it will be sufficient here to note that the pertinence of money to the actions of economic agents in a commodity economy arises from the circumstance that their sales and purchases are separated in time; the act of sale does not involve the seller in a simultaneous act of purchase, and vice versa. It is precisely these temporal discrepancies which require that we distinguish the prices of means of production at the beginning of a production period from their prices at the end. There can be no monetary pertinences in a Sraffan economy since, as we have seen, there are no effective temporal discrepancies and the value of capital advanced is determined simultaneously with the prices of the commodities it helps to produce. Furthermore, monetary exigencies arise in the conditions of circulation between economic agents. Not only does the time of circulation have no pertinence to a Sraffan economy, but there are no strictly determinate economic agents between whom circulation could be said to take place since there are no determinate and effective economic boundaries between processes which may be partitioned and combined by algebraic manipulation.

Analysis of price formation in the absence of monetary exigencies can be of no direct help in dealing with price formation in monetary economies. The industrial capitalist, for example, makes wage payments at regular intervals in accordance with the institutional conditions governing wages on the one hand and the composition of his labour force on the other—e.g. the division between salaried and non-salaried staff. His sales and his purchases of means of production will be governed by technical properties of the production process, e.g. the period of production, and by the characteristics of the markets in which he buys and sells. Thus, technical differences between the sectors of production and the regularities of wage payments ensure that the sales and purchases of capitalists will be separated in time and that the patterning of that separation will be different for enterprises in different branches of production. Much of Marx's discussion in volume 2 of *Capital* is devoted to these points. To suppose that Sraffan analysis is pertinent to the analysis of price formation and distribution under capitalism would be to suppress the effects of the temporal discrepancies between the sales and purchases of economic agents and, in particular, the costs that those discrepancies impose.

Finally, if there are no enterprises but only processes then the question of the forms and conditions of existence of effective possession of the means and conditions of production in capitalist enterprises cannot arise. If there are no capitalists then there can be no capitalist calculation and no problems of the direction and supervision of the labour process by the capitalist or his agents. The forms and effectivity of capitalist calculation, direction, and supervision are not given in the fact of capitalist possession itself. They are always subject to definite conditions, e.g. the conditions of capitalist calculation discussed in this volume, the effects of legislation, and the outcomes of struggles between capitalists and wage labourers. If there are no enterprises then such conditions have no pertinence for the analysis of the conditions of production, price formation, and distribution.

Conclusion

Marxism and strategy

The purpose of this concluding discussion is to outline and assess the political implications of the theoretical arguments and positions we have developed in this text. We began this project because of the role played by debates about the condition and prospects of the British economy in determining the political stance and positions of sections of the Left in this country. A specification of the structure of British capitalism and its likely paths of development was conceived by us as a necessary basis on which to begin the analysis of the present conjuncture. In view of the importance attached to economic questions on the Left we found the absence of any substantial body of Marxist analysis of the British economy a striking paradox. This absence was and is a real one. Despite the renaissance of Marxist economic writing alluded to in the introduction, there is in modern Marxism no serious analysis of the structure of definite advanced capitalist economies. Marxist economic theory here and elsewhere is dominated by debates concerning problems of the architecture and interpretation of *Capital*. Our return to *Capital*, to fundamental questions of Marxist theory and not merely economic theory, has been no diversion from the task of 'concrete' work which others are undertaking. This 'concrete' work simply does not exist. Many texts purport to be about Britain or 'contemporary capitalism', but that reference is only possible if one accepts the pertinence of a certain mode of theoretical discourse, that is, of the abstraction of the concrete in thought and the existence of the concrete in the form of the generalities in thought. The nature of the entities constituted in discourse is a theoretical question. Thus the problem of the structure of definite capitalist economies is impertinent, a non-problem, if all capitalist countries can be considered as exemplars of an essentially common structure, the capitalist mode of production. It follows that in such a form of discourse debates about, for example, the nature of the conception of the effects of the accumulation process in *Capital* can figure as debates about the nature and consequences of capitalist social relations.

No Marxist discussion of capitalist social relations is possible without taking a position on certain problems as to their nature as relations, for example the status of the laws of tendency. These problems can only be theoretical and they must centre on the crucial text of Marxist economic theory, *Capital*. The absence of substantial Marxist analyses of the British economy must seem paradoxical unless we accept the notion that *Capital* is the appropriation of the concrete in thought, that what is thought therein is the concrete in essence. If one does accept that notion then resolving problems of the architecture and interpretation of *Capital* is to resolve questions about the nature of capitalism itself.

We began our work in the conviction that the resolution of definite problems in *Capital* was necessary in order to begin any analysis of the British economy. As indicated in the Introduction, we conceived this examination of *Capital* as a necessary precondition for two reasons: (1) to counter the theoretical effects of evolutionist and historicist misreadings of *Capital* in the field of economics; (2) to rectify areas of *Capital* which were erroneous or insufficiently developed and which constituted an obstacle to the analysis of certain important aspects of contemporary capitalist relations (e.g. money, credit, finance capital, etc.). As a result of the theoretical work we have undertaken, we now find our point of departure problematic and insufficient. As we have attempted to demonstrate in the body of this text, the problems with *Capital* go far deeper than those of certain limited errors or of areas requiring development. They concern the very conception of the capitalist mode of production as an entity whose effectivities are necessary and are given in the concept of its basic structure. They go beyond propositions within the field of 'economics' and concern the necessity of antagonistic contradiction between classes of economic agents as political forces.

The depth of these problems reveals the extent to which historicist and evolutionist readings of *Capital* are not 'misreadings'. They render, sometimes accurately, sometimes as travesty, certain central elements of the discourse of *Capital*. We have stressed and must repeat that *Capital* is not a unitary discourse governed by a principle of coherence (as emanation of an author-subject or a problematic-subject). The discourse of *Capital* establishes positions which it subverts, contradicts, and fails to substantiate; often a proposition and its contrary can be found within a few pages. The elements of the discourse of *Capital* that we find problematic are not peripheral to the text as it is written; equally, they do not exhaust it. Our criticism of *Capital* is not a rejection of the discourse as a whole. What *is* most emphatically rejected is the discursive entity, the capitalist mode of production. This is an entity conceived as existence appropriate to abstraction, which makes possible, i.e. non-paradoxical, the paradox of the centrality of economic relations for Marxist political discourse and the absence from that discourse of any specification of the determinate economic structures of capitalist countries.

What is specified (and is not seen as paradoxical) is a concept of the capitalist mode of production. Capitalism forms the pages of *Capital*. The relation of this capitalism to political analysis and strategy is a particular one. Definite economies are conceived as exemplars of capitalism; the degree of development and crystallisation of the effectivities of capitalism-as-generality is the form in which specifity is accorded to economies in such an analysis. It is here that debates between Marxist economists about capitalist economic relations have centred. The discourse of *Capital* leaves the tendencies of the capitalist mode of production, their nature, interrelation, and effects, as an open and unresolved field of debate. It is these debates on the nature of tendency which give Marxist economic theory the semblance of vitality and of bearing on contemporary capitalist relations. Debates on the nature of 'monopoly' or 'late' capitalism concern the degree of maturity of the tendencies and their effects. Reference to definite economies concerns the question of the operation of these tendencies, the extent to which concrete conditions modify or defer them. Thus, for example, Mandel's *Late Capitalism* consists, in essence, in an attempt to argue that the terminal tendencies of capitalism have merely been counteracted temporarily and have in fact been reinforced by the unprecedented expansion and development of capitalist economies since the Second World War.

This role of the concept of the capitalist mode of production should not surprise us; it is no recent degeneration of Marxism into economic scholasticism. This conception of capitalism as a set of terminal tendencies has had a very definite political pertinence within the Marxist movement. A pertinence which has been established by conditions which are not themselves theoretical and which this theoretical position did not determine.

Our model of analysis of a definite national economy was Lenin's *The Development of Capitalism in Russia*. This text, as an interconnection of economic analysis and political implications, served as the benchmark of what we thought an appropriate investigation of a national economy should be. Here we encounter two paradoxes. First, Lenin's work has no flawed and undeveloped rival, let alone an equal, in writing on a developed capitalist economy. Second, Lenin's text is in essence negative, a demonstration of *what is not going to happen*. It is a refutation of the economic foundations of Narodnik and Legal Marxist political strategies. It counters economic theories as a means of conducting and resolving the terms of a political argument, it does so with a formidable battery of means from Marx's theory of reproduction to Zemstvo statistics. As Lenin's writings on capitalism in agriculture in Russia developed, so did the thesis, made possible by his critique of populist and Legal Marxist economic and political essentialisms in *The Development of Capitalism*, that there was no necessary and inevitable economic resolution of the class struggle into a definite political form. Lenin's analyses opened up a field of potential bases for political struggle and the construction of an anti-Tsarist and anti-big-bourgeois political movement. But Lenin's work provides no alternative economic theory distinct from Marx's. Consider Lenin's later writings pertinent to developed capitalism. Texts like *Imperialism* and *Imperialism and the Split in Socialism* generalise the analysis of the degeneration of capitalism to a world scale. Imperialism defers and accelerates the terminal contradictions of advanced capitalism, making its existence in the metropoles of capital ultimately impossible as a result of the effects of imperialist war on the mass of the proletariat. Lenin explains the absence of a successful revolutionary movement in the metropoles of capitalism by the deferment of the class polarisation which ought to be produced by the tendencies of 'parasitic and decaying' monopoly capitalism. This deferment is made possible by the use of imperialist super-profits to corrupt the aristocracy of labour. Chauvinist social democracy is the product of this corruption. In these analyses Lenin continues to found the political analysis of metropolitan capitalism on the necessity of class polarisation, a necessity generated by the economic tendencies of capitalism and induced through the medium of war.

Nevertheless, despite the theoretical foundations of the strategy in a necessary polarisation to be generated by the economy, it is war and national crises which create the field of action for revolutionary socialism. War and national crisis create a specific field of political calculation and practice, a field the specificity and complexity of which Lenin insists upon even if he does not explain it:

> To imagine that social revolution is *conceivable* without revolts by small nations in the colonies and in Europe, without revolutionary outbursts by a section of the petty bourgeoisie *with all its prejudices*, without the movement of politically non-conscious proletarian or semi-proletarian masses against oppression by landowners, the church and the monarchy, against national oppression, etc.,—to imagine all this is to *repudiate social revolution.* So one army lines up in one place and says, 'We are for imperialism' and another, somewhere else and says, 'We are for socialism', and that will be a social revolution! . . . whoever expects a 'pure' social revolution will *never* live to see it. (*The Discussion of Self-Determination Summed Up*, pp. 355–6)

Political calculation must act on and respect this complexity. This complexity provides, moreover, the *means* for revolutionary struggle and insurrection, e.g. the basis for political alliances forming a revolutionary bloc, for splits in the political line, policy, and armed forces of the ruling political bloc and the state.

In essence, three dominant strategic conjunctures have dominated the Marxist movement in this century.

 1 Revolutionary struggles have had the objective of an insurrectionary seizure of power, the conditions for this objective being created by a national crisis, a crisis classically taking the form of war, either inter-imperialist wars or wars of national liberation. Generally such struggles have been successfully conducted in relatively backward and peripheral capitalist states, or in the colonial and semi-colonial regions of world capitalism.

 2 Essentially defensive struggles have attempted the preservation of parliamentary democratic forms and freedom of organisation of the labour movement, and have been conducted with or without an alliance with non-Marxist democratic forces

against an ultra-rightist threat.

3 Conditions in advanced capitalist countries have been such that relatively stable parliamentary democratic forms prevail and there is no national crisis which splits the ruling bloc.

In the first two strategic conjunctures conditions of political calculation and practice are created which have only a marginal connection with the theoretical positions advanced in *Capital* (however these positions are conceived). Thus, while anti-imperialist and national liberation struggles are connected to the theory of the capitalist mode of production by the theses of the theory of imperialism (that 'parasitic and decaying' monopoly capitalism in the metropoles depends on the export of capital, etc. to its colonial and semi-colonial satellites, that the competition for division of the world between the capitalist great powers produces imperialist war which operates to sever the 'weakest links' in the chain of capitalist states), the strategy of these struggles does not directly depend on that theoretical connection. The objects of calculation and struggle exist and can be acted on whether or not the classical Marxist-Leninist theory of imperialism is correct. The theory of the capitalist mode of production is paralleled by the theory of national liberation struggle or people's war. Mao Tse-tung, in a text like *On Contradiction* (cited by Althusser as exemplification of the conception of 'complex totality'), attempts to theorise this parallel. What he does is to *parallel* the theoretically untransformed necessary political polarisation of bourgeoisie and proletariat as an effect of the capitalist mode of production by a complexity existing outside those effects; a complexity which is due to the existence of feudal, semi-feudal, and quasi-capitalist forms.

Where Marxism has confronted the problems of the structure of definite national economies it has been in the form of registering the effects of imperialism and the development of capitalism. It has registered these effects in the strategic field of the national crisis. These crises provide a definite strategic field of action; struggles and battle lines drawn without direct reference to the confrontation of two classes of economic agents as political forces, bourgeoisie and proletariat.

Under conditions where such a national-political crisis is absent, developed capitalist relations of production and relatively stable parliamentary democratic forms prevailing, Marxism has faced its classic political dilemma. Either forms of political struggle and

Conclusion 239

political issues that can be developed and realised within these economic and political forms predominate (forms of struggle and issues which can never be except in agitation and sloganising ones of a simple opposition, capitalism versus socialism, bourgeoisie versus proletariat); or the necessity of the revolutionary and insurrectionary road is insisted upon, and the possible political issues which could be fought and perhaps won are discarded as 'reformist'.

For Bernstein socialism provided morale, the motivation to struggle for reforms which could never equal the goal. For Trotsky reformist demands were merely a means to demonstrate the necessity of the revolutionary road to the workers, capitalism versus socialism. It is in relation to this dilemma that Marxist economic theory has entered to play a definite political role. The tendencies of the capitalist mode of production have been deployed to produce a 'guarantee' of the revolutionary/insurrectionary road. The necessity of capitalist collapse served Kautsky as a means of defense of the 'orthodox' position in the SPD no less than it has served modern Trotskyism as a guarantee of the necessity of a specifically 'revolutionary' stance. Here the nature of the tendencies of the capitalist mode of production is central to *political* debate. Thus the debate between Bernstein and Kautsky is in large measure a debate about the reality of terminal tendencies in capitalism. Bernstein counters one evolutionism and essentialism with another, modern capitalism has evolved beyond the sphere of the classic contradictions of *Capital*.

In this book, on the contrary, in challenging the essentialism of necessary tendencies in capitalism we are not arguing for any necessary stability of capitalist economies or for any logic of evolution into a benign form. Some variant of the necessary effects of the tendencies of the capitalist mode of production in creating the conditions for socialism (although this need imply no technical 'breakdown' of the economy) serves as the foundation for most revolutionary strategies for struggle under conditions of capitalist political stability. Such strategies are dominated by economism even if they are not 'economist' in the simple sense of giving primacy to trade union struggle (although it *is* this latter 'economism' that most of these strategies amount to in practice). This economism is central because it dominates the conception of the means by which the conditions of revolutionary *political* struggle can be created. Developments in economic relations (maturation of the tendencies) create the conditions for the economic polarisation of classes, for economic crises. This economic polarisation and these economic crises induce political polarisation and political crises. The evolution of the economy guarantees the revolutionary left its strategic class bloc and its revolutionary *point d'appui*.

This position explains the possibility of the political rationality of SPD's strategy of non-cooperation in the Reichstag and building the organisation and support of the party. It also explains the rationale for various Trotskyist strategies of 'raising consciousness', building the movement, and denouncing all attempts to win and exercise power within the political conditions of parliamentary democratic states. This is a possible strategy only if it is supposed that other political conditions are possible and necessary. The tendency of the capitalist mode of production to evolve in a certain direction (however conceived in detail) therefore serves as the direct theoretical foundation of a certain range of political lines. It is the condition of their plausibility. Denying the effectivity and existence of any *necessary* tendencies in the capitalist mode of production is therefore a radical challenge to the foundation of certain political positions widely influential on the Left. This is where questions of Marxist theory and economics directly intervene in current political debates. Where, as in *The Development of Capitalism*, the challenge to certain economic theories undercuts the political strategies based upon them.

Few groups on the British Left would attempt to argue that the classic Leninist theory of the national crisis and the possibility of an insurrectionary conjuncture is applicable to this country today. There are no such planes of fracture evident in the bloc of ruling political forces (including the Parliamentary Labour Party), nor any division in the armed forces of the state (and the population is almost wholly disarmed). No one in his right mind would consider that the conditions for a revolutionary seizure of power exist in this country (even on the criteria of such an ultra-leftist text as *Armed Insurrection*, the idea is absurd after a quick inspection of the conditions). If, however, the theory of the economically determined political polarisation of classes is also inapplicable, then the position of 'revolutionary' politics (that conditions of a revolutionary conjuncture will be created by the development of the economy) is untenable. Such an inapplicability indicates the need for radical strategic rethinking. The central problems to be thought out are the *construction* of a strategic power bloc in the absence of its necessity, and the seizure and the exercise of power under conditions other than those of armed insurrection. This dilemma has confronted British revolutionary socialism at least since the last war and the Labour Government of 1945. Economism has served as a means of evasion of it.

In later sections of this conclusion we will deal more directly with questions of political strategy in Britain today. Before we do so we will examine in some detail the more specific theoretical-political consequences of our interventions and analyses.

Theoretical/political implications

We will begin by reviewing the theoretical effects of our critical work on *Capital*. Volume One develops four main lines of critique of *Capital*.

1 It challenges the conception of mode of production as a totality which has inscribed in its structure certain necessary effects, these effects being assimilable in a general concept.

2 It challenges the 'law of value' (arguing that this 'law' has no rigorous formulation or unambiguous effects in *Capital*) and the theory of exploitation and accumulation.

3 The concept of 'tendencies' as necessary and progressively developing effects of the totality or structure is challenged; this concept of tendency is made possible by the conception of totality criticised in 1 and the relation of its phenomena as processes deriving from the effects of the fundamental process of the totality (determination of production by labour-time → exploitation → accumulation) summed up in the concepts connected with 'value'.

4 We reject the classic concept of classes as categories of economic agents/human individuals ultimately impelled to political unity and action by the effects of the economic structure of the totality and crystallising as political forces around 'interests' which are imposed upon and given to the agents by the structure.

The conception of mode of production as a totality, with certain effects inscribed in its structure and the specification of those effects in certain necessary economic processes (processes ultimately determined by labour-time in production and its specifically capitalist form of expression in the accumulation of profits deriving from exploited labour), creates a homogeneous field of realisation of those effects. The economic conceived as the 'total social capital' is this homogeneous field. All capitalist economies are exemplifications of this field of effects, all are equally determined by those basic processes and tendencies which express themselves as movements within the 'total social capital'.

The 'society' of this 'total social capital' is an abstraction, a concrete abstraction ever-always appropriate to its effects. It is a 'society' composed of human subjects acting as agents or personifications of elements of the structure. All capitalists are merely bearers of capital, moments of its totality in movement. Workers appear as subordinate agents, whose labour-power is purchased by representatives of portions of this totality and by means of a definite 'variable' portion of the total capital. Ultimately, all capitalists and all workers are ever-always identical, bearers of the same 'character masks'. How they function as bearers depends upon the conditions imposed by movements in the totality itself. Classes, like the 'society' they support, are concrete generalities. They are also concrete generalities composed of individuals who are acted through by the structure, they are the sphere of realisation of its necessary effects. This realm of individual human subjects as bearers of places in the structure is a necessary correlate of the way the structure itself is conceived.

Thus, the composition of the totality dominant in *Capital* creates an essential general structure of which all forms of capitalist social relations must be exemplars, and reduces the economic agents to being 'personifications' of movements within the totality. Several consequences follow from this.

1 The conditions of existence of the economy must be conceived (if this conception is to be consistently realised) as effects of the totality/economy itself. Thus, the calculations agents engage in are derived from the structure. The supply of labour-power is regulated by the structure itself—capitalism, therefore, has an inbuilt tendency to create 'relative surplus population' which forms an 'industrial reserve army'.

2 The composition of social production, its division into branches of production and the relative importance of the different branches, is discounted as a significant determination of the system. It is placed outside the theory, as it must be if the capitalist mode of production is to be conceived as a

generality with determinate and necessary effects (this composition is merely the object through which the basic processes, operating irrespective of the type of branches and their relative weight, act).

3 The relationships between the different forms of capital, industrial, commercial, financial and landed, are conceived as necessarily given—structured by the dominance of production (labour-time) and as merely sharing in a totality of surplus value created within the sphere of production.

The rejection of this conception of totality creates the condition for the appearance of entities with a new discursive status and a change in their theoretical pertinence. These entities are: (1) 'national' economies; (2) the structure of branches of production and their constitution into enterprises; (3) classes of economic agents. We will consider each of these entities and their theoretical pertinence in turn.

'National' economies

Capital creates the possibility of conceiving the capitalist mode of production as a general and homogeneous structure. Ultimately the 'total-social-capital' level of analysis is that of the totality of capitalist relations. The conditions of existence and operation of this general and homogeneous structure are to be found within the field of its effects. Marx argues in the '1857 Introduction' that it is necessary *not* to begin with the definite forms of an economy, its population, trade, etc. Rather it is necessary as the result of a process of formation by means of abstraction of the concepts of the economic relations pertaining to show how these definite forms are determined by and a function of basic economic laws. Plainly we are not going to argue that the alternative to *Capital* is the numbering of people or pigs. The problem is the mode of effectivity of the basic economic concepts in the method proposed in the '1857 Introduction'. As we have argued, this creates the problem of a 'privileged' domain of causes, the effects of the generality-structure, and the mode in which this domain is related to definite social formations. As we have shown, either privilege obliterates or subordinates any determinations outside itself, or privilege is subverted and negated by these determinations.

A classic example is the law of 'relative surplus population'.

Portions of the discourse of *Capital* suppose a necessary tendency toward the creation of an industrial reserve army, a permanent pool of unemployed labour as a reserve for expansion and a means of regulation of wages. However, the working population and the total labour-power it can supply are in no way determined by the actual or potential demand for labour-power nor are they determined exclusively by any 'laws' of the capitalist mode of production. The number of workers, the hours they can work, are determined as much by custom, legislation, emigration, and immigration as by anything else: this pertains to the labour supply of a definite capitalist country. The 'capitalist mode of production' has *no* determinate labour supply. That is because only capitalist national economies establish the conditions of determination and these conditions are in large measure 'non-economic'. Marx recognises this:

> if . . . labour generally were reduced to a rational amount, and proportioned to different sections of the working class according to age and sex, the working population to hand would be absolutely insufficient for the carrying on of national production on its present scale. The great majority of the labourers now 'unproductive' would have to turned into 'productive' ones. (*Capital*, vol. 1, p. 637)

Marxism has consistently neglected 'national' economies as units of analysis, rejecting the economic-policy standpoint of mercantilism and classical political economy. Marxists argue that phenomena at this level merely create the basis for theoretical illusions and obscure the reality of capitalism as a general phenomenon. Thus, while nations may obtain wealth through merchants' capitalist trade they merely redistribute the values produced and in no way add to that totality.

What are 'national' economies as a level of analysis? They are the level at which certain crucial parameters and conditions of operation of an economy based on capitalist relations of production are determined; these determinations are various and are by no means necessarily 'economic' (in the classic sense). The concept of 'national' economy does not designate an essence (any more than does the concept 'nation'—moreover the term 'national' is merely one of convenience). What defines such an economy are the factors which operate to determine and delimit the forms and conditions of economic performance within a region. These factors are not given and may vary. Take money: under conditions where money takes a commodity form, public policy can determine the status of this form (coining, weights, debasement, etc.) but it cannot control the *supply* of the money commodity (except by having a monopoly of the appropriate metal mines). Under conditions where the money function effectively operates through the capacity to create and restrict credit the money supply is a function of the monetary and fiscal policy of the state, and of the degree to which it can limit the generation of credit within the financial system. Similarly, the level of analysis pertinent may change with respect to a given region. In the next thirty years possible trends in the direction of economic integration and the growth of institutions of European state power in the economic sphere may make the EEC, rather than the United Kingdom, the relevant unit of analysis for the determination of certain crucial conditions of economic operation.

Central in determining the conditions of operation of an economy based on private property and the production of commodities by means of wage labour have been the activities of the state. State power was essential in creating the conditions of existence of generalised commodity production and exchange, the separation of a significant portion of the producers from effective possession of the means of production. Let us briefly list certain of the parameters of operation of capitalist forms of economy which can be determined through or affected by state policy.

The regulation of the supply of labour-power. Central here is the creation of a definite state territory closed by frontiers, the population being assigned a 'nationality', being regulated, identified, and numerated. In Europe this process began with the absolutist monarchy of Louis XIV. Similarly, state policy, in establishing a necessity to work and measures for the relief of the incapable and unemployed, can create a labour force. At the same time as the French state created a national territory and frontiers, it attempted to create a labour force, consigning beggars and indigents to the Hôpital-Général. Through policies on nationality, the regulation of immigration and the encouragement or discouragement of emigration, policies on population, incentives or disincentives to produce children, policies for the regulation of labour, who must and who need not or must not work, the hours and conditions of work possible, states can regulate the size and composition of the labour force and can limit the total of labour-power it can give.

Clearly, the state alone does not determine by policy all the conditions of supply, nor are policies necessarily effective. Population policies have had notoriously variable success. Other factors determine the supply of *wage* labour. Thus non-working wives and non-commodity and non-wage sectors of the economy, or regions outside the state territory, may constitute potential labour reserves. It is from these sectors, rather than the reserve army of unemployed, that the labourers necessary for the unprecedented growth in European industrial production and the accompanying expansion of non-manufacturing employment and public service since the last war were drawn. These conditions of supply are affected by the specific features of the regional territory in question; custom may strongly resist wives going out to work, for example, non-capitalist farmers have different commitments and capacities to resist the 'attractions' or necessities of wage labour. In no way, however, can the labour supply actually or potentially available be made simply an effect of the capitalist mode of production.

The form and supply of money and credit. The relation of money to public policy has been extensively discussed in the body of the text and we will not return to it here. We will merely stress two points.

1 Non-commodity money makes public policy a vital determining factor in economic performance, the state's monetary and fiscal policy becomes a vital issue of political division. This is, of course, also true under conditions where the money function is performed by a produced commodity, but here questions concern either the state's *regulation* of that commodity, state monopoly versus private mints, debasement, import and export of bullion, etc., or the *choice* between one 'precious metal and another, for example the controversies over the demonetarisation of silver in the USA at the turn of the last century.

2 At stake in these controversies is the fact that the form of money, and the conditions of its supply and regulation involve *distributive* relations; money does not merely 'represent' social wealth, it is a means of its appropriation, thus the return to the

Gold Standard at pre-war parity against the dollar in Britain was a rentiers' charter (the distributional effects in question stemming from the need to fix interest rates at such a level as would defend the exchange rate given the 'overvaluation' of sterling—Keynes recognised these distributional effects very clearly in 'The economic consequences of Mr. Churchill').

Taxation. Taxation has a variety of possible forms, policy objectives, and economic effects. We will simply give some examples here. Taxation is almost universally recognised as having distributional effects: direct versus indirect taxation, the degree of progressivity of direct taxation and its effects, the relative incidence of tax between different categories of income earners and wealth holders—all these questions have provoked political controversy and struggle. The forms of taxation of corporate wealth affect both economic calculation and performance; the nature of 'depreciation' allowances account to a considerable extent for the relatively high ratio of internal funding in British companies. These allowances amount to a tax subsidy to capitalist enterprises, and the ratio of internal funding thus produced does not generally reflect a high profitability. There is little evidence that these allowances induce additional investment in manufacturing, as they singularly fail to differentiate between forms of capital or forms of investment. Taxation policy can create 'privileged' conditions of operation for certain classes of enterprises; the exempt nature of building-society interest attracts the funds of small savers and maintains the present structure of the housing market in this country (it should be noted that this form of privilege does not unduly injure the clearing banks since in a closed financial system deposits interconnect and flow through them). Particular forms of tax have been designed to serve as the attempted instruments of specific economic policies, for example, SET. 'Demand management' in the period 1945–60 worked largely through the manipulation of tax levels, through rates of purchase tax and other indirect taxes.

The law of property and company law. Marxists have classically considered law as being merely the juridical expression of the relations of production and the relations of actual possession involved therein. We have indicated at length that the problem of what a 'capital' is cannot be separated from questions of legal definition. The legal subject of property as a natural person endowed with rights of disposal over things is hardly an adequate concept to deal with modern forms of property rights. The concept of 'capitalist' and the modern Roman Law concept of the subject of property right as possessions do indeed correspond in large measure. The creation of corporate forms of possession by legislation has broken that correspondence. In the legal regulation of companies and rights to claims over them (bank deposits, insurance policies, dividends, etc.) is a sphere of effectivity of public policy which Marxism ignores at its peril. The minimal legal regulation and policing of financial capital in this country may go some way to explain the failure of British Marxists to comprehend the importance of this area of struggle, but it does not fully explain it.

Marxists have tended to treat the development of limited liability as a function of development of the forces of production. This legal form appears as a necessary 'expression' of the concentration of capital. Such an analysis is naïvely apolitical; law becomes an 'expression', a recognition of what is, rather than an arena of struggle, a form with potential effects. The legal conditions prior to the Companies Act of 1844 were the product of a political struggle to try to *limit*, by unlimited liability, the forms of speculative organisation of capital. It was intended thereby to protect the creditor and also the investor against himself, and to ensure the stability of relations of loan and credit. The Bubble Act of 1720 sought (and failed) to prevent speculative financial crises and the disruption of trade by hitting at the organisational forms of speculation. By 1844 investors were at the mercy of speculative projectors using the existing forms. The Acts of 1844, 1855–6, and 1862 were primarily devised to protect the investor and to secure the integrity of the invested capital. They were in essence a by-product of the 'unacceptable face' of the railway and mining share booms. But in no sense were they made *necessary* by the forms of organisation of production and finance then dominant. Individual possession, partnership, and mortgage were adequate organisational forms for industrial capital (manufacturers did not press for incorporation of limited liability).Institutions like Lloyds demonstrate the capacity to organise complex financial enterprises without the joint-stock legal form.

This is *par excellence* an arena where the 'productionism' of classical Marxism has blinded it to the reality of the political struggles involved in the legal regulation of the organisation of capital and the definition of property right. Companies Acts are not merely a matter for capitalists or a *fait accompli* enforced by the level of development of the forces of production. The economic consequences of the joint-stock/limited-liability legislation have been very important and in no sense confined to the objects envisaged by the drafters of the legislation. Currently we face a position where the investors, possessors of the share capital of a company, can if sufficiently united initiate a motion for its winding-up at the annual meeting. Similarly, the shareholders may nominate the management board of the company. The share capital and the assets possessed by many companies bear no relation to one another. In the British Leyland crash a fraction of the shareholders sought to dispose of these assets. Company legislation could limit shareholders' rights in this matter (a radical restriction of shares to what they tend to be in fact for the individual investor, a marketable financial asset with a yield, would make the company in effect the possessor of itself; proposals to limit shareholders' rights in a less radical way are advanced in the Bullock Report). This is becoming a crucial question as the operations of financial institutions and holding-companies in the secondary market are changing the meaning of 'shareholder' (that the institutions supported the Board in the Leyland case demonstrates nothing, one could equally cite the case of Crittal-Hope). Maverick petty-bourgeois small investors and asset-strippers can operate in the way they have and pose a threat to the jobs of thousands of workers not by any logic of the capitalist mode of production, but by reason of the legal form in which companies are organised. Company organisation and the rights of 'property' have been changed by legislation and can be changed again. The legal concept of 'property' is not homogeneous. The capital of a company in which shareholders' rights in respect of the constitution and 'winding-up' are radically restricted (as they are for example in the American states of Delaware, Illinois, and New Jersey) is no less an exclusive 'private' possession, but it is possession with different rights. In like manner the capital of a company partially or wholly owned by the workers is still an exclusive private possession.

We have merely indicated four fundamental conditions of economic operation which can in some measure be determined by state policy: the supply of labour power, of money and credit, the distribution of categories of income, the form and rights of possession of capital. These indications are just that, examples, they are not meant to be considered as exhaustive. We have chosen these four for a very good reason. Marxist literature has been considerably occupied recently with the role of state intervention in the economy, with the rise of the 'welfare' state, and economic management. This literature predominantly sees the state as a functional mechanism made necessary by the development of monopoly capitalism, and as an instrument to counteract the effects of the basic underlying tendencies of capitalism, its policies being directed toward the deferment or melioration of crisis. As a result the effects of state policy are conceptually re-assimilated to the necessary logic of the capitalist mode of production. The *differential* effect of the policies of states on the conditions of economic performance tends to be neglected as a result. Also, the effectivity of state policy on the economy tends to be considered as in large measure a recent innovation.

The pertinence of the four examples chosen is that they are equally conditions established by the so-called *laissez-faire* state. These four conditions are crucial parameters for any economy operating by commodity production and exchange. Thus, for example, the attempt to *return* to the Gold Standard was a public policy with definite economic conditions of its operation and very wide effects on the operation of the economy. Public policy had to *create* the conditions for the operation of an apparently 'automatic' commodity-money system, this system had implications for the domestic credit supply and for foreign trade which could only be enforced by public policy (it is interesting to note that these implications were most clearly recognised and resisted not by the Labour movement but by sections of *banking* capital).

To take another example, the creation of a 'labour force' always implied as a counterpart of the regulation of labour the regulation of idleness and poverty. The 'welfare' state reflects a change in policy objectives, not a change in the economic parameter to which policy is directed. The *laissez-faire* New Poor Law involved a massive investment in its institutions and their operation (it was moreover an investment which singularly failed to achieve the policy objectives set). We do not wish to imply that the state has always been with us and that there have been no serious changes in the means and objects of state policy. We have noted a central change produced by the transformation in the form of money.

Economic 'management' changes its form with a credit-money system and a developed 'closed' financial system (a universe of transferable deposits and accounts; loans and credit expanding the universe). In a similar fashion the dependence of a significant portion of sales and purchases on consumer credit creates the condition for management of demand by means of regulation of the credit system.

It is just as important to stress that while state policy and state power *can* affect these fundamental conditions of operation of an economy not all states have the capacity to do so and not all effects correspond to policy objectives. The concept of 'national' economy is not an essence. The effectivity of states in establishing the parameters of economic operation is variable and can vary between one dimension of policy and another. The existence of a state in no sense guarantees the existence of a 'national' economy; this depends on the effect of many determinants. Mexico, in the latter part of the nineteenth century, had for a considerable period no internal control of its public debt and finances, no effective regulation or numbering of its population. Luxemburg's economy has been almost wholly dependent on the conditions established by the European Coal and Steel Community, the EEC and its larger neighbours. Policies may in no sense correspond in their effects to the objectives to which they were directed, and Colbert's economic *dirigisme* is a case in point; the instruments of policy were indeed established, but they tended to limit rather than promote French colonial and commercial expansion, linking commerce with the state's demands for revenue and all too directly with military power and conquest. Another more spectacular example of the effect of state policy on the conditions of economic performance in Paraguay's war with the Triple Alliance (1865–70), fought in the first instance to acquire more favourable territory from Uruguay. The effect of this war was to decimate the population of Paraguay, reduce its territory, and turn it into an economic backwater.

The importance of 'national' economy as a concept is twofold:

1 The concept of national economy specifies what determines the conditions and forms of capitalist production within a definite territory (thus both Sweden and South Korea have laws regulating the supply of labour-power, but their nature and effects are rather different), and state policy affects the economic

conjuncture within that territory—factors like degree of unemployment, balance of trade, distribution of income, etc., fall within the domain of conditions subject to public policy at least in part. To the extent that economic conjunctures establish conditions of political conjunctures the 'national' economy is a level of determination which must be considered. The national economies of, say, Japan and Spain by no means have the same structure or the same determinations of their economic-political issues of struggle, yet both operate predominantly by means of capitalist relations of production.

2 The 'economic' policy of the state is an arena of political struggle and dispute; for example, the Immigration Acts restrict the labour force in a definite way. Opposition to their racist basis cannot ignore the fact that control of the labour force through nationality is a precondition of any element of planning of labour supply whether devoted to capitalist or socialist objectives. The fact that the UK is a national economy imposes constraints on the positions which can be struggled for. An unlimited right of entry and residence for Commonwealth citizens radically limits manpower planning and involves an element of *laissez-faire* in labour supply. Manpower planning, however, does not necessitate racism, the cynical denial of citizenship rights to oppressed (black) minorities abroad or the exclusion of (black) dependants of citizens. We have taken this example to show that the national economy level of political calculation does not concern merely 'economic' issues. It further indicates that one objective may constrain another, that attempting to maintain full employment and permit free right of entry to an indeterminate number of people must evidently involve problems.

National economy is a concept the pertinence of which is politically determined. It locates a range of determinants of and constraints on socialist policy and practice. It locates an arena of struggle and a range of issues of struggle concerned with the economic and political effects of state policy and state power. We have attempted to show that this range of effects is *specific*, that it is determined in part within the parameters of a definite territory by state policies which are open to struggle and is not merely a necessary effect of the basic structure of the capitalist mode of production. We have also attempted to show that it is important.

Companies Acts, Immigration Acts, etc., are an essential field of struggle for the Left; at stake is the determination of conditions of operation of the economy which can affect both the livelihood of the mass of the working people and the political prospects of struggle for socialism. It is this level which is not only not theorised in *Capital* but to which certain of the forms of theorisation in *Capital* (forms which are not secondary aberrations) constitute an obstacle.

Although we have concentrated in considering the 'national' economy level on the effects of state policy, this concept is not confined to these effects. Within definite state territories and regions there are other specific determinants of economic-political conjunctures. Significant in this respect are: the relative dominance of forms of capital, the differentiation into branches, degree of dependence on foreign trade, migrant labour, etc. These factors do not simply differ between 'developing' and 'advanced' capitalist regions (the categories imply a unity and linear process which does not exist). So-called 'advanced' or 'industrial' capitalist economies differ radically in this respect and in the political-economic problems they confront. Relations of centralisation of function and division of labour are of central significance, but we would argue that they cannot be reduced to the determinations of the classic Leninist theory of imperialism nor to any uniform range of effects stemming necessarily from 'monopoly capitalism'. Many of the most important specialist agrarian and primary-commodity-producing regions can hardly be called 'satellite' economies, and have developed capitalist industry (Australia, Canada, South Africa); others are moving rapidly in that direction (Spain, Brazil, etc.). 'Metropolitan' or advanced industrial states differ widely in the structure of their national economies and in the forms of centralisation. Both England and Switzerland are major centralisations of banking and financial capital. The role of this centralisation in the national economy and the problems of these economies are radically different. These forms of centralisation, industrial structure, and relation to foreign trade can all too clearly affect the conditions for socialist political struggle. The dependence of the British economy on foreign trade and its long-term unfavourable balance of trade entails a connection with the capitalist world market that cannot be dispensed with (prospects for trade with socialist countries on a non-commodity basis are dismal). This dependence on foreign trade means the continued adjustment of the products made and the conditions of production to the necessities of competition in capitalist world markets.

The structure of branches of production and 'enterprises'

Capital postulates (and provides the means to contradict as a *realised* tendency) a tendency for the 'organic composition of capital to rise', the progressive concentration and centralisation of capital, and the 'socialisation' of production. These tendencies have formed the basis for the conception of monopoly capital based on large-scale industry. In this system the surplus value produced by the industrial capitalist sector is circulated and distributed to the other sectors of capital. We have argued theoretically against the foundations of these tendencies and therefore the conditions of their composition into a concept of 'monopoly capital'. We have, in contesting the pertinence of the theory of value, challenged the basis for any argument for the tendency of rising organic composition of capital. In challenging the concept of 'surplus value' and the notion that profit has a single source in the functions performed by agents in production we have opened up a range of questions about the determination of profits of enterprises. These questions are no longer bounded by the problem of the source of profit in 'exploited labour'. It follows that the determinants of commercial capitalist and financial capitalist profits are open to radical reconsideration. We have argued that concentration and centralisation are not conceivable as linear processes of reduction of a given universe of capitals, that changes in the composition of branches of production constantly change the universe (some branches being added and old ones shed), and that the prevailing scale of organisation in one branch by no means need be extended to another.

We maintain that these critical positions make it possible to investigate the actual composition and organisation of the economy into branches of production and forms of specialisation of capital function and to consider their possible effects. The classic concept of monopoly capitalism submerges these problems in questions of the nature and temporality of the fundamental tendencies. Radical developments in recent years, the growth in non-manufacturing employment and in public expenditure and employment, are analysed either as forms of deferment of the crisis of employment and investment generated by monopoly capital, and/or as forms which must ultimately intensify this crisis by accelerating industrial concentration and the decline in the rate of profit.

If one considers certain changes in the composition of capitalist enterprises and in the structure of employment in Britain since the last war without the comforting thought that they evince signs of a deepening crisis with its effect of objective class polarisation, then they offer disquieting food for thought for socialists. One might sum these changes up as follows:

1 A decline in employment in heavy industry (coal, steel, shipbuilding, aircraft construction, etc.), and the relative or in some cases catastrophic decline of these industries in their contribution to national production.

2 A general decline in employment in manufacturing coupled with a corresponding growth in employment in commerce, 'services', and the public sector.

3 The development and intensification of financial capitalist penetration of all spheres of commodity relations (conversion of wages into bank deposits, development of pensions and insurance, etc.); connected with this is growth in employment in this sector.

These changes are not the necessary effects of some 'post-capitalist' or 'post-industrial' logic (the sociologists' own small and dismal counter-Marxist historicism). They are, however, forms connected with the continued development, extension, and mutation of capitalist commodity relations rather than signs of their senescence. The expansion of retailing, catering, entertainment, tourism, etc., as sectors of employment means the development of a labour force which encounters massive objective obstacles to unionisation, which generally enjoys low wages and little security or stability of employment. Increasingly organised industrial workers able to bargain effectively for increases in wages and changes in the conditions of work are becoming a minority of the labour force. The public-sector unions can seldom so bargain and masses of other workers are separated by industrial conditions from unionisation. Trade union politics has its limits, and in this country these limits have had devastating effects on the Left. Nevertheless, it has been classically the form of politics most immediately accessible to the working people. The effects of inflation and the attempt to defend free collective bargaining show us how potentially dangerous this situation is. It threatens a radical division of the standards of living and conditions of control of these standards between a unionised minority and the rest of the labour force. This division can be and has been exploited to impose a wages policy and in effect to hobble trade unionism. We have drawn out this point to illustrate the fact that the composition of production and employment, a composition which has no necessary structure, can have consequences which are of importance for political calculation and political struggle.

Throughout the text we have laid considerable stress on the fact that *Capital*'s conception of the representation of the social process to the agents corresponds to the conception of totality as one in which necessary effectivities are given in its structure. The agents are 'personifications' of their functions; thus the capitalist is a mere 'aliquot part' of the total social capital, a moment through which that totality is operative in motion. We have argued, on the contrary, that there is no necessary process of 'representation', that calculation is not governed by the structure. We have also argued that the 'capitalist' as 'personification' tends to obliterate the fact of the organisation of capitalist production in enterprises, whilst the reduction of all capitals to mere 'aliquot parts' of the total social capital ignores the problems involved in the differential effectivity and success of enterprises. The political pertinences of these critical points are varied.

Marxists have tended to ignore and to dismiss the effectivity of calculation and management on the economic performance of enterprises. However, an important element of the determination of growth and profitability does lie in the area of investment, production, and marketing strategy. To take one example (significant because the survivor of this story is the struggling Meriden workers' co-operative), no explanation of the spectacular collapse of the British motor-cycle industry is possible which ignores the effects of calculation and strategy. Wage differentials, costs of production, and market structures do not explain the failure (Japanese wages were not significantly lower in the key periods of competition), or are in considerable measure a function of strategy (the Japanese revolutionised their cost structure by technical innovation). The radically different forms of calculation of profit and investment strategy are clearly outlined in *Strategy Alternatives for the British Motor Cycle Industry* (the report commissioned by Tony Benn as Minister for Industry from Boston Group Associates). A similar tale can be told about British

Leyland. These determinants reveal the extent of the danger of the theses of the secular decline of British capitalism or the inevitability of its defeat by the bigger battalions in international capitalist competition. Questions of the determinants of the performance of particular industries are clearly vital for specific reforms and interventions and for any strategy which bases the removal of the obstacles to the construction of socialism in this country on 'industrial regeneration'. Socialists must be able to intervene on an informed basis on questions of capitalist organisation and calculation (the government's supervision of British Leyland and the motor industry generally is a case in point)—the classic Marxist conceptions of these questions are of no value whatever.

Classes

In our analysis of classes of economic agents we have criticised and rejected two fundamental elements of the classical Marxist concept of 'class':

1 We have rejected the definition of classes by reference to the labour contributions they are supposed to make to the product. It follows that all conceptions connected with the concept of 'surplus value', in particular the division between 'productive' and 'unproductive' workers, are no longer pertinent. Classes of economic agents are defined and differentiated by these relations of possession of and separation from the means and conditions of production.

2 We have argued the necessity of a general separation between classes as categories of economic agents and the social forces and political organisations involved in political struggle. There is no necessary general correspondence between economic classes and the forces articulated in political struggle. This *general* non-correspondence does not exclude the possibility of specific relations. It does mean, however, that the specific relations cannot be investigated on the basis of a theoretical/ political position which assumes a general and necessary form of correspondence. Classes are not unities of human individuals occupying the same 'place' in the system of social relations and capable of being unified as a class by the effects of these social relations represented to them in experience. Economic agents do not necessarily correspond to human individuals. There is no

necessary structural process of representation of determinate 'interests' to the agents.

In our conceptions the 'working class' is a category of economic agents, which includes all wage workers separated from the means and conditions of production. This category of agents in no sense corresponds to the classic *political* usage of 'working class' in the Marxist and Labour movements to refer to industrial manual workers and the other workers associated with them in definite communities.

It should be added that the Marxist concepts of proletariat or exploited labourer do not correspond to this political usage either.

This category of economic agents is fissured by numerous divisions with various determinations and effects (differences of income, working conditions, type of occupation, 'race', nation, and region, to name the major ones). There is in capitalist social relations no necessary process that subjects this category of agents to tendencies toward homogenisation or unification *at the political level. It follows that the basis of support for socialist politics must be created by the effects of the political actions of socialists themselves.*

There is no basis of definition of what socialist politics should be in the given 'interests' of the working class. Socialist politics cannot be derived from class experience or from the nature of the capitalist mode of production. We emphasise the dependence of socialist politics on socialist ideology and organisation, a point made by Kautsky and Lenin, but which we seek to emphasise in a theoretical context radically different from that of the orthodox Marxism within which they worked. There are no 'socialist' issues and areas of struggle *per se*, assigned as 'socialist' by class interests and experience. Socialism is a political ideology. The basis for support for socialist politics is whatever issues and struggles from which it can be made. These issues are diverse and always specific to the economic and political conditions of definite nation-states. The key question of the issues from which socialist politics can be made is whether they further the struggle for non-commodity, co-operative, popular, and planned forms of production and administration. The answer to this question depends on political calculation, on the context, and the forces involved. Marxists and non-Marxist socialists have lived under the illusion that the 'working class' must ultimately be unified against capitalism by the effects of the capitalist system itself. Regrettably, capitalism has never obliged by creating of itself the political unity of the masses and the political conditions for the construction of socialism—that remains the task which socialists must undertake.

Two points should be made before we proceed, in order to clarify our standpoint; the first concerns the concept of 'national' economy and the second the concept of enterprise.

Our adoption of the concept 'national' economy to designate a vital level of analysis neglected by Marxist economic theory should not mislead the reader into thinking we have adopted the standpoint of national 'economic management'. This standpoint has varied with the different schools of political economy and the conditions of its application—from mercantilism to neo-Keynesianism. Its object, to make capitalist national economies function more 'efficiently' *as capitalist economies* under the prevailing conditions of international competition, is not our object. Equally, for all of these schools the *national economy* is an extra-economic category as it is defined by the techniques of economic intervention which are the means of management. Thus the school of Lizt (*Nationalokonomie par excellence*) identifies the unit of analysis with the extra-economic concept of Volk and the objects of discussion with the various techniques of management (protective tariffs, etc.). For us 'national' economy signifies not a pre-given unity of a people or the state as the horizon of a paid or vocational state functionary, but a series of precise effectivities with a limit. There is no essential unity or necessity in the concept. Its pertinence, as we have said, is *political*. The conditions at this level constrain and condition the forms of struggle for socialism. Its pertinence is not capitalist 'management' but the deconstruction of the entities to be managed.

Our concern with the 'enterprise', with questions of capitalist organisation and calculation, does not signify the adoption of a 'managerial' standpoint. The reason for our concern is not the promotion of company growth and profits, but an understanding of the role of 'management' in these phenomena and the political consequences they have for the struggle for socialism. An anti-capitalist standpoint need not imply ignorance of the role of management or inability to intervene with a definite position on questions of capitalist organisation or calculation where there is political debate and a question of public policy. The negative attitude toward proposals for the regulation and organisation of capitalist enterprises by the Left is an effect of political obstacles: the concentration of the Trotskyist and ultra-Left on questions of revolutionary collapse and direct action by manual workers; the concentration of the Labour Left on nationalisation as the primary means of resolving questions of the regulation and organisation of capitalist enterprises. In the case of 'monopolies' and 'multi-nationals' the Left confines discussion to the question of negative regulation and is primarily concerned to demonstrate their malign and all-pervasive power. These are discourses of resignation in the face of capital. Capital is not a monolith and it would be possible to score significant ideological and practical victories in questions of reorganisation and state aid if the Left developed the means and analyses necessary to do so.

In concluding this discussion of the theoretical/political implications of our work we will draw out two further implications of our opposition to the notion that there are in the structure of capitalism any necessary and general 'tendencies' creating the economic conditions of existence for, and political preconditions of, socialism. This opposition to the notion of necessary and realised tendency as an effect of the structure, is to all its variants, and not merely the thesis of a terminal collapse or breakdown of the conditions of functioning of the capitalist economy. Catastrophism is only one variant of the kind of evolutionism we are challenging. The two implications we are concerned with here are: the relation of socialist *political ideology* to the conception of the necessary transformation of capitalism into socialism; and the role of strategies which, although not catastrophist, do nevertheless depend on the effects of certain necessarily realised tendencies of the capitalist mode of production.

To begin with the question of socialist political ideology. Socialism is a political ideology which bases itself on the objective of constructing a planned and non-commodity form of production and distribution; popular democratic forms of socialism insist that this system should be based on the co-operation and administration of the people themselves. What is the pertinence of a planned, non-commodity, co-operative, and popular economy? Marxism has consistently refused to answer this question on an abstract and ethical basis. Marxism has defined its position as *scientific socialism* in opposition to ethical and utopian socialism. Socialism is not a desirable 'goal' which men can be persuaded to aim for, a goal which will be realised because of its human rationality. The classic Marxist conception of opposition to utopian socialism is based on the conception of the socialist mode of production as the necessary continuation of tendencies developing within capitalism. Socialism will be the product of the 'laws of motion' of capitalist production and of the class struggle between bourgeoisie and proletariat generated by these laws. The construction of rationalistic utopias is unnecessary and absurd. Socialism in some form is an historical necessity. In consequence, it is of no purpose to convince 'reasonable men' by utopian preaching but to operate on the actual historical movement, to develop the existing forms of the class struggle. It is also absurd to assume that an historical process involving titanic struggles and taking place under conditions not chosen by the participants can be legislated in advance: socialism will never correspond to the dreams of the 'ethical' petty bourgeois.

Marxism's opposition to the politics of utopian socialism and to the construction of rationalistic social blueprints was correct. Socialism cannot be achieved except by political struggle against opposing forces. It can only be achieved under conditions of constraint—constraints legislators on paper never encounter. The problem is the extent to which this correct and healthy opposition to utopianism and rationalism has been theoretically combined with evolutionism and the extent to which that evolutionism has threatened the power of appeal of socialist political ideology.

How is it possible to sustain the pertinence of socialist forms of economic and political organisation if it is argued that there are no necessary 'laws of motion' of capitalism? The foundation of a non-ethical 'scientific' socialism has been the *historical necessity* of this social form. One deceptively simple answer is that scientific socialism is the product of mechanistic Marxism and that what is needed is a return to a socialism not based on an abstract ethical ideal, but on a concrete anthropology, on the satisfaction of real human needs. The notion that socialism represents a 'better form of society' because it meets the real needs of man is a *non sequitur*. Are these 'needs' indeed met and whose 'needs' are they? The answer supposes a human nature the needs of which can be known. Other 'needs' and their defenders are not fully human, they are the mutilated reflections of the alienating social relations they live as truth. 'Socialisms' which do not meet these needs are socialisms in name alone. The ethical has returned in the form of an anthropological absolute.

This is not just a matter of the theoretical banality of philosophical humanism, it is a question of its political banality also. These very 'needs' serve as the main basis for the *humanistic critique* of socialism. Are they not daily thrown in the face of the USSR and other socialist countries by capitalist ideologues? To adopt this position of 'human needs' as the definition of socialism is to place oneself on the weakest possible *political* ground. On questions of popular participation in socialist construction and democratic control by the masses no serious socialist defence can be made of the existing situation in the USSR. Indifferent to philosophical anthropology and its 'needs', the mass of ordinary workers in this country prefer the elements of civil liberty and freedom from state political constraint which are possible under the existing parliamentary democratic forms to the conditions prevailing in the USSR. Humanist ethical ideals will, however, *always* encounter definite socialist formations, and not merely the USSR, as their contradiction or negation. These formations, constructed under definite constraints, can never result in a realm of freedom and the realisation of the human essence. A popular socialist regime, in which the masses play an active part, is no less the subject of a humanist critique. Is not the regimentation of the mass and the negation of the individual a persistent theme in the Western literature on China (a theme echoed in the 1950s even by progressive writers like Sartre)? To base one's defence of and argument for socialist construction on the humanist notion of man's needs or nature is to expose oneself willingly and naïvely to the ideologies which can only oppose the reality of any socialism.

Marxism has been correct to insist that the content of socialist political ideology cannot be defined by the writings of *philosophers*. The ideological victories against socialism in Britain and the West have been made possible by its defeats in practice; central in this respect has been the development of the USSR since the late 1920s. Equally, the best possible case for socialism will be made by practical achievements in political struggle and socialist construction. Marx was correct to seek to learn what he could about the nature and problems of socialist construction from the experience of the Commune. The most valuable writings of Marx, Lenin, and Mao on socialism are precisely attempts to learn from, account for, and to digest existing forms of socialist struggle.

But here we encounter a serious difficulty. In Britain the Left movement is weak and ghettoised, the lessons to be learned are those concerning its weakness and lack of impact. Further, the process of construction and the political ideology which defines socialism in China is remote from the conditions of struggle for socialism in this country. One has only to see the ludicrous antics of those who blindly ape and caricature Maoist practice in the West to recognise the dangers of any attempt to build too directly on the practices of the Chinese.

If socialist political ideology in Britain cannot be given its pertinence by necessary 'laws of motion', by anthropology, or by advances elsewhere, then how can this be done? It is not merely a theoretical problem and it cannot be resolved by presenting an abstract 'case' for socialism. Two answers seem to offer themselves: to learn from and build on the experience of the socialist movement in this country; to build up through political critique and agitation bases to argue the practicality of measures of a co-operative and planned nature and their superiority to existing capitalist/commodity forms. To learn in this way means to learn primarily from the experience of the struggle of the Labour party: the role of the Marxist Left has been insignificant and paltry. One can learn only of its exclusion from any real part in the dominant political struggle. To struggle in this way is to fight for the practicality and viability of socialist forms of organisation. No amount of preaching socialism as a 'solution' to the current crisis will alter the massive scepticism of the masses (demonstrated in absentism and apoliticism) and the non-representation of socialist positions in the dominant political debates.

This involves a more limited base of the construction of socialist political ideology, one that will never be able to justify the 'necessity' of socialism but which will be able to fight for the content of its political programme. If capitalism has no evolutionary tendencies in general and takes the form of specific national economies subject to differing problems and constraints, then *socialisms must differ*. The pertinence of planned, co-operative, and non-commodity forms will differ and there will be different roads to their construction.

To return to our two answers. First, it is necessary to learn from the experience of the struggle for and implementation of non-commodity forms in this country. Second, it is necessary to identify the key areas in which the fight for non-commodity forms as the basis of which socialist struggle can be continued and can be successful. This implies taking what is often called 'reformism' seriously. It is the dominant experience from which we have to learn. 'Reformism' pertains to the *politics* which articulate reforms and programmes, not necessarily to the programmes themselves. The question of the road to power is crucial here. If there can be no revolutionary seizure of power under existing conditions one must work toward a 'parliamentary' seizure of power (if that is possible). If there is no revolutionary conjuncture, the process of socialist construction must first take the form of building the economic and political conditions for a socialist economy. These conditions are not given by the evolution of the capitalist economy itself.

It is in this context that we may consider the forms of non-commodity and planned relations introduced by the Labour movement and Labour party. There are two salient lessons here.

1 That the products of the Labour movement (TUs, friendly societies, the Co-operative movement) and of the 1945 government (NHS, nationalisation) were in no sense the creation of strategic conditions for advance. The nationalised industries, billed as the 'commanding heights of the economy', were and are, in the absence of any strategy with regard to the private sector, merely state-owned commodity producers subject to the logic of demand and growth in the private sector.

2 That the absence of any strategic perspective of constructing bases for socialist advance is evident in the absence of any detailed attention, from a socialist position, to questions of the organisation and effects of the non-commodity relations. The Labour party has adopted a consistently statist and managerial conception of organisations (this is even more true of Left figures like Aneurin Bevan).

The 'failure' of the Labour movement and Labour party should not form the basis for the invalidation of all political strategies which involve the creation of limited non-commodity forms as one of the conditions of socialist advance. This is because the 'failure' in question was in no sense a failure of this type of strategy; it reflects rather the absence of any strategy for socialism. However, there is in this 'failure' a basic lesson to be learned. Such limited non-commodity forms cannot survive possible electoral defeats and changes in state policy consequent upon them if they are merely the product of legislation and the province of professional management. Without popular involvement and control, the encouragement of extra-parliamentary mass organisation, such measures of reform are lost in advance. For example, the NHS was from the first surrendered to doctors and bureaucrats; the results are all too clear to see. The Health Service ancillary workers, excluded from administration and decision-making, represent the only current basis of socialist ideology and struggle within this organisation.

In the absence of necessary class polarisation along lines of class 'interests' it is essential to create by involvement and practice the basis for mass support of socialist political ideology. In the absence of their taking part in and being surrounded by socialist political organisation and activity, there is no reason why workers should adopt socialist political ideology. The USA is the classic demonstration of this. The socialist movement can only gain ground by bringing masses of the working people into activities which organise matters of consequence to the way they live (TUs, NHS, etc.). Oppositional campaigns and 'revolutionary' abstentionism can never have this effect and by and large the best they can achieve is to articulate discontent (and the Right can be just as successful at this). Trade unions have been the classic medium by which workers, through practical questions of organisation, have been brought into contact with socialist political ideology. This political form and effect of trade union organisation is not a necessary one (it does not occur in the USA). It must be fought for and maintained. Trade unions are a limited form in two senses. First, there are tendencies within the practice being organised in the absence of constant practical pressure to the contrary, for defensive issues and questions of wages to predominate over and even virtually to exclude forms of struggle which advance socialist political ideology. Second, masses of the working people are excluded from this practice. Forms of organisation of important and necessary activities on a non-commodity and non-statist basis, in which socialist political ideology can be a practical political force, are necessary to begin to involve masses of non-unionised, non-manual, and non-employed working people. These forms will necessarily be varied and partial, from workers' participation schemes to the self-administration of council housing estates. 'Workerism', the belief in the spontaneous unity of the working class around its 'interests' and of the necessary privilege of manual labour, is a major obstacle to the conception of the problem of how to build the popular organisational foundations of commitment to socialist political ideology and the forms of political unification of the masses.

These forms of organisation, which cannot be destroyed without struggle, merely by the results of an electoral defeat, or changes in the political composition of the government, are an essential complement to a struggle which must be waged through parliamentary forms. They complement and constrain this struggle for electoral victory and governmental power. They can be built and rebuilt piecemeal, through local electoral victories, pressure toward policy concessions on a government which is not implementing a socialist strategy programme but is open to Left constraint. Any view of the struggle for socialism that is not insurrectionary in its immediate form and does not rely on the spontaneous movement of the economy must pay close attention to organisational questions of this sort.

Here the second of our two answers becomes important. Such attention to organisation must be coupled with a careful selection of the areas of the specific capitalist social relations in question that are open to campaigns for reform on a planned and/or non-commodity basis and where such reforms can be implemented as viable alternatives. These areas must vary with the conditions in question and no general answers can be given. One important comment might be made here, however, that it is necessary to differentiate between *institutional forms and effect* when considering the implementation of planned or non-commodity relations. Nationalisation is a classic case in point. Planning control and regulation do not require a change in the form of property in the first instance, nor does the development of a state sector require the acquisition of capitalist enterprise. Financial capital is a sphere ripe for political challenge, reform, and control. It by no means follows that this should take the form of nationalisation and acquisition by compensation. The state, in determining the form of money and some of the conditions of its supply, the form of property, and the relative privilege of institutions in respect of taxation, rates of interest, etc., has a massive battery of means of regulation and means to create or reconstruct parallel state financial institutions with a 'privileged' (and economically attractive) status. Socialist struggle conceived as a 'protracted war' without arms requires careful consideration of the elements of state coercive power which can be used to achieve its aims. Socialist struggle as a 'war of position', a succession of investments and sieges, must make use of the fact that *capitalism takes the form of national economies*, that an element of the existence of these economies is the effectivity of the state in determining the parameters of economic operation. Labour regulation, the form of property and commercial laws, taxation, monetary and credit regulation all take on a new significance as potential instruments of policy. These instruments will vary in their effectivity, in the opposition they encounter, and in the political conditions of their exercise. But it is important to insist that *state power is not homogeneous*. State apparatuses and their powers have differential degrees of utilisation in the promotion of socialist policies, they do not form 'one reactionary mass', any more than the 'state' forms a single entity (except in a constitutional sense). The calculation of the extent to which these powers can be used, the specific forms of their use (legislation or administrative action, nationalisation or regulation, etc.), and the extent to which they can be doubled by or coupled with popular pressure forms a large part of the determination of which reforms and interventions are viable and practical alternatives to the existing statist or commodity forms.

This discussion of socialist political ideology has taken us beyond the realm of justifications for the pertinence of socialism and into questions of socialist strategy and the road to power. We would maintain that it is at this level that the questions of the pertinence of socialist forms and the content of socialist political ideology can be answered, that they are always answered in specific ways which confront the problems of the movement and the constraints it encounters. These answers will differ and in consequence socialism will differ. Support of a necessarily non-insurrectionary struggle of a prolonged nature does not imply its universalisation as the sole appropriate strategy, even in countries where advanced capitalist industry predominates. Universalisations of the 'necessary' road, the only revolutionary position, and so on, immobilise no one but the Left. The opposition of revolution and reform is a creation of Left sectarians and reactionary social democrats; the chosen universal and necessary paths confront one another. Just as nineteenth-century Marxism needed to challenge utopian socialism, and did so by creating the opposition utopian or scientific, so socialism today needs to deconstruct another opposition, revolution or reform.

As we indicated above, another implication of our opposition to the conception of necessary 'laws of motion' of capitalism is the questioning of non-catastrophist strategies based on the operation of these laws. A classic example of such a position is the strategy of 'anti-monopoly alliance'. The political pertinence of the notion of 'monopoly' is that it is the distillation of all the effects of the basic capitalist tendencies of concentration/centralisation/accumulation. Monopolies become the dominant forms of modern capital, exploiting workers, cheating consumers, and expropriating dependent small businesses alike. This common range of effects becomes the basis for the unity of those who suffer these effects, the economic foundation of a political alliance between the workers and the petty-bourgeois 'middle strata'. Even if the monopoly did have this unitary form and this unambiguous unity of effects, it by no means follows that it unites politically those who suffer these effects. The conditions of resistance to expropriation by small businesses, to 'monopoly' pricing, and poor conditions of service by 'consumers' (whoever they are), and exploitation by workers can by no means evidently be seen to be incorporable into a single political programme. Unless, that is, the programme itself is ambiguous and opportunist, appealing to distinct sectors in the hope that they will back it.

We have argued that the processes of concentration and centralisation of capital as presented in *Capital* do not produce a uniform and linear range of effects. We would also argue that there is no evidence that the *scale* of a company operating in one definite group of branches of production leads it to have any policies in common with another (having, say, the same percentage dominance of a different market) in another group. The effects of different companies in different industries and markets are not necessarily the same, nor is the effect of the dominance of a larger company over smaller ones unambiguously against the interest of its possessors or workers. Socialists should by no means oppose large enterprises and support those capitalists who happen to be threatened by them *per se*. The notion of an anti-monopoly alliance supposes the political and economic homogeneity of 'monopoly capital' (meaning enterprises of a certain scale). This homogeneity and the homogeneity of the resistance to it needs to be demonstrated. This economism writ large, an economism which does not merely concern the workers, was hitherto the theoretical basis for the PCF's political strategy and was influential with sections of the CPGB. It legitimates an attempt to break out of a narrowly workerist basis, to attempt to win electoral success by winning the 'middle strata'. The essentialism of the theoretical foundation couples the unargued opportunism of the groups aimed at and the composition of the programme. There is nothing wrong *per se* in attempting to construct a broadly based electoral alliance—the PCF may be in concrete terms more or less successful in this—but what is at stake is tying the strategy and its objectives to the evolution of the economy and the resolution of the political forces into the appropriate positions by these effects. What makes the 'anti-monopoly' alliance theoretically possible as a socialist programme is the classic economistic and evolutionist notion that the very process of concentration can only give economic and political dominance to the working class as the one partner in the alliance favoured by history itself.

So far we have been concerned to demonstrate the connection between questions of Marxist theory and economics and political and strategic issues. Our central point has been that the 'laws of motion' of capitalism have served as a talisman for the maintenance of insurrectionary/revolutionary positions under conditions of parliamentary-political stability, particularly where this is coupled with capitalist economic expansion. This political outlook has served as a massive obstacle to the fundamental strategic rethinking and theoretical changes that are necessary if socialists are to adapt to the conditions of struggle which confront them in countries like Britain. Economic crises are the religious festivals of sectarian Marxism, the promised moments of epiphany when the totality reassures us that it and its tendencies are still with us. It is in the current period that it is all the more necessary to stress and to criticise the obstacle this evolutionism poses to socialist struggle with any prospects of success.

Marxist theory and Britain

The theoretical/political implications we have developed from our work so far apply equally well to most industrial capitalist countries dominated by relatively stable forms of parliamentary democracy. The central political problem for socialists in such countries is how to build the *political* conditions for socialist construction within the limits set by parliamentary forms, and in particular how, within those limits, to build a mass base of popular organisations and practices which can support and extend the struggle for socialism. Whilst the problems and dilemmas of the basic strategic situation are similar, the means at the disposal of the socialist forces are not. It is these means which set the terms of strategic calculation in the particular capitalist countries in question.

In France and Italy, for example, there are Communist parties with mass support which show some recognition of these strategic problems and a willingness to come to terms with the limits set by parliamentary democratic forms (whether this recognition will lead merely to electoral opportunism and this willingness to slavish legalism is an open question, a question that can still be decided by the political practice of these parties and political struggle within them). In the USA, in contrast, socialist forces of any kind above the level of doctrinaire sectlets do not exist. In Britain the situation is different again. The Marxist Left lacks a mass base, is excluded from or has excluded itself from effective participation in representative bodies, and in consequence it is consigned to the sidelines of the dominant forms of political struggle and effectively ghettoised. The Labour party, on the other hand, has in effect become the dominant party of government since 1964. Its parliamentary majority has for a long time committed itself to the management of the capitalist national economy, and yet it requires as one of the crucial conditions of its electoral support the pretence of ultimately pursuing the party's own (nebulous) conception of socialism. This ambiguous position of the Labour party is not necessarily unadvantageous to socialist forces. The Left in the party organisation and rank and file remains a considerable force, if confused and fragmented; the parliamentary majority is electorally dependent on the party organisation and lacks within itself the means of generating political programmes with a popular appeal; and, most important of all, the party retains a mass electoral base both *as a socialist and popular party* (a base whose decline would be halted if it were one in its practice), and *as a party of government* (a vote for which has some prospect of determining issues in current politics). This combination of openness to socialist ideology and a mass electoral base means that the Left can struggle *within* the Labour party and that the object struggled for is worth winning, that it offers the prospect of political power.

The political means available for socialist struggle are the key determinant of definite strategic calculation. In going beyond the more general implications of our work and in considering how our analysis bears on the political conjuncture in Britain the constraints imposed by the means available limit and condition our (and any) analysis. We cannot offer here a ready-made political programme. A programme for whom? Strategic analysis must be placed in terms of the forces available or which can be constructed. The existing forces and the potentialities of construction are constrained by political conditions which cannot be changed by analysis alone or by the content of a programme. Analysis and political ideology must adjust to these conditions of existence, work toward socialism through the forms enforced by the political conditions, and not seek to promote some 'privileged' conception of struggle independent of these conditions. Political 'parties' and sectlets are constantly being created around programmes based on such 'privileged' conceptions of socialist political struggle and political ideology. This constant addition to the diversity of the Left ghetto is pointless. Political interventions, if they are to amount to anything, must be based on those organisations and practices which are actually capable of altering the existing balance of political forces. This means acting in the arenas where this balance is set. Absence of electoral success and absence of politically effective support tend to reinforce one another. Political programmes cannot be effective if they are not voted for and they will not be voted for if they offer no prospect of intervening in the existing political struggles (thus in practice the CPGB defines itself as a junior partner to the Labour party, recognising its own limited prospects of electoral success and adapting its politics to *acting on* a party still capable of mass support).

Marxist-Leninist sects espouse a particularly developed variant of this privilege of the programme.* They depend on the rationalistic illusion that there can be a 'correct line', a political position which because of its correctness gives the organisation, however insignificant, strategic advantage and renders obsolete all other organisations on the Left. If, however, there is no class as political subject to whom this line will, ultimately, have the effect of sirens' song, then this whole enterprise collapses into a rationalism of Proudhonian dimensions.

To have political effect is predicated on the possession of the organisational means to implement the politics which have that

---

* The group with which the authors were previously associated, Theoretical Practice, was strongly committed to the notion of strategic intervention based on a correct line. It never, however, committed itself to the rationalistic position that it itself was a sufficient medium for the realisation of that line and never constituted itself as a political party.

effect. Given the continued dominance of parliamentary forms as the basis of organisation of political issues and the determination of struggles, the question of political effectivity leads to one answer: questions of socialist strategy in Britain depend crucially on the prospects for the transformation of the Labour party. The prospects or the mode of transformation cannot be settled by any analysis we offer here. Given the ambiguous nature of the party, they remain open questions. The role of struggle within the party and that of pressure through other political bodies (CPGB, trade unions, etc.) do not seem to us ones that can be assigned or settled in advance at the moment. What we will be concerned with here is to locate the *context* in which any socialist strategy based on the transformation of the Labour party and accepting the existing conditions of political struggle must operate.

It will be evident that in specifying this context we consider that any effective strategy must confront the problem of creating the conditions for *taking power* and doing so on the basis of the existing political and economic relations. These conditions must amount to the overcoming of the constraints imposed by those relations. It is in relation to this strategic problem that we would reject the two stances toward parliamentary forms of struggle dominant in the British Left.

The first we will characterise as 'insurrectionism'. This stance makes opposition to the possibility of a parliamentary road to socialism an issue of principle, a defining element of a revolutionary line. It bases this opposition on the evident difficulties of attempting to construct socialism on the basis of the legal and political forms of a capitalist state. It identifies its opponents as dogmatically legalist social democrats. The problem is that this insurrectionism becomes the basis for the critique and rejection of *all political practices* in which parliamentary struggle is the dominant form irrespective of the political conditions and the objects of struggle. Creating the *political conditions* for socialist construction and building socialism itself are not the same thing. Where the politics of a revolutionary seizure of power are not possible, then other forms of politics must predominate and become the means for advance of the socialist cause.

This is a necessity the insurrectionary Left fail to recognise in terms of strategy, yet are forced to concede to in their daily practice. The Left sects which espouse this principle (the WRP, SWP, and IMG) all combine an anti-parliamentarian *theoretical* stance with more or less extensive commitments to legal and parliamentary struggles. This is necessary if they are to engage with and have any practice of acting on issues which concern the mass of wage workers (the Tory Industrial Relations Act, incomes policies, etc.). However much emphasis they may place on the mass movement and mass mobilisation, the object of that mobilisation is almost invariably to influence a decision in Parliament. Furthermore, mobilisation is effective to the extent that issues *can* be defined and determined within the existing political forms. Given the absence of a national crisis, the relative stability of parliamentary forms and of mass support for them, the revolutionary line based on an insurrectionary seizure of power is stalled and forced into a state of making what it can of the existing conditions. We would argue that the conditions for an insurrectionary road simply do not exist in this country and that the supporters of this 'privileged' form of struggle are condemned to live in hope of an economic crisis that will make them a reality (for the present one will not).

Yet, despite the concessions of daily practice, the revolutionary crisis remains dominant in this politics, the basis of its strategy. This negates the reality of the concessions; it reduces participation in existing institutions and struggles to a tactical necessity imposed by the immediate conditions. This must necessarily limit the forms of participation involved to a strategically abstentionist opportunism, to the attempt to win supporters to the movement by articulating current concerns which are far removed from the revolutionary objectives of that movement, and to win mass conviction in the necessary limits of 'reformism' (equated with struggle within the conditions imposed by parliamentary forms). The privilege accorded to insurrectionary politics must negate the concrete practices and struggles engaged in by these movements; it severs these practices and struggles from being in any real sense part of the road to power. For all the apparent concern with the seizure of power, this politics is as far removed from the practices of taking power as the most timid and legalist social democracy.

The other stance we will characterise as 'oppositionism'. This is a chronic disease of sections of the Parliamentary Labour party and the Left organised around them. This stance entails, in effect, the absence of any strategy or practice directed toward taking power by using the existing political conditions. At the same time its struggles are entirely bounded by these conditions and the issues that arise within them. The Labour Left as a whole has abandoned the practice of fighting for power (something which Bevan, whatever his political limitations, did not do) and contents itself with being the channel of articulation of the grievances of sections of the Labour movement. This articulation is oppositionist because it is merely directed against existing policies and is in no sense part of a wider struggle for power. In effect the Labour Left articulates within the established political institutions the same discontents that the revolutionary Left attempts to articulate outside these institutions. The two compete to articulate these same discontents in a similarly negative and oppositionist manner; currently dominant are opposition to the EEC, to public expenditure cuts, and to an incomes policy. This opposition can achieve nothing in socialist terms because it is not linked with positive struggle for viable alternatives, nor is the opposition connected in any definite way with a socialist strategy. On the contrary, it is negative and a-strategic.

The extent to which the representatives of these two stances dominate the British Left and its politics makes those current political positions which are concerned to control and to exercise power toward socialist objectives, and on the basis of existing political and economic relations, all the more significant. These positions, developed on the left of the Labour party, are virtually all that there is in the way of practical socialist political programmes. We will consider here those political positions which seem to us to demand serious critical attention. These positions presuppose the Labour party as the vehicle for the implementation of this strategy. Of special significance are Stuart Holland's *The Socialist Challenge* and the various writings and speeches of Tony Benn. They deserve consideration because they played a prominent part in the formulation of Labour's 1973 policy proposals and because Benn has recognised the need to continue to struggle for power within the Labour government rather than withdraw into 'principled' opposition.

Both Holland and Benn attempt to confront the problems of socialist strategy in terms of the constraints on the realisation of socialist policies in contemporary Britain. Both define the primary constraints as economic ones. Both conceive the removal of these obstacles in terms of the state aided and partially planned 'regeneration' of capitalist commodity production. We may characterise the nature of these obstacles as follows.

1 Britain has suffered from a low rate of growth in manufacturing output relative to its competitors and a relative decline in its share of world markets; these processes have been especially marked in the phase of world capitalist expansion since the Second World War and with the end of Empire.

2 This fact is unimportant in itself. What makes this relative falling behind in relation to the conditions of international capitalist competition problematic is the dependence of the economy on its export performance, the significance of imported raw materials and foodstuffs, the increasing penetration of imported manufactures, and the resulting chronic tendency to deficit in the balance of trade.

3 This balance has not been financed by receipts from foreign capital holdings and imperial balances held in London since World War II, it has only been offset by other foreign earnings under favourable conditions, and this situation creates a chronic tendency to deficit in the balance of payments. Successive governments in the past two decades have attempted to resolve the problem of the balance of trade by the short-term expedients of manipulation of the balance of payments: through encouraging short-term foreign deposits, through foreign loans, and through defence of sterling. This has created the constraints of economic 'management' that have generally placed the control of the conditions which favour foreign deposits and loans (relatively high interest rates, defence of the exchange rate, etc.) before the conditions which would favour industrial growth. These difficulties are real ones and make any British government chronically dependent on the conditions prevailing in international commodity, capital, and money markets, and on the conditions of support required by foreign powers and international agencies. This dependence clearly constrains the economic and political policies that can be followed.

The type of strategy Holland and Benn propose would have three main merits.

1 If successful, it is claimed that it would remove a considerable amount of constraint on the type of policies the national government sought to pursue.

2 That the conditions of 'management' of the balance of payments immobilise any government with socialist pretensions and force more and more purely defensive struggles upon the

Labour movement (against falling living standards, unemployment, expenditure cuts, etc.—these struggles absorb the energy of the movement and form the real foundation for the oppositionist tendency we noted above).

3 A successful 'industrial regeneration' accomplished under a Left government would as a result create a position of strength for socialist policies and win new support, whereas the conditions of 'management' of the balance of payments have lost the Labour party mass support.

Both Holland and Benn make the conversion of a vicious circle of industrial stagnation into a virtuous circle of industrial growth the main precondition for and the primary means of attaining the conditions of socialist advance. Both are concerned primarily with the management of the national economy; their object is to manage it in a different and more progressive way than previous Labour governments.

Both Holland and Benn consider the essence of this management to be the state's constraining and facilitating the private industrial sector to a higher level of investment and growth in output. The battery of institutional innovations and reforms proposed— selective nationalisations, compulsory planning agreements, rationalisation through the NEB—are the means of this constraint. They represent a departure from the means employed in the Butskellite 'demand management' era of national economic policy—taxation, credit control, etc. The objectives of the two management strategies differ; rather than the essentially conjunctural management of demand level through consumers' purchasing power and commercial credit Holland and Benn are concerned with the management of what is conceived to be a structural shortfall in investment. Holland, who deals most explicitly with what he conceives to be the reasons for this 'shortfall', considers that 'Keynesian' policies at the level of the national economy have been subverted by what he calls the 'meso-economic power' of large multi-national firms.

We would argue that these positions which tie socialist politics to the success of a programme of 'industrial regeneration' are not a viable basis for socialist strategy. This is for two reasons: first, these strategies largely ignore the *political conditions of their implementation*, and second, they fail to answer the question of whether such a 'regeneration' is possible and whether, if possible, it

Conclusion 277

can take place under conditions which will be of benefit to socialist politics. Holland and Benn stake their politics on the prospect of particular outcomes of the practice of management of capitalist national economies.

Let us begin with the economic problems. Nationalisations are *selective* measures in these strategies, they are designed to give positions of leverage against the private sector as a whole. The enterprises nationalised are to be provided with levels of investment funds such that they will become efficient producers of commodities on a world scale. The elements of planning and constraint are designed to make the private sector do what it otherwise will not do, raise the level of investment.

The pertinence of investment and the extent to which the private sector as a whole can be constrained to perform in appropriate ways are the primary problems which need to be considered. The relatively low rate of growth in manufacturing output is by no means a simple function of the level of investment, nor are investment decisions by capitalist enterprises the primary *cause* of this low rate of growth. Neither Holland nor Benn demonstrate that a 'shortfall' in investment is responsible for Britain's lower rate of growth (that higher levels of investment would be needed for a significant increase in the level of output is true, but that is a different question). Holland takes it as evident that investment decisions by enterprises are the cause of a lower rate of growth and attributes this primarily to the activities of large multi-national companies siphoning funds and new production off to foreign countries. Holland's position verges on the absurd when he deals with multi-national companies; they appear to be engaged in a malevolent conspiracy to subvert the British national economy. Multi-national companies are not extra-terrestrial, and their differential levels of investment in different countries clearly have something to do with their calculation of the economic conditions which will pertain in those countries. This calculation may correctly determine obstacles to the expansion of the enterprise's production in a given country. To some extent a low rate of growth in the economy as a whole is self-reinforcing and acts to limit the growth of the manufacturing sector. A predictable expansion in demand will encourage expansion in output or extensions to capacity roughly coincident with it. What would determine a decision not to invest in additional capacity in Britain would not only be the relatively limited expansion of internal demand as a whole that could be anticipated but also the relatively unfavourable conditions of competition in foreign markets which may result from producing products here for export.

Holland ignores the fact that there are a number of factors which constitute obstacles to growth and to competitiveness in industrial production which cannot be obviated by constraining firms to invest in new plant. These obstacles *are* recognised by enterprises (often to an exaggerated extent, as in management literature on 'productivity'), however, and do affect their calculation. Since the Second World War the following factors have been of some importance in limiting growth in industrial production and capacity (we have no intention of adding to the literature on the determination of rates of growth by trying to assess them or attempting to rank them):

1 a relatively slowly growing and ageing population;
2 the absence of a non-commodity or non-capitalist sector of any appreciable size (non-capitalist agriculture or domestic production) in process of being incorporated into the capitalist economy;
3 shortages of skilled labour and the relative immobility of the labour force (especially the unemployed);
4 the relatively higher cost of borrowing (compared to, say, Germany and Japan) and generally lower profit margins than in other comparable countries;
5 a tendency toward lower productivity per worker in manufacturing (often with similar manufacturing technique, for example, the difference cited in *The Future of the British Car Industry* between plants of the same company in England and Belgium);
6 the resistance of sections of the organised labour force to changes in technique and in the organisation of labour;
7 relative openness to foreign manufactured imports (an effect of, among other factors, the absence of protective measures as in the USA or the kind of *de facto* import controls found in Japan, of shortages during credit-based short-run booms, of the complexity and level of development of commercial capital and its highly competitive nature).

These factors cannot necessarily be removed by government policy (1 and 2) nor easily dealt with by a socialist government in large measure dependent on the trade unions (3, 5, and 6). National economies are constituted in part by the way in which the parameters of economic operation are determined within a definite territory, and state policy plays a large part in this determination. But it by no means follows that state policies are necessarily effective in producing the particular results required.

It is not at all clear that the Holland/Benn strategy could coerce the private sector into the directions planned. The battery of instruments of control proposed by Holland is insufficient to overcome the resistance of companies to a programme of expansion beyond what they consider viable or to overcome the support for that resistance provided by political parties and organisations opposed to socialism. This resistance would have a real foundation and would not be merely the product of a lack of 'confidence'. A generalised programme of expansion in capacity in many sectors of engineering and manufactures would increase the dependence of these industries on performance in increasingly competitive and international markets. Many of the sectors particularly important for employment and exports are currently characterised by chronic overcapacity on a world scale (e.g. shipbuilding, motor vehicles, aeroplanes, etc.). The results of 'regeneration' (an ambiguous notion) would be neither attractive to the managements of particular enterprises nor a 'solution' to the problems of the national economy.

Far from an increase in the level of investment or an expansion in capacity, an effective response to the conditions of international competition for many managements may well be, on the contrary, a *reduction* in the overall productive capacity and a reduction in the labour force. 'Investment' is an ambiguous notion; investment which lowers the costs of production may well displace labour. What is good for Henry Ford or Arnold Weinstock is not necessarily good for the mass of working people. Holland attempts to constrain firms to invest, to expand in regions of high unemployment, and to retain their existing labour forces. These objectives are not necessarily compatible. Adapting to the conditions of international competition may well produce politically unacceptable results, seeking to meet objectives in regional and employment policy may produce nonsense in terms of competitiveness (the classic example is the Chrysler bail-out). The resistance of managements like Chrysler or GEC is based upon economic calculation at enterprise level, calculation which necessarily puts the viability of the enterprise in relation to its competitors first. Holland and Benn offer no serious means of coming to terms with the contradiction between the conditions of successful competition for enterprises and their policy objectives. Creating conditions for economic 'growth' which capitalist enterprises will find attractive is, in the case of many of the larger enterprises in manufacturing industry, very difficult, and in the case of other sectors—financial capital, commerce, services, and tourism (the current 'growth' sectors of the British economy)—such conditions are inimical to the political objectives of socialism.

If capitals cannot be induced to invest in the way required by creating conditions which are 'attractive' to them, then they must be compelled. The means that Holland envisages for controlling the 'commanding heights' of the economy, nationalising the key companies in a number of sectors, involve legislation, political opposition, compensation (which creates the basis for new capitals), and administrative reorganisation. On anything like the scale necessary, it presupposes a secure parliamentary majority committed to the line, and significant popular support. Even if these political conditions existed there is no reason to suppose that Holland's policy objectives could be attained by these nationalisations. Accelerated investment and growth in output will not necessarily 'solve' Britain's economic problems. Nationalisation will not necessarily produce even this expansion (the managers of a nationalised motor-vehicle industry would undoubtedly propose a contraction in units of production, employment, and output). Holland's entire battery of means consists in finding substitutes for decisions and actions capitalist managements are unwilling to undertake. Holland and Benn attempt to play, by means of state power, the part of capitalist entrepreneurs, making enterprises 'efficient' commodity producers. Enterprises like GEC or ICI have no shortage of funds for investment and their reasons for not investing have little to do with 'confidence'. Despite the attempt to recognise the significance of national economy as a level of analysis, Holland and Benn end up displacing it onto the behaviour of capitalist managers. Their strategies consist in forcing different decisions at enterprise level. That the managers to be constrained have 'good' reasons for their actions, that these reasons cannot easily be gainsaid if the enterprises are to produce for profit under conditions of international capitalist competition, is ignored.

This is not an attack on the possibility or desirability of socialist governments intervening to regulate or reorganise capitalist production *per se*. We are concerned merely to challenge the value of one particular form of that intervention, 'industrial regeneration', as a basis for socialist advance. We have tried to point out the dependence of this position on the success of enterprises in commodity production. We have tried to point out that even if this intervention were successful in raising the level of investment the result would be to make the British economy no less dependent on foreign trade and even more committed to certain highly competitive international markets characterised by overcapacity. This form of 'adjustment' to the conditions of international capitalist competition reinforces their internalisation in the structure of the economy.

Another response to the dependence of the economy on the international conditions of competition is the classic Left-Labour reflex of attempting to limit links with the world market. This reflex has drawn its strength from the period of physical controls in the post-1945 Labour administration. The virtual government monopoly of foreign trade was possible and necessary then because the conditions for the operation of world markets had not been restored and a substantial portion of foreign trade was conducted as bi-lateral barter between states. These conditions no longer apply. Import controls on a large scale bring with them the threat of trade discrimination and conflict with the rest of the EEC. More considered variants of this response are to be found in Spokesman pamphlets nos 44 and 47. The pamphlet by Eaton, Barratt Brown, and Coates (*An Alternative Economic Strategy for the Labour Movement*) proposes import controls, petrol rationing and, in effect, withdrawal from the EEC. This programme is proposed in the context of continuing dependence on private capitalist production. The effects on key sectors of manufacturing of the resulting discrimination against British exports is not considered, nor is the effect of the general dislocation of foreign trade that would result from withdrawal from the EEC. The Cambridge Political Economy Group pamphlet (*Britain's Economic Crisis*) proposes the resolution of balance of payments difficulties in the short run by the liquidation of British overseas assets; the value of these assets on the market and the willingness of foreign governments to accept their confiscation by a socialist government are never discussed. Both of these pamphlets offer 'solutions' to Britain's current economic crisis which in the short run would involve disruptions and sacrifices which would exceed the present economic difficulties by a good measure. Moreover, limiting contacts with the EEC cannot be easily reconciled with reducing dependence on world markets, and reducing dependence on world markets cannot easily be combined with a strategy of 'industrial regeneration' (if that strategy means continuing to expand the largest enterprises in manufacture and engineering whose markets are international and which require foreign raw materials and machine tools).

Both 'industrial regeneration' and the limiting of dependence on foreign trade through controls are economic schemes to 'solve' the problems of the British national economy. Whatever the economic possibility of these 'schemes' (and we consider there to be little), what is absent from them is any serious consideration of the *political* conditions of their implementation. Holland, Benn, Barratt Brown *et al.*, all address themselves to the Labour movement and consider the vehicle of implementation of the changes in question to be a Leftist Labour government. These schemes, while they leave capitalist relations of production intact (a nationalised ICI as in Holland's scheme would still sell commodities produced by wage labour and compete against equivalent producers in world markets, adjusting itself to the conditions necessary for this competition), would provoke enormous resistance. The level of resistance involved cannot be measured by the (relatively modest) goal; one has only to think of the activities of Mr Cube. Many managements, whether nationalised or not, would resist to the bitter end and do everything in their power to sabotage the policies because they would consider these policies dangerous for their enterprises. A government committed to the *success* of certain planning objectives directed at private enterprises is politically a hostage to sabotage and evasion. The policies proposed by the various Left-Labour strategists presuppose a massive exercise of state powers of coercion, inspection, and regulation. A government even with a substantial and committed majority would face legislative obstacles, judicial resistance, and the opposition of the higher organs of certain ministries (notably the Treasury). The normal means of legislative enactment and administrative action are unlikely to overcome the combined resistance of enterprises, political organisations, and the state machine. The creation of special state institutions and the support of extra-parliamentary organised forces (trade unions, workers' committees, etc.) not restricted by narrow constitutionalism or legality would certainly be required. In other words, to implement such programmes a Labour government with a Left majority in Parliament backed by strong organised mass support would be necessary. Given the existence of these means, it would be absurd to limit the political objectives of such a government to the schemes of Holland or the other Left-Labour industrial strategists.

The problem resolves itself into a question Holland *et al.* are silent about: how to construct the basis of a Left electoral victory and its backing by an organised mass movement. We do not believe these political conditions can be created around a programme of 'industrial regeneration' or any such economic 'solution'. Rather than scheming as to what a Left-Labour government should do, it is vital to consider the political basis on which such a government will become a possibility. We would argue that this means starting at a more basic level:

1 with the *political* obstacles to advance within the practices of the Labour Left and the labour movement itself;

2 by broadening the base of mass support, creating institutions and organisations which extend the socialist movement beyond the minority of organised labour;

3 fighting for specific reforms in the organisation of capital that will create new positions of struggle and control for working people (limitations of shareholders' and managements' powers, workers' representation, etc.), fighting for reforms in non-commodity areas such as health, education, and welfare that introduce elements of popular administration and control.

This means that instead of looking for an economic 'solution' to Britain's economic problems in a Leftist policy of 'management' or doggedly bashing one's head against the effects of these problems (falling living standards, cuts in public expenditure) in an ultimately fruitless opposition, the Left should look to preparing for a longer-term struggle for power. This involves identifying the areas where it can begin to win victories that lead on to something. It involves selecting, and fighting for those legislative and administrative measures which are attainable given the dominance of non-socialist governments. It also involves developing through government reforms and through non-state action areas of mass organisation and intervention in the affairs of enterprises and of the state.

We will begin by considering the *political* obstacles to socialist advance constituted by the positions and activities of the Labour Left and the Labour movement itself. We will identify four basic areas. In each case the Left has committed itself either to the immobile defence of certain given institutional forms or to dogmatic opposition to others. The institutions defended are in no sense essentially socialist or privileged as areas of struggle for the Left. The institutions and practices opposed, opposed beyond the point where the effort involved could change things or have any positive political effect, are in no sense necessarily arenas in which socialists cannot struggle to advantage. The removal of these oppositionist shibboleths which have consumed the energies of the left to no political advantage and without changing the existing states of affairs is a crucial precondition for effective political advance. We will consider these institutional arenas in turn.

The most futile of the Left's continuing struggles is its opposition to the Common Market. The central reason for this opposition is said to be that EEC control involves a loss of sovereignty and that this destroys the autonomy for socialist strategies of managing the national economy. As the Left is in no position to exercise these management functions, this opposition is as pertinent as that of a beggar opposing the nationalisation of the banks for fear of his assets. The EEC is a state power in the making. At present the constraints offered by Community policy could easily be challenged or evaded by a sufficiently determined national government. What makes the EEC a constraining power at the moment is not any directive from the Commission but Britain's *de facto* integration in and dependence on the European economy. This dependence would be no less even if Britain ceased to be constitutionally a member of the EEC. The EEC is still open in the direction of development it will take, and the form of its institutions and policies. Because of its opposition to these institutions *per se* the Left has abandoned any strategic consideration of how to attempt to influence or how to adapt its politics to these growing institutions. Opposition *to* the EEC displaces any discussion of policy *in* the EEC. Central in this abandonment is the stupid opposition to the creation of and refusal to participate in European representative institutions. The only way regularly to supervise and challenge the actions of the Council of Ministers and the Commission in Community matters is by creating effective representative institutions parallel to those organs of European state power. Direct elections and proportional representation offer the Left a new arena of struggle which the established political forces have not yet colonised. It is an area which might well be exploited given the fear and concern of large numbers of people about the role of the EEC. It is an area which is being abandoned without a fight to the pro-market Rightists and the careerists looking for yet another salaried gravy train.

Nationalisation is another area of unprofitable and immobile Left-Labour commitment. Nationalisation has been conceived by the non-revolutionary Left as the main answer to problems of the regulation and control of capitalism, and as the solution to problems of industrial decline and reorganisation. The Left's critique of existing nationalisation programmes is to demand workers' control as an element in any future legislation. The problem with nationalisation is that the change in the form of property and management organisation by no means involves a strengthening of non-commodity relations or creates a basis for future socialist advance. The 'failure' of the existing nationalised industries is probably the most effective plank in *anti-socialist* propaganda because the Labour Left has defended and pushed for nationalisation as a characteristically 'socialist' alternative. Nationalised industries remain commodity producers, dependent on their success and failure (measured in terms of capitalist calculation) in selling commodities to state, capitalist, and domestic consumers. At the same time the capital funds of these industries are identified with the state's finances. As 'efficient' commodity producers these industries need to be able to regulate their prices, costs of production, and investment in some planned way. But in fact nationalised industries' managements have generally suffered from conditions of calculation far more unstable and less subject to control than those in large private enterprises like ICI. This is because governments have intervened to fix prices and because the capital expenditure programmes of these industries have been a ready source of budgetary cuts. Short-term 'economic management' adjustments have predominated in budgetary policy over the concerns of planning in these sectors (this planning requires autonomy in decision-making and operates on criteria distinct from those of national 'economic management'). Public economic policy has actually militated against planned commodity production in these sectors. Workers' control would not remove this contradiction; it would merely pit workers and management against the state. Even if a socialist government provided a more stable environment for these industries it would only be to enable them to operate in a way similar to a large enterprise like ICI (i.e. it would have to accord them *more* autonomy in capital budgeting and pricing policies).

If a socialist government attempted to intervene through these industries in the operations of the non-state sector (the dubious doctrine of 'the commanding heights') it would be attempting to use the activities of one set of commodity producers to constrain another. The fuel, power, and steel industries do not 'command' other commodity producers, they *sell* to them. These industries are determined in large measure by the demand from the private sector and by its considerations of competitiveness and costs (a wood-burning electricity-supply industry would not be too popular). The nationalised aeroplane industry will sell its products primarily abroad to capitalist airlines and foreign powers; so will the shipbuilding industry. *Nationalisation is in no sense a non-commodity measure.* Public ownership does not remove the effects of commodity production and competition. Nationalisation or partial public ownership *can* enable governments to control enterprises and to regulate commodity production, but in a much more specific way than in the 'commanding heights' doctrine. Public ownership can attempt to unscramble management failures (like British Leyland) in order to make them more 'efficient' commodity producers—and it could also bring 'rogue' enterprises to heel (firms like RTZ, Consolidated Goldfields and Lonrho could be forced to end their active co-operation with the racist regimes in southern Africa by such means, for example). The regulation and planning of production do not *require* public ownership; an integrated fuel and transport policy would have far more effect on the activities of the fuel, power, transport, and steel industries than nationalisation and public ownership under existing policies has had. The Left should consider first and foremost in proposing the nationalisation of enterprises and industries what it wants to do with them, and it should recognise that what it can do is limited by the fact that they remain commodity producers dominated by the continued existence of the private sector.

In the case of opposition to any form of incomes policy and the defence of 'free collective bargaining', what the Left as a whole has done is to commit itself to the interests of certain unions and certain groups of industrial workers who are able to bargain effectively. Opposition to the Tories' industrial relations policies was both necessary and correct; it involved a defence of existing basic trade union rights. What that struggle and its successful outcome hides, however, is the fact that 'free' collective bargaining can only benefit those *able* to bargain. It ignores the majority of non-unionised and unionised workers, most of whom do not have the organisation or the industrial position for effective bargaining, or are employees of the state. As we have indicated earlier, this commits the Left to what amounts to a sectional interest among the working masses and creates the prospect of serious divisions if inflation continues in double figures. In effect the union leaderships have capitulated to an incomes policy *without effective concessions*. They have done so because certain of the most powerful unions will not accept the reality of an incomes policy. Accepting the necessity of state intervention in the determination and regulation of wages, seeking to influence the form of that intervention, and seeking a *quid pro quo* for the loss of 'free' collective bargaining (for example, the implementation of the Bullock Report which would more than make up for this loss in the powers of supervision of and intervention in the affairs of enterprises it makes possible) are the ways in which the Left should adjust to the realities of incomes policy and attempt to make political advantage out of it. Refusing to accept the reality and being unable to change it is a guaranteed path to political sterility and defeat. The tragedy is that the Left has let the moment when it could have made the maximum political capital out of adopting a wages policy slip from its grasp.

The question of public expenditure and public spending cuts again reveals the utter sterility of oppositionist politics. In effect almost all sections of the Left have committed themselves to a simple blanket opposition to *all* public expenditure cuts (with the exception of defence). The result is that, with the cuts actually taking place, the Left, in refusing to accept their existence, has refused the language of priorities. It has condemned itself to be unable to concentrate on the defence of certain sectors and accept (or even push for) the priority of cuts in others. But this blanket defence is merely a symptom of the absence of a serious position on the sources of public finance and the objectives of public spending. Whether or not the cuts are 'necessary' is not really the pertinent question. Trends in public expenditure, whether of expansion or contraction, should be evaluated in the context of a general political position on the composition of public expenditure, its objectives, and finance. The Left as a whole lacks such a political position; it has reacted to the immediate effects of a change of policy in a way that has placed the object of that policy beyond question. We will repeat an obvious truism here: *state* expenditure is no more privileged as such in socialist terms than the expenditure of private enterprises. This truism needs to be repeated because of the Labour-Left's tendency to regard the public sector as in some sense privileged and to see the expansion of this sector a sign of the increasing 'socialisation' of the economy. State spending does not as such contribute to the development of non-commodity and co-operative relations. Arguably, 'private' co-operative bodies and popular mutual aid may make more of a contribution in that direction.

The sources of the Labour-Left's illusions are easy to see: a reverse reflex to the Tories free-marketism and an identification of public spending with the reforms which placed education and health care on a (primarily) non-commodity basis. The expansion of the level and scope of public expenditure in the two decades or so since those reforms has been considerable, particularly in the local-government sector. What is significant about this expansion is that it has *not* been primarily in those areas which directly benefit the working people—public transport, housing construction, welfare payments, education, and health care—even when the money is nominally spent on institutions like the NHS. What is also significant is the extent to which this expansion has been the expansion of 'professional' administrative machines (this expansion has contributed far more to the increase in public employment than any other single category of workers, and the increase has continued even while the number of employees in certain useful occupations in the public sector fell or remained static—council direct construction, factory inspectorate, etc.).

Ignored by the Left in the question of public expenditure is its foundation in public finance. Taxation is considered by the Left predominantly in distributional terms (in terms of the degree of progressivity, tax subsidies to and evasion by enterprises and the wealthy) and not in terms of its place in public finance. The significance of the considerable dependence of the level of public expenditure on central- and local-government borrowing is largely ignored, that is, the extent to which the markets in public bonds are a crucial element in the expansion and continued strength of financial capital. One cannot simultaneously control financial capital, attempting to limit and regulate its role in the economy, and leave the present structure of public finance untouched. In the long run that means arguing for basing an increasing proportion of the state's expenditure upon taxation.

Manifestly, a combination of a continuing relatively high rate of inflation and the need to reduce the public borrowing requirement (whether to check its inflationary effects, to please the IMF, or to regulate financial capital—there are few good arguments for continuing to expand it) will continue to produce pressures on public expenditure for some time to come. Given the likelihood of continuing controls on wages and pressure to hold down prices, personal and corporate taxation cannot increase significantly. Financing public expenditure through the existing forms of borrowing has definite distributional effects, and it is of direct benefit to financial capital (particularly to the clearing banks). There is no easy way to continue to finance or to expand public expenditure on the basis of the real levels pertaining, say, in 1975. The Left should come to terms with this fact and try to take what advantage there is to be made from it. The Left should now be thinking beyond the immediate defence of threatened jobs toward a longer-term programme of struggle on questions of public expenditure and finance. We will outline some possible areas of struggle.

1 On the question of the reorganisation of public finance and taxation, a campaign to highlight the role of finance capital and proposals to regulate it, and a campaign to expose the uselessness of the present forms of tax subsidies and concessions to business.

2 On questions of the *composition* of public expenditure any redistribution in a period of contraction or stagnation must mean cuts somewhere along the line. Far from defending all jobs and services as it has tended to do, the Left should identify those areas it wishes to give priority in defence and also those areas of negative or negligible social usefulness which ought to be cut (simply listing the duties and salaries of many local-government functionaries would make excellent propaganda).

3 'Professional' administrative machines eat resources. It is perfectly possible in a period of reduction in expenditure to attempt to fight the reduction in *services* by campaigning to place those services on a co-operative and popular administrative basis. Depending on how this type of measure was carried out the

result might be of real benefit in terms of extending non-commodity and non-bureaucratic social relations.

The degree to which such detailed struggles over public expenditure will be effective is obviously open to debate. Even on a pessimistic assessment there is more to be gained from these struggles than the negative and futile refusal that is already happening. Where such struggles are most likely to be effective is at the local-government level and through the various 'consultative' bodies (like the Community Health Councils). The revolutionary Left has traditionally largely ignored and despised these institutions. It is, however, much easier to elect socialist local councillors than it is MPs and in many cases local authorities offer ample scope for agitation and exposure. The Left cannot hope to reform the public finances as a whole, but a political programme on this question energetically pushed could gain it a good deal of popular support. As it is the Left's positions on this issue, as on so many others, are easily defeated in propaganda and political struggle because they fly in the face of political and economic realities.

We have placed particular stress on these four areas because they have consumed, negatively in our view, so much of the Left's time and energy in recent years. If the socialist forces within and around the Labour party fail to come to terms with the realities of continued membership of the EEC, of the limits of 'free' collective bargaining, and of constraints on public expenditure then they will continue to commit what strength they possess to a series of losing battles. At the same time they will ignore, often in these very areas, issues on which victories of some value might be won and new fields of struggle opened up.

Accepting that creating the conditions for an attempt to exercise political power involves a prolonged struggle means coming to terms with the political apparatuses involved. Accepting that there is no necessary political majority given in the working class means that the issues and organisations out of which the foundations of a socialist electoral victory can be made must be determined by analysis. This involves two reorientations.

The first is coming to terms with the need to concentrate on struggle *within* political organisations, rather than broadcasting a political appeal to an imaginary working class-as-political subject. This means concentrating agitation and struggle on transforming the Labour party and other organisations of the Labour movement and accepting that this can be nothing but a long job. It also means treating the Labour party as an arena to be struggled in rather than as a vehicle for political action in any immediate sense. It also means breaking the hold of Left-Labourism and the 'Trotskyist' groups on the positions of offering political alternatives to the Labour party leadership.

The second is coming to terms with democracy as a medium and form of political struggle. We mean this not only in the limited sense of accepting the continued dominance of parliamentary forms but in the broader sense of recognising the role popular democratic forms can play in creating the mass base and means of struggle for socialism. Tony Benn is one of the few Left politicians to recognise the power and value of the appeal to popular democracy. This power is evidenced by the extent of the response to the movement for workers' control. Accepting the dominance of representative institutions at the level of the state does not mean limiting politics to the struggle for parliamentary representation. Given the weakness of the Left, that can only produce repeated disaster. There is no necessary contradiction between representative and popular democracy. The very limits of representative democracy make popular democracy a potent force where parliamentary forms are dominant and continue to enjoy mass support. This support means that insurrectionist or terrorist politics are doomed to be marginal or criminal. It does *not* mean, however, the acceptance of narrow constitutionalism and legalism by the masses. Struggle in relation to parliament and the state need not and must not be confined to seeking to elect socialist MPs and councillors; parliamentary and administrative decisions can be influenced without a strong direct presence in representative institutions. The Left should attempt to develop popular involvement in the administration and regulation of activities (encouraging tenants' associations to take over housing estates, backing workers who treat their enterprises as activities they should direct and control, like the Hawker Siddeley shop stewards). This type of popular organisation and involvement has developed spontaneously and on a mass scale in recent years, e.g. squatters' and tenants' associations, community and minority groups, issue and resistance campaigns. It has also involved a far wider base than manual workers. It has developed in large measure *against* the activities of 'constitutional' authorities (central and local government, public authorities and planning bodies, boards of directors, etc.). This in no sense implies a general rejection of representative democracy rather a commitment to influence its workings and to develop substitutes for its failures to represent popular demands.

The revolutionary Left, particularly the Trotskyist sects, has involved itself in those organisations of this type which it identifies as forms of spontaneous action of the working class. Its relation to them has been to use them as arenas for revolutionary political agitation. In effect this means attempting to change one form of struggle, concerned to fight over definite issues within the existing institutions, into another. To the extent that a 'revolutionary' politics is a non-politics, a politics of deferment and hope, success in this enterprise could only mean the effective demobilisation of these struggles. On the contrary, building a base for socialist support for these struggles means fighting them for what they are, winning where possible, and developing the popular involvement. The revolutionary Left's relation to such activities and organisations has been opportunist, exploitative, and largely unsuccessful.

We began our discussion by saying we cannot offer a strategy and programme. Our aim has been limited to indicating the *context* in which a strategy articulated around the dominance of parliamentary forms must operate. We have tried to indicate that the Left cannot hope to win power quickly by schemes for the management of the national economy, that it must carefully prepare the basis for struggling for power inside and outside the Labour party, that it must begin to win (however small the victories may appear), and that it must appear credible. We have also stressed the need to broaden the socialist forces beyond the traditional conception of the 'Labour movement'. Particularly urgent is the need to extend involvement beyond the traditional constituency of urban manual workers (not merely because it is shrinking but because large sections of that constituency are sunk in a semi-impenetrable political apathy and indifference). This must involve moving beyond workerism, beyond privileging the articulated interests of certain bodies of trade unionists. It involves taking seriously issues that may, superficially, appear remote from socialism and giving them a high order of priority in struggle. Issues such as civil rights, the position of women, the control of environment and living space, all involve moving outside of the traditional appeals of workerism. They also offer in many cases opportunities for co-operative activities and self-administrative organisations. 'Socialism' conceived either as an insurrectionary seizure of power by the workers, or as public ownership combined with planning by state officials *is* remote from these questions. That is the problem with the classic insurrectionist and labourist political ideologies. Determining the content of socialist political ideology involves recognising the conditions of struggle and learning from the successes and failures of the socialist movement. Workerism and statism are the two cardinal limitations of British Labourist socialism. Recognising the importance and potential role of other aspects of this socialist movement, co-operation, self-action, and self-administration may go some way to redressing the balance, and can broaden and develop the appeal of socialist political ideology.

It is on the basis of successful, broadly based practical activity and organisation that a positive attitude toward the struggle for power on a non-insurrectionary basis can be developed. It is this basic attitude, far more than any 'programme', which is what the British Left needs. A precondition for political programmes adapted to the conditions of struggle is a recognition of basic political realities and the limits they enforce. It is toward this end that this book is directed.

Bibliography

Benn, Tony, *Speeches and Writings* (London, Spokesman Books, 1974).
Benn, Tony, *Labour and the Slump* (Pamphlet no. 48, Institute of Workers' Control, 1975).
Benn, Tony, Morrell, Frances, and Cripps, Francis, *A Ten-Year Industrial Strategy for Labour* (Pamphlet no. 49, Institute of Workers' Control, 1975).
Boston Group Associates, *Strategy Alternatives for the British Motor Cycle Industry* (London, HMSO, 1975).
Bright, J. R., *Automation and Management* (Boston, Harvard University Press, 1958).
Bullock, Allan *et al.*, *Report of the Royal Commission on Industrial Democracy* (London, HMSO, 1976).
Burnham, J., *The Managerial Revolution* (Harmondsworth, Penguin, 1962).
Cambridge Political Economy Group, *Britain's Economic Crisis* (Pamphlet no. 44, Spokesman Books, 1974).
Central Policy Review Staff, *The Future of the British Car Industry* (London, HMSO, 1975).
De Brunhoff, S., *Marx On Money* (London, Pluto Press, 1977).
Dobb, M., 'The Sraffa system and critique of the neo-classical theory of distribution', *De Economist*, 118, 1970.
Done, K., 'Electronics advance', *Financial Times*, 19 October 1976.
Draper, P. M. *et al.*, *Money, Health and the NHS* (London, Unit for the Study of Health Policy, Guy's Hospital, 1976).
Eaton, J., Barratt Brown, M., and Coates, K., *An Alternative Economic Strategy for the Labour Movement* (Pamphlet no. 47, Spokesman Books, 1975).
Fishlock, D., 'The glamour goes out of technology', *Financial Times*, 28 February 1977.
Foucault, M., *The Order of Things* (London, Tavistock, 1970).
Godley, W. and Wood, A., 'Profits and stock appreciation', *Cambridge Economic Policy Review*, 1 March 1975.
Gregory, R. S. and James, D. W., 'Do new factories embody best practice

technology?', *Economic Journal*, 83, December 1973.
Hannah, L., *The Rise of the Corporate Economy* (London, Methuen, 1976).
Harris, A., 'Cross your fingers—and get them burned', *Financial Times*, 9 October 1976.
Harrod, R. F., *Money* (London, Macmillan, 1969).
Hilferding, R., *Finance Capital* (Vienna, 1910; Paris, Minuit, 1970).
Hirst, P. Q., 'Althusser and the theory of ideology', *Economy and Society*, 5, 4, 1976.
Hodgson, G., 'Marxian epistemology and the transformation problem', *Economy and Society*, 3, 4, 1974.
Holland, S., *The Socialist Challenge* (London, Quartet Books, 1975).
Hollis, M. and Nell, E. J., *Rational Economic Man* (Cambridge University Press, 1975).
Hume, D., *Of Money, Political Discourses* (Edinburgh, Fleming, 1752).
Hussain, A., 'Crises and tendencies of capitalism', *Economy and Society*, 6, 4, 1977.
Johnson, C., *Anatomy of UK Finance 1970–75* (London, *Financial Times*, 1976).
Kautsky, K., 'Gold, papier und ware', *Die Neue Zeit*, 31, 24, 1910.
Keynes, J. M., *The General Theory of Employment, Interest and Money* (London, Macmillan, 1973).
Keynes, J. M., 'The economic consequences of Mr. Churchill', *Collected Writings*, vol. IX (London, Macmillan, 1972).
Lenin, V. I., *The Development of Capitalism in Russia, Collected Works*, vol. 3 (Moscow, Progress Publishers, 1964).
Lenin, V. I., *Imperialism: The Highest Stage of Capitalism*, and *The Discussion of Self-Determination Summed Up*, both in *CW*, vol. 22 (Moscow, Progress Publishers, 1964).
Lenin, V. I., *Imperialism and the Split in Socialism, CW*, vol. 23 (Moscow, Progress Publishers, 1964).
Luxemburg, R., *The Accumulation of Capital* (London, Routledge & Kegan Paul, 1963).
Lynch, H. H., *The Financial Performance of Conglomerates* (Boston, Harvard University Press, 1971).
Mandel, E., *Late Capitalism* (London, New Left Books, 1975).
Mao Tse-tung, *On Contradiction, Selected Works*, vol. 1 (Peking, Foreign Languages Press, 1967).
Marshall, A., *Principles of Economics* (London, Macmillan, 1961).
Marx, Karl, *Capital* vols 1–3 (Moscow, FLPH-Progress) (different printings vary as to pagination, for part 1, 1965; for part 2, 1962; for part 3, 1966).
Marx, Karl, *A Contribution to the Critique of Political Economy* (with '1857 Introduction') (London, Lawrence & Wishart, 1971).
Marx, Karl, *Theories of Surplus Value* (London, Lawrence & Wishart, 1969, 1972).
Meek, R., 'Introduction to Second Edition', *Studies in the Labour Theory of Value* (London, Lawrence & Wishart, 1973).

Merrett, A. J. and Sykes, A., 'The real crisis facing British Industry', *Financial Times*, 30 September 1974.
Merrett, A. J. and Sykes, A., 'The industrial crisis after Mr. Healey's budget', *Financial Times*, 19 November 1974.
Morishima, M., *Marx's Economics* (Cambridge University Press, 1973).
Neuburg, A., *Armed Insurrection* (London, New Left Books, 1973).
Neumann, J. von, 'A model of economic equilibrium', *Review of Economic Studies*, XIII, 1945-6.
Parry, T., 'The international firm and national policy', *Economic Journal*, 83, 1973.
Patinkin, D., *Money, Interest and Prices* (2nd edition) (New York, Harper & Row, 1965).
Pigou, A. C. See R. Clower (ed.), *Readings in Monetary Theory* (Harmondsworth, Penguin, 1971).
Powles, J., 'On the limitations of modern medicine', *Science, Medicine and Man*, 1, 1, 1973.
Prais, S. J., *The Evolution of Giant Firms in Britain* (Cambridge University Press, 1976).
Pratten, C. F., *A Comparison of the Performance of Swedish and UK Companies* (Cambridge University Press, 1976).
Pratten, C. F., *Labour Productivity Differences within International Companies* (Cambridge University Press, 1976).
'Resources devoted to research and development by manufacturing industry', *Economic Trends*, March 1974.
Sandilands, F. E. P., *Inflation Accounting: Report of the Inflation Accounting Committee* (London, HMSO, 1975).
Scherer, F. M., 'The determinants of industrial plant sizes in six nations', *Review of Economics and Statistics*, LV, 2, May 1973.
Singh, A. J., 'Take overs, economic natural selection and the theory of the firm', *Economic Journal*, 85, September 1975.
Smith, A., 'Footwear under scrutiny', *Financial Times*, 14 December 1976.
Sraffa, P., *The Production of Commodities by Means of Commodities* (Cambridge University Press, 1960).
Steedman, I., 'Value, price and profit', *New Left Review*, 90, 1974.
Steedman, I., 'Positive profits with negative surplus value', *Economic Journal*, 85, 1975.
Wiles, P. J. O., *Price, Cost and Output* (Oxford, Blackwell, 1961).
Winter, S. G., 'Economic "natural selection" and the theory of the firm', *Yale Economic Essays*, 4, 1, Spring 1964.
Wolfstetter, E., 'Surplus value, synchronised labour costs and Marx's labour theory of value', *Economic Journal*, 83, 1973.
Wood, A., *A Theory of Profits* (Cambridge University Press, 1975).
Wooley, P. K. 'The economics of the UK stock exchange', *Moorgate and Wall Street*, Spring 1974.

Index to Both Volumes

This index is not arranged as a single alphabetical list of concepts, names and topics. This is because the discussions in this work are concerned with a limited number of key concepts and as a result we have thought it better to group the individual entries under the main concept to which they are connected rather than disperse them through the list. The entries grouped under each concept heading are not listed alphabetically but (in so far as this is possible) in order of generality and importance. The reason for this is that the names of many of the entries are far from obvious ones and in consequence they would probably be overlooked in an alphabetical list. We suggest that the reader look through the system of categories before trying to use the index. Where possible, when entries grouped under different main concepts are very closely related, cross reference is given (with the category number, followed by the entry heading). A separate list of names (primarily of authorities discussed or quoted and authors of works cited) is also given. The volume numbers, in bold type and enclosed in brackets, precede the page number.

Concept Areas

1 Analysis of discourse, critique of epistemology and general methodological questions
2 Social formation, mode of production
3 Agents and the structure of the social formation
4 Value and prices
5 Money
6 Classes
7 Economic calculation
8 Circulation, exchange and reproduction
9 Tendency, contradiction and transition
10 Financial capital, institutions and markets
11 Capitalist organisation and enterprises
12 National economies
13 Socialist political ideology and practice
14 Socialist politics in Britain

1 Analysis of discourse, critique of epistemology and general methodological questions

discourse/s (status of, and forms of analysis of), (1) 4, 5, 12, 20, 52–3, 67, 107–9, 114, 119–20, 122–4, 129–32, 157–61, 163, 180, 218, 228–9; (2) 130, 233–5
epistemologies/doctrines of method, (1) 109–13, 119, 122, 127, 159–61, 180, 211–17, 221, 228, 238; (2) 157
epistemological privilege/dogmatism, (1) 215–18
empiricist epistemologies/doctrines, (1) 212–15, 219–20
rationalist epistemologies/doctrines, (1) 211–15, 219–20, 223, 228, 238, 313
appropriation of the concrete in thought, (1) 110–12, 125; (2) 233
relation between discourse and its objects, (1) 211, 213–16, 218–20
science/ideology distinction, (1) 180, 213

causal doctrines/privileged causality, (1) 127–32, 164, 181–2, 213–14; (2) 243
historical necessity/economic determinism, (1) 124–8, 131, 135–42
determination by the economic in the last instance, (1) 169–70, 172, 176, 196, 207, 209–12, 220, 223–4
role of economic in Marxist discourse if determinism not assumed, (1) 229–30, 315–16
structural causality, (1) 159, 171, 199, 200, 202, 224, 314

totality (entity governed by organising principle), (1) 111–17, 121–4, 169–70, 178, 227–8, 231, 316–17; (2) 221–2, 229–31, 241–3
CMP as totality-entity (including total social capital and capitalist economy in general), (1) 3, 106, 113–14, 118–19, 121, 123, 152, 164, 172; (2) 111–12, 127, 129, 133–6, 147, 149, 154–5, 189, 235–6, 238, 241–2
'mapping', (1) 113, 121, 123, 133. (*See also* 9: tendencies)
conditions of existence of social relations, (1) 173, 208–10, 218–19, 221–3, 227, 239–41, 276, 278, 288, 290, 306, 314–15
philosophical anthropology as grounding social relations, (1) 69

2 Social formation, mode of production

structure of social formation, Marxist concept of, (1) 169–82, 196–7, 199, 222–3, 226–8, 230–1, 238, 313–14, 316–17. (*See also* 1: totality)
mode of production, general concept of, (1) 174, 196, 218, 222–6, 230, 238, 314; (2) 241
modes/relations of production:
    feudal, (1) 177, 243, 246–8, 254, 258, 277–8, 286
    slave, (1) 243, 251, 254, 257, 278
    pre-capitalist ground rent, Marx on, (1) 243, 245–8
relations of production, (1) 208, 225, 227, 241, 246, 254
relative autonomy, (1) 169–70, 172, 176. (*See also* 1: determination by the economic in the last instance)
means of production, definition of, (1) 251–3

3 Agents and the structure of the social formation

agents, general, (1) 173, 182, 239–41, 249, 256–7, 263, 266–7, 273–4, 278, 285, 288, 318–19. (*See also* 7: representation of economic process to agents by structure)
agents as subjects, (1) 267–70; (2) 187
agents as structure effects, (1) 270–2, 274
non-individual forms of agent, (1) 276–8. (*See also* 11: economic subject in capitalism, definition of; joint-stock company)
forms of recognition/constitution of agents, (1) 278–81
agents and the rationalist conception of action, (1) 269–70

ideology, (1) 202, 205–6; (2) 111, 122, 128. (*See also* 7: Economic calculation)
ideological state apparatuses, (1) 202, 265–8, 270

4 Value and prices

value, general, (1) 3, 4, 9, 11; (2) 241
value as measure/exchange as equation, (1) 12–19, 26, 35–6, 43, 54, 60, 86; (2) 17–18, 215
labour time as measure of value, (1) 11, 25
value-creating power of labour, (1) 36, 38–43, 58, 69
machinery, automation and value, (1) 39–43
value and division of labour of society, (1) 17, 21–3, 27–30, 37, 42–4, 69–71, 75–6, 80–6, 88, 90–1, 93; (2) 13–14. (*See also* 4: equilibrium—reproduction prices)
grounding of pertinence value, (1) 38. (*See also* 1: philosophical anthropology as grounding social relations)
value and use-value, (1) 38, 58–60, 67–8, 86–7, 91
abstract and concrete labour, (1) 55, 89–90
form of value, (1) 26, 37, 54, 74–5
problem of the source of profit, (1) 17–19, 31–5
surplus value, (1) 31–5, 295; (2) 254
exploitation, (1) 33, 35–6, 45–7, 254–5, 259; (2) 22
labour and labour power, (1) 38, 44–5; (2) 112
constant and variable capital, (1) 38, 44
value and classes, general, (1) 45–7
value in classical political economy, (1) 20
utility and theory of value, (1) 24, 43, 58–60, 67–9, 86–7
supply and demand and theory of value, (1) 60–2, 83–6, 88, 91–3
competition and theory of value, (1) 62
problem of labour reduction, (1) 63–6
values and prices, (1) 30, 36–7, 53–8, 73, 83, 94–5; (2) 12–13, 21–2, 86, 215

prices, theories postulating universal determinants and economic functions of, (1) 14, 19; (2) 86, 216–18, 231–2
functions of prices in economic discourses, (1) 61, 62
equilibrium—reproduction prices, (1) 70–1, 81–5, 87–8, 91–3, 98–100; (2) 216–18, 221–4

Sraffa model/Sraffa economy, (2) 217–18, 220, 227, 231–2
economy of processes, (2) 216, 218, 220, 227
standard commodity, (2) 217, 226–8, 230
joint production, (2) 224–6
consumption in Sraffa model, (2) 222–3
dated labour series, (2) 228
classical/neo-classical problem of distribution, (2) 219–21, 230–1

5 Money

money, general, (1) 2, 99–100; (2) 231–2
functions of money:
  general, (2) 1–10, 16–17, 24, 26–7, 29–30, 56–7, 59, 72
  medium of circulation, (2) 6–7, 9, 13, 16–18, 23, 25–6, 28–9, 56, 82, 87
  measure of value, (2) 5, 9–13, 29
  standard of prices, (2) 16–22
  means of deferred payment, (2) 16–17, 22–5, 56, 72, 74
forms of money:
  general, (2) 6–10, 12, 28–30, 103–4, 245–6, 266
  commodity, (2) 5–6, 8–12, 22, 25, 28–35, 45, 52, 103, 205–6, 245
  non-commodity, (2) 11–12, 29, 31, 246
  fiduciary, (2) 6, 28, 32–6, 43, 52
  credit, (2) 6, 24–6, 28, 30, 36, 52–3, 75, 103–4, 106, 245, 251
money as sign, (2) 13–15
money and problem of representation of wealth, (2) 84–7
orthodox monetary theorists' analysis of money, (2) 56–7, 60–1, 72–4, 78–81, 84–7
supply of and demand for money, (2) 78–9, 81
the quantity equation, (2) 82–7
circulation of money, (2) 77–82, 85, 87
velocity of circulation money, (2) 80
monetary exchange contrasted with barter, (2) 56–63, 65–9, 71–4, 81, 102
money and problem of financing, (2) 77, 81–4, 87–8
money as a distributive relation, (2) 30–1, 52–4, 246–7
legal tender, (2) 33–6, 41–2, 53
effects of wages taking money form, (2) 19–21, 126
money, gold and foreign trade, (2) 32–3, 35, 41–6, 54–5. (*See also* 8: foreign trade)
gold standard, (2) 31, 44–5, 47, 51–2, 247, 250
money and socialism, (2) 15, 67

6 Classes

classes, general, (1) 4, 169–71, 231, 260–1, 289; (2) 241–3, 257–8
theories of classes:
  class as intersubjective unity, (1) 186–95
  counterposition of subject and structure, (1) 171, 185–6, 203–6, 234–5, 263–4
  class as structure effect, (1) 171, 185, 195–9, 201, 263–4

classes/human individuals, (1) 173, 182, 286-8, 319-20
class interests, (1) 236-7, 239
classes and labour of supervision, (1) 299-303
productive and unproductive labour, (1) 47, 257, 291-9; (2) 257
non-class forms of division of labour force, (1) 261-2, 290-1

possession/separation, (1) 46-7, 177, 182, 208, 240-61, 275-6, 289, 291, 312, 324-8; (2) 121, 230-1
communal possession of means of production, (1) 319-23
labourer and non-labourer, (1) 243-5, 254-61, 291, 302-3
social and technical divisions of labour, (1) 182, 255-61, 289, 312
class relations between agents other than direct producers, (1) 250-1, 253
class relations and systems of circulation/reproduction, (1) 252-3
political representation of economic classes, (1) 170, 172, 183-4, 222, 231-7, 242, 314-15, 328; (2) 257-8

7 Economic calculation

calculation, general, (1) 117-19, 240, 273-7, 281-4, 307-11, 318; (2) 19-21, 26, 87-8, 106-7, 111, 128, 232, 256, 279-80
representation of economic process to agents by structure, (1) 4, 116-18, 239, 264-5, 305; (2) 111-12, 128, 242, 256
fetishism, (1) 3, 27, 75-80; (2) 13-15
economic ideologies—false sources of value, (2) 112-23
theories ascribing universal forms and functions to calculation, (2) 129-33, 141
subjects of universal forms of calculation, (1) 274; (2) 129-31, 141-2, 154, 189, 196
domains of application of theories of calculation, (2) 129-31. (*See also* 1: CMP as totality-entity)
rationality, (1) 283-4
marginalist theories of calculation, (2) 129
profit maximisation, (2) 132, 141-8, 190
'economic natural selection', (2) 146-9
measurement of returns/accounting practices, (2) 131-3, 144, 155
measures of profit, (2) 132, 134-40
accounting treatments of stocks, (2) 135-7, 156
'managerialist' calculation, (2) 144-6, 189-90, 192-6, 220-1
'going concern' concept of enterprise, (2) 130-40, 143, 145, 163
concept of enterprise as a parcel of assets, (2) 143, 145
calculation of financial conglomerates, (2) 142-3, 145, 213-14
calculation of multi-national enterprises, (2) 160-2
calculation industrial enterprises and sources of finance, (2) 140, 142, 145, 168, 202-4, 205-14
mergers, enterprise finance and calculation, (2) 197-8
time periods of calculation, (2) 149-52, 203-8
comparison of calculative strategies in British and Japanese motorcycle industries, (2) 150-2, 163-4, 166, 169-72, 178, 203, 256

mechanisation of production methods—calculation of costs and profits:
  general, (2) 164–6, 173–8
  technical determinants of choice of production methods, (2) 167–8
  'technical' calculation, (2) 168–9
  delivery of products and supply of raw materials as questions affecting mechanisation, (2) 166–7, 171
  limits on mechanisation posed by structure of consumption and markets, (2) 179–85

8 Circulation, exchange and reproduction

production and circulation in *Capital*, (1) 48–9
role of circuit concepts in *Capital*, (2) 63–4
commodity circulation (properties of), (2) 56–9, 62–5, 73–5, 77–82, 87–9, 90–1
effects of multilateral exchanges in capitalism, (2) 67–70. (*See also* 5: Money)
money balances of agents and circulation, (2) 68–71. (*See also* 5: money and problem of financing)
problem of realisation of surplus value, (2) 88
reproduction, (1) 96–101; (2) 185–6
foreign trade, (2) 49–51, 281–2. (*See also* 5: money, gold and foreign trade)
free trade, (2) 44, 49

9 Tendency, contradiction and transition

tendencies, general, (1) 1, 4; (2) 179–82, 185, 231, 234–6, 239–40, 241, 254, 259–60
concept of law of tendency, (1) 105–6, 114–15, 119–20, 132–4, 153, 158–65; (2) 111–12, 123–8, 179, 188, 234, 268–9
forces and relations of production:
  correspondence and contradiction, (1) 135–9, 143–8, 200, 207–8, 220, 226
  grounding of process development of productive forces, (1) 140–2. (*See also* 1: philosophical anthropology as grounding social relations)
  transition from feudalism to capitalism, (1) 143–6
  transition from capitalism to socialism, (1) 147–54
specific tendencies in capitalism:
  concentration and centralisation, (1) 147–53; (2) 93, 127, 268–9
  decline in rate of profit, (1) 120, 133–4, 157–64
  formation of industrial reserve army, (2) 125–6, 180–1, 244, 246
  rising organic composition of capital, (1) 162–3; (2) 22, 123–5
  socialisation, (1) 147–8, 150–1, 154
crises in capitalism, (1) 99
monopoly capital (as product tendencies), (1) 1, 2, 4, 105–6; (2) 236, 254, 260, 268–9
imperialism (as product tendencies), (1) 1; (2) 50, 236, 238

10 Financial capital, institutions and markets

finance capital, general concept of, **(1)** 1, 2, 4, 306–8, 311; **(2)** 89, 92–3, 212, 226

financial institutions, general, **(2)** 3–4, 24–5, 28, 34, 36–46, 51, 89–90, 94, 98, 101, 103–8, 142–5

differentiation of financial circuit and commodities circuit, **(2)** 23–4, 91

credit:
    general, **(1)** 154–55; **(2)** 22–4, 51–2, 87, 89–90, 92–4, 106, 204–7
    lending and borrowing, **(2)** 90–1, 94, 101–4, 196–8
    trade credit, **(2)** 22, 102

developed system of interrelated deposits in financial institutions, **(2)** 38–9, 42, 90, 257

credit creation by financial institutions/system, **(2)** 39, 43

financial assets and money, **(2)** 74–5, 90

market in financial assets, **(2)** 25–6, 94, 96–8, 100

stock market, **(1)** 154–6; **(2)** 96–101, 154, 211–14

rate of interest, **(2)** 97–8

speculation, **(2)** 26, 94–6, 213–14

conception of financial institutions as intermediaries, **(2)** 104–5, 107–8

central bank:
    general role in monetary systems, **(2)** 33–4, 36, 39–43, 45, 53–4, 106–7, 162
    monopoly in issue legal tender, **(2)** 33–4, 36
    role in credit regulation and control, **(2)** 37, 39, 43

public expenditure/public debt, **(2)** 40–1, 49, 53–4, 100–1, 289–90. (*See also* 14: cuts in public expenditure)

monetary policy as means of economic management, **(2)** 45–8. (*See also* 12: National economies)

11 Capitalist organisation and enterprises

a capital, definition of in the absence of a theory of value, **(1)** 307–9

economic subject in capitalism, definition of, **(1)** 306–7, 309–11

capital as a relation of production, **(1)** 156

organisational forms of capital/enterprises, **(1)** 154; **(2)** 92–3, 256

capitalist management, **(1)** 304–8, 309–12. (*See also* 7: 'managerialist' calculation)

joint-stock company, **(1)** 153–6, 182, 249, 276–7, 281, 285–7, 311; **(2)** 120–1, 249

divorce of ownership and control, **(1)** 154–5, 306, 311; **(2)** 120–1, 144, 189–90, 192, 200

Companies Acts/company law, **(2)** 152, 155, 247–9

neo-classical theory of firm, **(2)** 190–2, 196

industrial enterprise and sources of finance. (*See also* 7: Economic calculation):
    internal sources, **(2)** 204–6
    share issues, **(2)** 205–6
    loans, **(2)** 206–7
    sources finance UK and US companies, **(2)** 209–11

12 National economies

concept of national economy, (1) 2; (2) 93, 127, 130, 160, 185, 187, 233–5, 238, 243–5, 250–3, 259, 266–7, 274–80, 282–3
structure of branches of production and, (2) 243, 254
'managerialist' conception of national economy, (2) 259
role of state in setting parameters economy/economic policy, (2) 250–3, 266–7, 279
taxation, (2) 48, 138, 247
regulation of labour force, (2) 245–6, 250
unemployment as an economic problem, (2) 41, 45–52

13 Socialist political ideology and practice

political calculation, (1) 237–8; (2) 186, 237–8, 258, 267, 270–1
socialism, (1) 323–8
capitalism and socialism contrasted, (1) 49–50, 151; (2) 67
scientific and utopian socialism, (2) 260–2
socialist political ideology in the absence of essentialistic reference to classes, (1) 316–18, 328; (2) 258, 260–3, 265, 267–9, 292–3
non-commodity relations and socialist ideology/politics, (2) 264
role of means of political struggle in conditioning socialist strategies, (2) 270–2
'national crisis', as object of Leninist politics, (2) 237–8, 240
'economism', (2) 239–40, 268
'reformism'/reform-revolution opposition, (2) 264, 267, 273
socialist strategy/political struggle under conditions of dominance of parliamentary democracy, (2) 238–41, 264, 269, 272, 291–3
'insurrectionism' and 'oppositionism' as left responses to this dominance, (2) 272–4

14 Socialist politics in Britain

British economy and socialist politics, (2) 233–4
'industrial regeneration' strategies, (2) 274–82
Labour Party, (2) 263–4, 270–4, 290–1
Labour left, (2) 274, 282–5, 288
CPGB, (2) 268, 271–2
political obstacles constituted by practices of left, (2) 284–90
trades unions/TU policies, (2) 255–6, 265
Industrial Relations Act (1971), (2) 273, 286–7
incomes policies, (2) 273–4, 287–90
cuts in public expenditure, (2) 274, 287–90
nationalisation, (2) 260, 264, 277, 280, 282, 285–6
National Health Service, (2) 184, 265
European Economic Community, (2) 274, 281–2, 284–5, 290
multi-national companies and British economy, (2) 276–7

Name Index

Althusser, Louis, **(1)** 79–80, 108, 110, 122–3, 159, 171, 180, 185, 196–7, 199, 200–3, 207, 213, 217, 223–5, 263, 265–8, 270–2, 286–7; **(2)** 238
Anderson, Perry, **(1)** 247

Balibar, Étienne, **(1)** 79–80, 159, 223–5
Barratt Brown, Michael, **(2)** 281–2
Benn, Anthony Wedgwood, **(2)** 256, 275–7, 279–80, 282, 291
Berle, Adolf, **(1)** 311
Berlin, Isaiah, **(1)** 124
Bernstein, Edouard, **(2)** 239
Bettelheim, Charles, **(1)** 50, 323–5
Bevan, Aneurin, **(2)** 264, 274
Böhm-Bawerk, Eugen von, **(1)** 9, 43, 51–67, 72–4, 92, 283
Boston Consulting Group, **(2)** 150, 207
Braverman, Harry, **(1)** 44, 304
Bright, J. R., **(2)** 170, 172–5
British Leyland, **(1)** 151; **(2)** 249, 256–7, 286
Brunhoff, Suzanne de, **(2)** 3, 8
Bukharin, Nikolai, **(1)** 1, 51
Bullock, Alan, **(2)** 249
Burnham, James, **(2)** 189

Cambridge Political Economy Group, **(2)** 281
Carchedi, G., **(1)** 297, 301–4

Central Policy Review Staff, **(2)** 183–4, 278
Chayanov, A. V., **(1)** 283–4
China, People's Republic of, **(2)** 262–3
Classical political economy, **(1)** 74–5; **(2)** 84, 219, 244
Colbert, **(2)** 251
Commune of Paris (1871), **(2)** 262
Corn laws, **(1)** 250

Deborin, Abram, **(1)** 78
Dobb, Maurice, **(2)** 221
Done, K., **(2)** 183
Draper, P. M., **(2)** 184

Exchange Equalisation Account, **(2)** 45
Engels, Friedrich, **(1)** 69, 141, 157, 179, 190, 322
    letter of to J. Bloch, **(1)** 125–6, 130

Federal Reserve Bank, **(2)** 45
Feuerbach, Ludwig, **(1)** 141
Fishlock, D., **(2)** 184
Ford, Henry, **(1)** 259; **(2)** 279
Foucault, Michel, **(2)** 84

Godley, W., **(2)** 136–8, 156
Gramsci, Antonio, **(1)** 234
Gregory, R. S., **(2)** 169

Name Index

Hannah, Lesley, (2) 168–9, 182
Harris, A., (2) 162
Harrod, Roy, (2) 45
Hegel, G. W. F., (1) 15–16, 69, 75, 122–3, 141, 153, 305
Hilferding, Rudolf, (1) 1–2, 9, 17, 36, 43, 51–3, 56–60, 63, 64, 66–8, 70–2, 85, 98, 100; (2) 3, 6, 11–12, 28–9, 31, 89, 91–4, 96, 108
Hindess, Barry, (1) 108, 153, 180, 213, 269, 273, 324
Hindess, Barry, and Hirst, Paul:
  (*Pre-Capitalist Modes of Production*), (1) 47, 143, 177, 179, 199, 223–5, 227, 243, 245, 248, 253–4, 257, 259, 320
  (*Mode of Production and Social Formation*), (1) 5, 108, 158, 171, 213, 215, 316
Hirst, Paul, (1) 201, 265, 271; (2) 187
Hodgson, Geoff, (2) 215
Holland, Stuart, (2) 274–83
Hollis, Martin (and Nell, Edward), (2) 157–60, 186
Hume, David, (2) 6
Hussain, Athar, (2) 125, 185

Inflation Accounting Committee, report of, (2) 133

Johnson, C., (2) 209–11

Kant, Immanuel, (1) 214
Kautsky, Karl, (2) 11, 239, 258
Keynes, John Maynard, (2) 5, 26, 46–8, 72, 76, 153–4, 177, 247
Keynesianism, (2) 40, 259, 276

Lecourt, Dominique, (1) 123
Lenin, Vladimir Ilich, (1) 1, 152, 179, 184, 230, 232–3, 237, 263; (2) 3, 12, 46, 50, 91–4, 101, 108, 236–7, 240, 253, 258
Lukács, Georg, (1) 171, 185, 189–95, 203, 205–6, 234, 263
Luxemburg, Rosa, (2) 88
Lynch, H. H., (2) 213

Mandel, Ernest, (2) 11–12, 235
Mao Tse-tung, (1) 237; (2) 238, 262
Maoism, (2) 263
Marshall, A., (2) 84
Marx, Karl
  Works other than *Capital* discussed in text:
    1844 Manuscripts, (1) 43, 140; *Communist Manifesto*, (1) 186–7; *18th Brumaire*, (1) 183–4, 186, 187, 192; *Grundrisse*, (1) 40–1, 43, 107, 142–3; *A Contribution to the Critique of Political Economy*, (1) 31–3, 45, 48, 260: '1857 Introduction' to, (1) 107, 110–12, 122, 124, 174–5, 179; (2) 243; '1859 Preface' to, (1) 124, 135–48, 153, 164, 174–5, 179, 197; *Critique of the Gotha Programme*, (1) 31–3, 45, 48, 260; *Theories of Surplus Value*, (1) 25–6, 292, 293, 296, 298; (2) 122
  Letters to:
    Kugelmann, (1) 28–9; Otechestvenniye Zapiski, (1) 125; Weydemeyer, (1) 182, 197, 323
Medvedev, Roy, (1) 78
Meek, Ronald, (2) 215
Meillassoux, Claude, (1) 320
Merrett, A. J., (2) 136–40, 156, 212
Mill, James, (1) 24
Morgan, Lewis Henry, (1) 322
Morishima, M., (2) 225

neo-Darwinism, (1) 69
neo-Kantianism, (1) 189–90, 193
neo-Ricardianism, (1) 10; (2) 215–16, 220, 224
Neumann, J. von, (2) 216–17
New Poor Law, (2) 250

Partie Communiste Français (PCF), (2) 268–70
Patinkin, D., (2) 87
Pigou, A. C., (2) 84
Popper, Karl, (1) 124
Powles, J., (2) 184

Poulantzas, Nicos, **(1)** 171, 185, 197, 203–6, 244, 263, 289–90, 295–7, 300–1, 303–4
Prais, S. J., **(2)** 177, 182, 197, 199–200
Pratten, C. F., **(2)** 161

Rancière, Jacques, **(1)** 305
Revai, Josef, **(1)** 191
Rey, Pierre-Philippe, **(1)** 320
Riasanov, David, **(1)** 78
Ricardo, David, **(1)** 20–1, 24–6, 74; **(2)** 11, 14, 49, 84, 220–1
Robbins, Lionel, **(2)** 158
Rubin, I. I., **(1)** 9, 17, 36, 43, 60, 66, 68, 70, 72, 73–8, 80–7, 94–5, 98

Samuelson, Paul A., **(1)** 98
Sandilands, F. E. P., **(2)** 133–5, 144, 154, 156
Sartre, Jean-Paul, **(2)** 262
Say, Jean-Baptiste, **(2)** 62
Scherer, F. M., **(2)** 179–80
Singh, A. J., **(2)** 193

Smith, Adam, **(1)** 20–5, 27, 29; **(2)** 11, 84, 114
Social Democratic Party (SPD) (German), **(2)** 239–40
Sraffa, Piero, **(1)** 10; **(2)** 215–32
Stalin, Joseph, **(1)** 78, 148, 171, 198, 207, 225
Steedman, I., **(2)** 215, 225

Taylor, Frederick, **(1)** 259
Terray, Emmanuel, **(1)** 320
Theoretical practice, **(2)** 271
Trotsky, Leon, **(2)** 239
Trotskyism, **(2)** 240, 260, 291–2

Union of Soviet Socialist Republics (USSR), **(1)** 50, 323–8; **(2)** 262

Walras, L., **(2)** 72–4
Weber, Max, **(1)** 146, 185, 234, 263
Wiles, P. J. O., **(2)** 141–2
Winter, S. G., **(2)** 146–8
Wolfstetter, E., **(2)** 215
Wood, Adrian, **(2)** 144, 196–9, 209
Wooley, P. K., **(2)** 195